W9-BHY-134

mk

The
TWELFTH VICTIM

The Innocence of Caril Fugate
in the Starkweather Murder Rampage

Linda M. Battisti
John Stevens Berry

Addicus Books
Omaha, Nebraska

An Addicus Nonfiction Book

ISBN 978-1-950091-56-0 / TV/Media Tie-in Edition

Typography and cover design by Jack Kusler

Cover photo by United Press International

Library of Congress Cataloging-in-Publication Data

Battisti, Linda M.
 The twelfth victim: the innocence of Caril Fugate in the Charles Starkweather murder rampage / Linda M. Battisti, John Stevens Berry.
  pages cm. — (An Addicus nonfiction book)
 Includes index.
 ISBN 978-1-950091-56-0 (alk. paper)
 1. Fugate, Caril Ann. 2. Starkweather, Charles Raymond, 1938-1959. 3. Criminals—Biography. 4. Mass murder—Nebraska. 5. Trials (Murder)—Nebraska. I. Berry, John Stevens, 1938- II. Title.
 HV6248.F83B38 2014
 364.152'34092—dc23

                                        2013047677

Addicus Books, Inc.
P.O. Box 45327
Omaha, Nebraska 68145
www.AddicusBooks.com

Printed in the United States of America
10 9 8 7 6 5 4 3 2 1

*To Caril and all those
who have believed in her*

Contents

ACKNOWLEDGMENTS

I wish to acknowledge my beloved Aunt Jeanmarie for all the prayers she said and the candles she lit for me during this endeavor; I thank my beloved brother Gino for educating me in criminal law and for his encouragement. I thank my dear friends for their abiding and unselfish interest in the years I spent researching and writing this book. I thank my bulldog, Christine Dior ("Chrissie"), for chewing on her toys rather than on my toes while I worked on my rewrites.

I wish to acknowledge James McArthur, Esq., son of Caril Fugate's attorney, for his devotion to Caril, for his selflessness, and for sharing with me the work of his late father, John McArthur. I have developed the deepest respect and admiration for John and for Jim; the apple doesn't fall far from the tree. I thank my coauthor, John Stevens Berry, Esq., for his dedication to this book, for his eloquence, and for his passion for justice.

Finally, I must express my complete gratitude to Caril Fugate, for her heroism, her triumph over tragedy, her courage, her patience, and her trust in me. I especially thank you, Caril, for choosing me, out of many other journalists and writers who have approached you over the years, to tell your story. You always believed that God would send you the right person to tell *your* story, and it is He who brought us together.

Linda M. Battisti

Firstly, I wish to acknowledge Caril Fugate, who began our friendship when she first called into my radio show in 1996. I also thank Jody Pitsch, who supplied me with recordings of my radio programs with Caril. I thank Caril for allowing me to record our conversations together in Lincoln, Nebraska, and for her hard work in going over documents and records with me. I want to thank my wife, Margaret Berry, for her support and her kindness to Caril.

A special thank you to Linda Battisti for appearing on my radio show. She ignited my interest in the book she was writing about Caril. I appreciate her inviting me to be her coauthor.

Linda and Caril recorded many interviews during the years Linda worked on this book. Linda has facts and memories of Caril that are not available to anyone else. Linda has been an inspiration and pleasure to work with. I've always admired her championing of Caril over the years.

I acknowledge my son, John Berry, Corporate President of Berry Law Firm, who was kind in making the secretarial staff available to me any time I needed them. I particularly appreciate the efforts of Cassidy Hasty, a paralegal with the firm who, despite her duties compiling trial books at Berry Law Firm, always found time to assist me.

John Stevens Berry

INTRODUCTION

My coauthor, John Stevens Berry, and I are aware that the murderous rampage of Charles Starkweather left wounds that will never heal in Nebraska. It is not our intention to renew the terrible suffering of the victims' families, or to force recall of the terror and horror in Lincoln and surrounding areas during that time. However, in the interest of both truth and justice, it is our intention to demonstrate how a fourteen-year-old Nebraska girl was treated unfairly both legally and ethically in the aftermath of the Starkweather murders.

We ask our readers to set aside long-held opinions, to suspend disbelief, and to join us in this inquiry, which we have been pursuing for many years. We would have not written this book if we had not become convinced that Caril Fugate had, indeed, also been a victim of Charles Starkweather. She was never a willing accomplice, and she did not receive a fair trial. Several factors convinced us of this. We've learned intimate details of Caril's story through conversations with her over many years. Knowing her story, studying the trial record in light of our own experiences as attorneys, and doing historical research has led us to these conclusions.

As an attorney and longtime reader of true-crime stories, it seems inevitable that I would become interested in one of this country's most brutal and terrifying events—the tale of Charles Starkweather's slayings of ten adults and a little three-year-old girl.

I have read every book about Starkweather that I could find. I have watched the movie *Badlands,* and sat glued to the television series *Murder in the Heartland,* both based on the Starkweather murder rampage. Starkweather's guilt in the killings is undeniable—he admitted the slayings and paid the ultimate price with his life at the young age of twenty.

The real story of his alleged accomplice, fourteen-year-old Caril Ann Fugate, was much more mysterious, and, until now, remained untold. Most books written about the killings assume that Caril was a willing participant, a smart-mouthed, thrill-seeking, blue-jeaned punk—crazy about Starkweather and his leather jacket, hot rods, and guns. In the 1950s, she was also considered a little tramp who had engaged in sexual intercourse outside the bonds of matrimony. In that era, Caril Ann Fugate's reputation was as low as a girl's could get.

I wasn't satisfied with the public's perception of Caril Fugate. I wanted to know just what role, if any, she really played in the Starkweather spree killings of early 1958. I ordered the trial transcripts of Starkweather's and Fugate's trials. The prosecution's case against Starkweather was a given because he admitted committing all the killings himself, although he stated it was self-defense. The real impetus for the prosecution was to prove that Starkweather was sane at the time of the killings and ensure his execution. Starkweather's lawyers needed to prove his insanity in order to save his life. As was widely expected, the jury gave him the death penalty. On June 25, 1959, Starkweather died in the electric chair.

Caril Fugate pleaded not guilty to the murder of Robert Jensen, Jr. She took the witness stand in her own defense. She testified that she never knew her family had been murdered until after Starkweather's capture, that she was his hostage, and that she only accompanied him on his spree killings in order to save her family. The jury didn't buy her story. They found her guilty and sentenced her to life in prison.

In my opinion, Caril's defense lawyer, John McArthur, convincingly explained Caril's actions and refuted the prosecution's claims of her complicity in the murders. Why, then, did the jury find her guilty? I had to delve deeper. The more I researched, the more I became convinced that Caril's conviction wasn't just. I researched not only the trial transcripts, but also the newspaper articles written during Starkweather's killing rampage. I interviewed various witnesses who were either directly involved in the investigation and trial, or were close members of their families and had lived through the ordeal with them.

I also read the book, *Caril,* written by an Omaha reporter after Caril had spent years in prison, and *The Murderous Trail of Charles Starkweather,* by criminologist James M. Reinhardt, who spent numerous hours with Starkweather while he was on death row. I learned two important things. First, I learned what was inside the mind of Starkweather, and second, I learned what was inside the minds of Caril's jury members. It was then that I came to the conclusion that Caril Fugate was a victim of a terrible injustice.

Certain events just didn't make sense to me. I thought if I could find the answers to these lingering doubts I had, maybe it would clear Caril's complicity in these crimes.

Over the years that I have studied this case and written this book, I have had exclusive access to Caril Fugate. She never trusted others who approached her throughout the years to write her story. She wanted somebody she trusted to write it, and she prayed for the right person to come along; she told me she knew God would let her know who the right person was. When I approached her, she knew I was the one. I had researched her case for more than two years before I approached her sister, Barbara, about contacting Caril to talk to her about writing a book. Early on, I was convinced that Caril, too, was a victim of Charles Starkweather.

Caril never wanted to make money through telling her story for a book. She never asked to have approval over what I wrote. She said she had nothing to hide from me. In fact, she told me to write only the truth, even if it reflected poorly on her. I agreed and told her she would read the book only after it was published.

Linda M. Battisti

Our purpose in writing this book is to show how brutally and unfairly Caril was treated by the judicial system in the state of Nebraska, in ways that would not be allowed under today's laws, and also to demonstrate her innocence and her actually having been another victim of Starkweather.

I met Caril Fugate, quite by chance, in August of 1996, when I was hosting a drive-time radio talk show on KLIN radio in Lincoln. Before I was hosting the show, I was a guest on the program. I had been invited to talk about that day's not guilty verdict in the O.J. Simpson trial. The audience response to my guest appearance apparently impressed the radio station manager. He offered me the job of hosting the drive-time radio program. I was pleased to accept the position and hosted the show for a number of years.

On August 8, 1996, my radio guest was James McArthur. He had been Caril Fugate's attorney and had recently tried, unsuccessfully, to get a full pardon for Caril. He was appearing on my show to talk about Caril's case and his attempt to get her a pardon.

It took me by surprise when Caril called into the show. It was the first time she had spoken publicly about her case. The switchboard lit up with supportive callers. We stopped all commercial breaks so that we could hear more from Caril. As she began telling the story of her life on my program, I was astonished by the number of telephone calls that came in from listeners who were convinced that she could not have known that her family was dead when Starkweather kidnapped her. Moreover, they believed that she couldn't possibly have participated in their killings.

I remember one caller saying she went to high school with Caril and had seen Charles Starkweather pull Caril off a bus. Another caller remembered seeing Caril trying to hide from Starkweather at school. Other callers said that they were in school with Caril, and were convinced of her innocence, but their parents would not let them testify. Others felt the police had ignored them.

At the end of the program, Caril agreed to be my guest again the following day. Altogether, she spent four hours on the air with me. I was most struck by Caril's statement, "I have never been able to tell my story."

As a result of Caril's appearance, her attorney, James Mc-Carther suggested that I invite an attorney, Linda Battisti, from Ohio, to be a guest on my radio show. Linda was writing a book about Caril's case. Linda came on the show as a guest, and by the time we had finished the interview, Linda asked me to collaborate with her on her book. Having had a book published, I had some insights about writing a book and getting it published. I gladly joined Linda as her coauthor. The more I learned about Caril's case, the more convinced I became that she was innocent and that she had been treated unjustly by the state of Nebraska.

Back when the murders occurred, I, like many people in Nebraska, accepted the fact that Caril Fugate was guilty of murder by her association with Starkweather during his mad killing spree. Caril was seen by the general public as a combination of Bonnie Parker (of Bonnie and Clyde) and Lolita—a girl-woman caught up in the thrill and excitement of the murderous rampage of her boyfriend, Starkweather.

I was as uniformed as the rest of the state of Nebraska as to the courage Caril exhibited while she was his hostage, the heroism she displayed the few times Starkweather was out of sight; she may have had the opportunity to escape him but decided to remain for the sake of her family's lives.

She had returned home from school one afternoon and was met by Charles Starkweather pointing a shotgun at her. He told her to do as he said, or he would have her parents and her three-year-old sister, Betty Jean killed. And so, she obeyed Starkweather's every order.

After her arrest, Caril was under the impression that her family was alive. It was while she was being held in a jail cell in Gering, Nebraska, that she found out about their deaths through a casual remark made by a jail staffer.

I had not realized at that time that Caril was a true victim. She was not only the victim of being a juvenile charged and tried as an adult, but also the victim of being convicted under archaic laws that were in play prior to the passage of the *Miranda* decision which requires police to advise an arrested person that they have a right to remain silent and the right to legal counsel.

In 1958, she had no such rights. She was the genuine victim of a monster, and then was further victimized by ruthless, ambitious, and relentless prosecutors who deliberately concealed evidence that could have helped her defense.

As a trial lawyer I suspect that Caril Fugate could not have received a fair trial in Lincoln, Nebraska, at that time. It is unlikely, in today's criminal justice system, that Caril Fugate would have been prosecuted as an adult. In fact, she most likely would be treated as a victim witness.

After witnessing the murder of farmer August Meyer, one of Starkweather's first victims in his murder spree, Caril—like any other fourteen-year-old girl, and in fact most adults—would have been in such a state of shock and disbelief as to be rendered numb.

Most of the people who have condemned Caril have never been under the kind of stress she was under as a hostage. Some combat-trained adults, after seeing just a fraction of the brutality Caril saw, have undergone personality disintegration; some have been diagnosed with post-traumatic stress disorder, a condition that had not been heard of at the time Caril was tried. Many adults have become confused and disoriented while going through the process of a murder trial. Yet Caril, who had failed a grade in school, who had come from a disadvantaged background, and who was not yet fifteen at the time of the gruesome acts of Charles Starkweather, was criticized for her courtroom performance and her statements to police as though she had awkwardly stumbled during a ballet recital. Some people seemed to enjoy immortalizing Starkweather's lies about her guilt.

Through the years, I have become friends with Caril Fugate. I have spent many hours with Caril when she and her husband, Fred, visited me in Lincoln. Her passion for getting the truth told is contagious.

Thinking that her story must be told, and remembering Russian author Dostoyevsky's admonition that a universe without justice is unthinkable, I felt compelled to help write this book. I wanted the truth to finally emerge from the blizzard of lies, misconceptions, and inaccuracies that surrounded this prosecution, trial, and conviction of an innocent Nebraska girl.

John Stevens Berry

PART I

CARIL FUGATE'S STORY:
The Beginning

CHAPTER 1

Oh, I took my girl a-skating
I sat her on my knee
She lit a fart
Broke my heart
And shit all over me
Ohhhh, it ain't gonna rain no more, no more
—William Fugate

"If I've told you once, I've told you a thousand times not to sing those songs to the girls!" Velda Fugate stopped what she was doing and marched herself down the hall to where the entertainment was taking place.

Her little girls, Barbara, seven, and Caril Ann, four, were rolling on the floor laughing. The sound of their ringing laughter made their mother relent. Laughter was a treat Velda could allow her children—it didn't cost anything.

Velda returned to her task of packing; her bedroom floor was strewn with boxes, clothing, and what little odds and ends her family owned. They were being evicted from the small one-bedroom house they rented in a poor section of Lincoln, Nebraska. Velda wanted to have everything ready before the sheriff came this time.

She carefully took down from the wall her cherished porcelain-faced Chinese doll and wrapped it in newspaper. That doll always hung on a wall well out of reach of her two curious little girls who had no dolls of their own. That's because the Fugates were not only poor, but poorer than they needed to be. The head of the house drank his paycheck away and

3

neglected such things as food, rent, and a forty-hour workweek. Velda found out about her husband's penchant for spirits after she married him. Being a devout Nazarene, she never drank, swore, or took the Lord's name in vain. She did take seriously the words, "No man shall put asunder" and tried to make the best out of a bad situation. Velda was just one of those born optimists who, when given lemons, made lemonade.

Velda was also a realist who refused to fill her children's heads with that Santa Claus and Easter Bunny nonsense. She realized early on in her marriage that William Fugate would never be able to provide his family with basic necessities, let alone toys and chocolate Easter eggs. Velda didn't want her children to grow up expecting such things only to be disappointed later on when the treats didn't arrive. Faith in the Lord would do her children more good than any foolish beliefs in a tooth fairy.

Velda realized there was something very odd about William Fugate; he never mentioned a mother or father, or where he came from. No other Fugates lived in Lincoln. It would have been helpful to have known something about Fugate's background—it might explain his "Jekyll and Hyde" personality. When he was sober, Fugate was a fellow who could pull a penny out of your ear and entertain you all night with his guitar. When he was drunk, he was venom on two shoes. Velda was relieved when he didn't find his way home at times. When the girls asked their mother where Daddy was, Velda knew he was in either one of two places—a seedy bar or jail—but she never said so.

In contrast to their father's absence, Barbara and Caril only had to look up, and there Velda would be. Her pretty face was the first thing they saw in the morning because Velda would wake them up; her voice was the last thing they would hear at night because Velda sat by their bedside and told them stories until they drifted off. When Barbara came home from school, it was Velda who opened the door for her; and when Caril took her afternoon nap, it was Velda who held her in her arms and slept, too.

There was only one time when the little girls couldn't reach out and physically touch their mother—when Velda hid them in the closet. She did this as soon as Fugate came home.

If she opened the door and found him sober, she called her children out at once. If she found him drunk, they had to stay in the closet until he went to sleep it off. Barbara and Caril would sit huddled on the closet floor, holding onto each other and crying while they listened to their father call their mother names you wouldn't call a dog. As soon as Velda got rid of him, she called them out from the closet and they would run crying into her arms.

"Oh mommy, are you all right?" they would cry.

"Of course, I'm all right, darlings," she would say. Then, to send them to sleep with sweet dreams, she would give them each a graham cracker with frosting Velda made out of milk and powdered sugar.

The Chinese doll was wrapped and boxed. The singing had stopped, and Velda's reverie was called off by little Caril Ann.

"Mommy, won't you draw me Betty Boop?"

"Sure I will, Honey. Find me a crayon. I haven't packed up everything yet."

Velda's entire family, the Streets, lived in Lincoln. Barbara and Caril were especially close to their grandmother, Pansy Street. Pansy was a big woman who could sit both the girls on her lap at the same time and rock them in her arms. Her favorite things in the whole world were grapefruits and chocolate-covered cherries, which she would smash and eat in a sandwich. The cherries, not the grapefruit. Pansy also crocheted the most beautiful doilies with delicate handkerchief edging. She tried to teach Barbara and Caril how to crochet and tat, but they never got the hang of it. Especially Caril Ann. If she couldn't learn to do something in five minutes, it wasn't worth doing. Pansy would try to instill patience in Caril when she would quit in frustration and throw her work on the floor. Just why should she have to learn how to make a bunch of dumb knots on a dumb piece of string anyway?

"Young lady, I don't like your tone of voice," Pansy would say as she walked away to begin another task.

Left alone to sulk, Caril would cry out how Grandma didn't love her anymore.

And her grandma would say, "I love you, Caril Ann, even though I may not like how you behave. There's a big difference."

Caril Ann gave her grandmother many opportunities to hate the sin but love the sinner when she cussed like a sailor. She learned how at a tender age from her father. This habit remained a shameful family secret until Caril was five years old. The girls' Aunt Lola took them one Saturday afternoon to the University of Nebraska football field to listen to the marching band practice. They ran into some friends, and Caril remained with the friends while her aunt and sister walked around the crowd. In a little while, Barbara flew excitedly across the cobblestone street in search of her little sister.

"Look, Caril! See what Aunt Lola let me wear," she cried. It was lipstick! Lipstick that turned Barb's lips as red as an apple!

"Me, too," Caril cried, not paying attention to the fast-approaching pickup truck. As she darted across the street, the truck knocked her down flat on her back and she found herself staring up at an exhaust pipe.

"Don't move, little girl," a voice warned.

Not listening, Caril rolled out from underneath the truck, made a fist, and hollered, "You dirty, goddam son-of-a-bitch truck driver! You runned over me!"

A rush to the nearest hospital revealed no broken bones or internal injuries. Even though the next day she was very sore and bruised black and blue, Caril insisted on going to church that morning. While Velda brushed her daughter's hair, a big chunk fell out. Velda warned Caril not to expect any cookies and milk after bible school because by now Reverend Proffit had heard all about the bad words she used yesterday. But when Caril returned home from church, she informed her mother that not only did she get cookies and milk like all the other children, but she got double for being an example of how you can get run over by a truck and still live through it —all by the grace of God!

There was one person in their family the girls didn't like. It was their great-grandmother, Grandma Hitchcock, or, as the girls called her, "Grandma Witchcock." Grandma Witchcock lived in a big spooky-looking house in Havelock, a suburb of Lincoln. She always dressed in long black dresses and was just down-right weird in her beliefs about dead spirits. Pansy and Velda would take the girls across town on a bus to visit her sometimes. Before they got there, Velda would warn them to be sure to mind their manners and not ask their great-grandmother for anything. Then she'd tell Caril she had a smudge on her face, lick her index finger, and wipe it off.

Grandma Witchcock had waiting for them foul-smelling potions of herbs she concocted and made the girls wear in a tobacco pouch tied around their necks. She said it would prevent them from catching colds and measles from the neighborhood kids. And it worked, too, because none of the neighborhood kids wanted to play with the malodorous Fugate girls whenever they came to visit. As soon as their visit ended and they left her house, the girls would toss their tobacco pouches into the nearest bushes.

At the top of the stairs, Grandma Witchcock had a room that she always kept locked. Caril and Barbara used to dare each other to peek through the keyhole, but neither one ever did. They were terrified of what might be behind that door and figured they were better off not knowing.

The very last move the family would make with Fugate landed them at 410 North 10th Street in Lincoln, a tenement house run by a kind landlady, Mae Holley. Also living at Mae's were Velda's mother Pansy, and her sister, Lola, and Lola's husband and their twins, Timmy and Tiny. Caril was eight years old and in second grade. She failed first grade because the family moved five times in two years. Barbara hated school, and she hated moving. She could not count the number of times she came home to find the house packed in boxes. Changing schools so often never allowed her to make friends. What's the use? And why bother to catch up in school? She knew they would only be moving, and she'd get behind again.

Living at Mae's was like living with an extended family. Barbara especially liked living there because she finally made a friend her own age, Franny Ortiz. Franny's family came from Mexico, and at times the most tantalizing aromas emanated from inside their apartment, so much so that Barb and Caril often found themselves beckoned to the Ortiz door, usually around dinner time. Barbara developed a passion for Mexican cooking and would sneak hot dogs to Franny in exchange for some of her mom's tortillas.

Their tenement house was close to the State Theater, and on Saturdays Velda, Barbara, and Caril walked to the matinees. Velda was like a kid herself and walked so fast to get there that her daughters had to yell, "Hey, mom, wait for us!" Kids got in for free if they showed five milk-top cartons to the cashier. They would tie them together on a string, holler "five," and walk on in.

Trips to the closet didn't stop after they moved, and now Fugate's fights with his wife were heard by the whole tenement house. The last time the girls hid in the closet they heard something more than the usual tirade. Blows, a scream, and then a thud against the kitchen table brought the girls out of the closet in time to see their father's hands squeezed around Velda's throat. Barb got a butcher knife and brandished it in the air while Caril found a hammer, got down on her hands and knees, and tried to hit her father's toes. Both girls were screaming, "Don't hurt our mother! Let go of our mother!"

When Pansy burst through the door she witnessed a macabre scene of four Fugates going around in a circle performing what looked like some kind of a war dance. Pansy grabbed the knife out of Barb's hand, Fugate ran out the door, and the four of them held onto one another for how long they didn't know.

Finally, Velda said, "That does it. He goes."

Later that year, for the first time in their lives the girls had a Christmas tree. A spindly, brittle tree, faintly smelling of pine, was standing proudly in a tree holder borrowed from the Ortiz family. The girls transformed it into something magnificent. They spent hours making decorations fashioned from foil wrapping taken from Velda's Camel cigarettes. They ironed out the foil with their nails and wrapped it around pencils to form make-believe icicles. They fashioned chains out of colored crepe paper. When they finished, Velda oohed and aahed and said it was the prettiest tree in all of Nebraska. It didn't matter a hoot if any Christmas presents turned up under it.

Suddenly, William Fugate stormed through the door and ran straight into the bedroom without saying a word to anybody. Nobody had seen him in over a week since he tried to strangle Velda. In less than ten minutes, he emerged carrying a suitcase and ran out of the apartment so fast that he knocked over their beautiful Christmas tree. Caril ran over to the window and saw a taxicab parked underneath a streetlight. It was dark and snowing. As her father approached the cab, a woman got out of the backseat and held the door open for him. The driver started the ignition and Fugate drove out of their lives.

It was just the three of them now. Velda's divorce from Fugate left her with nothing but the clothes on her back and a fierce determination to provide for her children without the aid of any welfare, which she was too proud to accept, and without any help from Fugate, which she knew she would never get.

Velda found a job, and the girls adjusted to being latchkey kids. Living at Mae's turned out to be a plus; there was always Aunt Lola, Mrs. Ortiz, and Mae to whom the girls could run in emergencies. Pansy worked all day.

All three pitched in to do the cooking, wash the dishes, make the beds, and clean the house. Doing the laundry was an all-day affair reserved for Saturdays. Two large buckets had to be filled and emptied over and over again, one with hot water to wash, the second with cold water to rinse. Items needed to be wrung and then hung on a clothesline to dry. Living together in a peaceful environment made these domestic tasks seem fun.

Velda developed a passion for jigsaw puzzles, which she would only work on after the girls went to bed. She looked forward to an hour or two of quiet time alone before turning in for the night. However, the impish Caril often made it difficult for her mother to concentrate on her hobby. The girls still slept in the same bed; Barb was skittish in the dark and always covered her head with the blanket and faced the wall. Caril took shameless delight in whispering, "Oooh, Barb. There's someone looking at you through the window."

"Stop it, Caril," Barb would snap while Caril giggled. "Quiet down in there, both of you," Velda warned.

"Oh, yes, there is. He's gonna get you," Caril continued. "Did you hear what I said?" Velda warned again.

"He's opening the window now."

Barb started to cry.

"Don't make me have to come in there," Velda said for the third time, which meant she was coming in.

"All right, both of you! I want you to be quiet and get to sleep, do you understand me?" Velda yelled in exasperation, to which Barb retorted that she couldn't get to sleep with Caril Ann scaring her about some man looking in the window.

Velda assured her elder daughter that no man was tall enough to look through a second-story window. And nobody could get into the apartment, either. Every night before going to bed, Velda slid a long, black-handled kitchen knife sideways between the crack in the wood molding which ran parallel to the front door so it would serve as a bar on the door.

The movie *The Thing,* staring James Arness, was playing at the State Theater, and everyone was raving about it as being the spookiest movie ever. Arness, who later gained fame as "Marshall Dillon" on the popular *Gunsmoke* TV series, played the seemingly indestructible monster that terrorized a group of scientists doing research at the North Pole. Barbara and Caril cried that they would just die if they couldn't see this movie.

A flying saucer crashes at the North Pole. The only thing remaining at the crash site is a body frozen in ice. The research expedition transports the body in a giant ice cube back to the laboratory to study it. An electric blanket inadvertently thrown over the ice cube melts the ice and frees the monster. The explorers stare out a window in horror as the escaped monster fights off and kills a few of their sled dogs, but not before one dog tears off the monster's arm. The monster runs away— where to, nobody knows. The arm is being studied to determine what it consists of when, lo and behold, it starts to move. It's alive! The explorers huddle together terrified in a long corridor at the end of which stands a door to the greenhouse.

They slowly approach the door, open it, and out lurches the monster in all his menace! It has grown another arm!

This scene in particular badly frightened nine-year-old Caril Ann. Ever after seeing the movie, she was afraid to open the door to their apartment. She would knock on the door, yell, "It's me," and run down the hall until her mother or sister opened the door for her. She aggravated her mother and sister with this ritual for months.

"Never again to another scary movie," Velda muttered.

A stranger had entered their lives in the form of fifty-something Marion Bartlett, a veteran of World War II, who worked with Velda. Despite the twenty-year difference in their ages, Velda and Marion fell in love and got married. Marion moved in with them, and things suddenly seemed crowded. Initially, it was a difficult adjustment getting used to living with a woman and two energetic daughters. However, Marion was a good-natured man who loved his wife and from the very beginning treated Barb and Caril as his own. Never once did Marion refer to them as his stepdaughters; they were his daughters.

Soon after they were married, Marion spotted a dust mop on the kitchen counter and told Caril to put it away.

Caril retorted, "If you want the damn mop put away, put it away yourself."

Marion grabbed Caril by the arm, pulled her over his knee, and gave her a few good swats. He then sat her on his lap and kissed her and said, "I'm sorry I had to do that, Caril, because I love you, but I'm your father now. So when I tell you to do something you better mind me."

Their new father was hardly a pushover and imposed certain restrictions the girls didn't like. He wouldn't let them wear lipstick, sleep over at friends' houses, or eat potato chips and ice cream. When they complained, he said that it would give them worms and rot their teeth.

"Not true!" they retorted. Everyone they knew who ate potato chips and ice cream still had all their teeth!

On February 11, 1955, Velda sent Marion, Barbara, and Caril over the moon by presenting them with a baby girl, Betty Jean Bartlett. However, for the longest time, Caril referred to her baby sister as "Patty" because that's what she would have named her.

Whenever Caril came home from school, she'd open the door, stick her head inside, and yell, "Patty, Patty, Patty!" And little Betty Jean would squeal in delight because her big sister was home. From the moment she was born, Betty Jean became like a live doll for Barbara, fourteen, and Caril, eleven. They would dress and undress her, which would prompt their mother to remark, "Why is it every time I look up, little Betty Jean is naked?"

Marion decided living at Mae's was no longer adequate for his growing family and, shortly after Betty Jean's birth, they moved to a house on Belmont Street in Lincoln. The house consisted of three rooms: a living room, a kitchen, and a bedroom. There was no plumbing in the house, and the family had to use the outhouse in the backyard. Barbara and Caril shared the bedroom, while Marion, Velda, and the baby used the living room as their bedroom. Immediately after they moved in, Marion started adding on to the house. By the time 924 Belmont would make the headlines in the *Lincoln Journal*, Marion had added on a dining room, a master bedroom, and a bathroom. Caril was eager to help remodel and one day badly cut her finger on a half-moon knife while she was cutting linoleum for the bedroom floor. Marion rushed Caril to the hospital where she was given a few stitches. The scar left by this wound would one day be used to identify Caril in an all-points bulletin put out by the FBI.

One Saturday afternoon Marion hollered, "Come on, girls. Let's all go for a ride." Marion drove them downtown and parked the car in an alley, telling them to wait for him. He walked through the back door of a store and came out carrying a television. The family's very first television! Caril Ann thought she had died and gone straight to heaven.

Their first summer on Belmont Street, Marion canned vegetables he grew himself in the backyard. Caril loved everything but his pickles. Every time company visited, Caril foisted upon the departing guests as many jars of pickles as they could carry, always insisting that she couldn't allow anybody to leave her house empty-handed!

Because a chicken coop was already on the property, they decided they might as well get some use out of it. First, Marion brought home a few hens. But hens alone aren't of much use to a hungry family. When they first brought a baby rooster home, Velda said it was so cute it had to live in the house. But, when it grew up, Velda put him outside to perform his manly duties. That's when the rooster got mean and vindictive toward Velda. Whenever she would go outside, the rooster chased her and pecked her ankles. Velda was at her wits' end and threatened over and over that if he ever nipped her again, she would turn him into fricassee! One day, Caril Ann noticed the rooster was missing and asked her mother what happened to him.

"Last Sunday's dinner," Velda admitted.

Daisy the duck became the friend and protector of baby Betty Jean. For the little girl's first summer, Velda would place her on a blanket in front of their back porch off the kitchen to enjoy the summer breezes. Daisy always slept between Betty Jean's legs and rested her chin on the baby's stomach. Whenever the baby would stir, Daisy would quack. When Betty Jean learned to crawl, Daisy would follow from behind, pecking her diaper, which made the baby scream with indignation but sent her family into howls of laughter.

William "Bill" Fugate resurfaced and invited Barb and Caril one afternoon to visit with him and his new wife, Dot. They did not want to go, but their mother made them. Marion drove Barb, Caril, and Betty Jean over to Fugate's and told them he'd pick them up at 4:00 sharp. Barbara chatted with Fugate in the kitchen while Caril sat with Dot in the living room and played with Betty Jean. Betty Jean was big enough to crawl up onto the coffee table and, when she did, Caril would laugh and say if she fell down, she wasn't going to pick her up. But, every time Betty Jean pretended to fall, Caril picked her up. Fugate, feeling ignored by his youngest daughter, decided to play a little ditty on his guitar for old times' sake.

> *The bear went over the mountain*
> *The bear went over the mountain*
> *The bear went over the mountain*
> *To see what he could see.*
> *He stuck his head in a dark hole*
> *Filled his belly with charcoal*
> *The smoke blew out his ass-hole*
> *And blew his tail away.*

It turned out to be a very long afternoon. When they heard Marion's horn toot at 4:00 and headed for the door, Fugate asked the girls if they wanted to come live with him. Caril answered, "Hell, no!" and ran out the door.

When Barbara Fugate turned sixteen she found a steady job after school as a babysitter for five children who lived down the street. When she wasn't babysitting, she was usually visiting with her friend, also named Barbara—Barbara Griggs—who lived a block or two away from Caril and Barbara. Barbara Griggs was dating a very nice boy named Rodney Starkweather. Rodney introduced Barb Fugate to his younger brother, Charlie. Together, they completed a foursome and would hang around the Griggs' house together and sometimes go out to a movie.

One day Charlie brought his best friend, Bob Von Busch, over to the Griggs' and introduced him to Barb. It was love at first sight for both of them. Bob's conscience stung him for falling for his best friend's girl. Neither Barb Fugate nor Bob wanted to hurt Charlie. Thinking this would solve her problem, Barb suggested that they introduce Charlie to her younger sister, Caril. Caril was only thirteen years old, and Bob wondered whether she was too young to date an eighteen-year-old boy. Don't worry, Barb assured him. She was certain that if she and Bob always went out with them, her mother would let Caril date Charlie. After all, Charlie was such a nice boy. He was handsome, polite, funny, and just plain cool. She felt certain that Charlie and Caril Ann would really hit it off.

14

CHAPTER 2

Charles Raymond Starkweather was born in Lincoln, Nebraska, on November 24, 1938—the third of seven children born to Guy and Helen Starkweather. Their ancestry could be traced back to 1640 when a man named Robert Starkweather sailed to America from the Isle of Man in the Irish Sea, settling in Roxbury, Massachusetts. Starkweathers fought in the Revolutionary War and at Bunker Hill. A Colonel Starkweather commanded the first regiment of soldiers to leave Wisconsin for the front in the Civil War, and he is depicted in a mural in the executive chambers in the State Capitol in Madison. There was never a hint of insanity or lawlessness in the Starkweather clan. In fact, streets located in Detroit, Michigan and Cleveland, Ohio were named after Starkweathers who had distinguished themselves in some kind of public service in this country. The town of Starkweather, North Dakota was named in honor of an early settler there.

Charlie's father Guy was a handsome man who was considered a jack-of-all-trades. His mother Helen was a small, red-haired woman with hazel eyes and finely cut features who, underneath a fragile-looking exterior, was the strength behind the family. In fact, she often supported the family; she had held a job since 1946, when her husband developed arthritis. Guy often worked as a carpenter, but could rarely work full time because of the arthritis.

The neighbors liked the Starkweathers and appreciated how well behaved their children seemed. The children always ran outside to meet their father as soon as his car hit the

15

driveway. Guy and Helen were especially kind about helping neighbors when they were sick.

Charlie's early years were happy ones. He grew up in South Lincoln in a small, white, one-story house with a big front porch overlooking a large lawn made shady by numerous cottonwoods. He loved to listen to the birds singing in the trees and made believe he lived in an enchanted forest. Using imaginary guns and bow and arrows, Charlie and his two older brothers, Leonard and Rodney, played cowboys and Indians in this tree-filled yard, pretending to be Daniel Boone, Crazy Horse, Roy Rogers, the Lone Ranger, and Wild Bill Hickok. When his older brothers went off to school, Charlie was content to spend his days feeding the chickens in the backyard and helping his mother can vegetables.

On weekends, Guy would take the children to the zoo and tell them the name of every animal there and what they were thinking when the children looked at them. To little Charlie, Guy could do anything. He could fix a shoe, put a new roof on a house, and even run a bakery. He took the children camping and taught them how to build a campfire and how to put it out. When he took the children fishing, Guy always walked ahead of them carrying a stick and would hit the grass and undergrowth with it to scare away any lurking snakes. While his father and brothers went off to bait their hooks, Charlie stayed behind on the riverbank because he never took to fishing. Guy told Charlie that when he was older he would teach him how to hunt with a gun.

Charlie seemed to function well within the protected confines of a closely knit family circle. His early years were the happiest of his life. To his family he seemed normal, but when he was eight or nine his teachers began to think he was mentally slow. Little did they know the troubling issues he had simmering inside of him.

According to James M. Reinhardt, noted nationally known criminologist and author of *The Murderous Trail of Charles Starkweather*, Starkweather concealed a hidden hatred of others and a murderous lust for power that festered within him.

It is difficult to pinpoint when this hatred started. According to Reinhardt, it manifested itself on Charlie's first day at school where, away from his family, he discovered, at least in his own mind, how different he was from other people. Reinhardt had no question in his mind "as to the unrealistic nature of much of Charles Starkweather's thinking about himself and the world around him; and there was a delusional quality in many of his responses to the language and behavior of other people."

Charlie told the following story about his memory of his first day at school. After his brothers dropped him off, Charlie was frightened. His teacher, Mrs. Mott, asked all the children to introduce themselves to their classmates. Because they went in alphabetical order, Charlie was one of the last to stand in front of class and tell his classmates how he spent his summer. When it was his turn to walk up to the front of the room, the other children giggled at him. Charlie had a speech impediment and bowlegs. When he started to talk about canning vegetables with his mother and family Sunday picnics, the children laughed at his speech impediment. He would say "wouse" for "house."

During recess, as soon as Charlie walked over to the playhouse, all the other children walked out. When it came time to play Charlie's favorite game, soccer, nobody picked him for their team. He had to be a substitute and stay along the back stop near the bench, and if someone got hurt he would take his place. The children mocked him further by yelling, "You think you can kick with those bowlegs?" They continued to poke fun at his speech impediment and imitated his bowlegs. Charlie started to cry.

"Look," the children mocked, "he's going to cry!"

When it came time to walk home from school, the children followed him, chanting, "bowlegged, red-headed woodpecker" over and over again. When Charlie paused to cross the street, someone shoved him into oncoming traffic. Suddenly, Charlie was lying in the street. He remembered the driver's eyes opening as wide as silver dollars.

As he got up, a boy yelled, "What happened, bowlegs? Can't you stand? Won't those bowlegs hold you up?"

Then, someone jerked something out of Charlie's hand. It was a picture he drew in school for his mother. The boy who grabbed it called it a piece of junk and tore it in half.

Charlie started to cry.

The children then chanted, "Bowlegged, red-headed woodpecker is a crybaby!" Charlie ran home as fast as his legs would take him.

A sad first day in school, indeed. Only James Reinhardt is doubtful it ever happened. In Reinhardt's interviews with Charlie's former teachers and fellow students, he discovered that teachers tried to help Charlie overcome his terrible low self-esteem. They gave him special tasks to do. They tried to encourage his artistic ability. Reinhardt concluded that Charlie was miserable, and, like most miserable people, he did not know the source of his hatred, so he exaggerated the event in order to justify his hatred against the world. He gave himself the right to hate by exaggerating what he considered the cruelty of others.

After kindergarten, Charlie quit crying and being afraid of other children. As Reinhardt stated: "Slowly, fear was transformed into hate...hate, like a consuming passion in the bloodstream—invaded every tissue and interstice of his being. Hate and a quenchless hunger for a servile respect: these were the psychic twins that impelled Charlie to develop a complex chain of self-defenses. He had to justify his utter failure to meet the ordinary, everyday demands that life imposed. So he constructed a self-illusion and he made it an object of derision. It was all a defensive form of make-believe."

Charlie developed a reputation of being a bully. He once said, "I began to love fighting, and would walk a mile just to fight someone."

Grade-school teachers remembered him as being timid; getting along well with boys, but not getting along so well with girls; and not liking to participate in games with other children. He was fond of his mother and two older brothers but didn't often speak about his father.

His sixth-grade teacher found Charlie "very eager to work and to please."

Another teacher reported: "Low achievement in general, but on the whole has a good attitude and has never been a disciplinary problem."

Charlie was suspicious of the kindness of his teachers. He spoke about one of them to Reinhardt, a woman whom Reinhardt described as "very fair and very kind." "Oh, yes, she would snap her fingers at other children sometimes, but what's that...I was the one she didn't like and I knowed even when the teacher talked nice to me, it was just words."

Nobody back then ever could have suspected that Charlie would become a killer.

"He had a temper, sure, but I would never have thought he could ever kill a human being," reported a former teacher.

"He had his faults but I thought he was a pretty good kid," stated a boy who knew Charlie in school.

"I always felt sorry for the kid, he seemed so lonely...I couldn't imagine that he would kill anybody," a girl said.

However, one teacher who described Charlie as "cold and feelingless," recalled: "Once I came upon the scene of one of his fights just in time to see his antagonist, a boy somewhat older than Charlie and a little larger, being helped to his feet. The fight had taken place in a crushed rock driveway in front of the schoolhouse. Charlie had churned the boy's face into the bed of ground rock and it was bleeding badly. The boy was crying, but Charlie seemed totally unmoved by what had happened."

Charlie liked to read comics whose protagonists used knives, and he watched television shows where cowboys and mobsters used guns. Early on in his childhood he fantasized about seeing imaginary people dead at his feet; this image "gave him an inexpressible secret satisfaction," Reinhardt would later say. Above all, Reinhardt noted, Charlie acquired an "inhibited, remorseless, power-hunger."

After failing several grades, Charlie got kicked out of Irving Junior High, having earned a reputation for being one of the meanest, toughest kids in Lincoln, a reputation of which he was proud. In ninth grade, at the age of sixteen, Charlie transferred to Everett Junior High. It was here that he met his best friend, Bob Von Busch. Bob, stocky and bigger than Charlie, also had a reputation for being a tough kid. It was inevitable that the two would clash. Their fight started right in the classroom and ended in the hall where they beat each other until they both collapsed from exhaustion. Neither one could claim victory, but, after the fight the two young men became fast friends and stayed that way for years.

In his book, *Starkweather: The Story of a Mass Murderer,* author William Allan quotes Starkweather's friend Bob Von Busch as saying, "Charlie could be the kindest person you've ever seen. He'd do anything for you if he liked you. He was a hell of a lot of fun to be around, too. Everything was just one big joke to him. But he had this other side. He could be mean as hell, cruel. If he saw some poor guy on the street that was bigger than he was, better looking, or better dressed, he'd try to take the poor bastard down to his size. But I didn't think too much about it at the time. We were all a little like that then. We all had a lot of growing up to do."

As a teenager, Charlie had become a rather handsome young man. He wore his thick red hair in a "ducktail" style that had become popular, and smoked Kool cigarettes. He belonged to what he called a "gang," and dressed like the other boys in the gang—wearing blue jeans, cowboy boots, and a black leather jacket. He was a virtual James Dean, the movie star.

On Saturday nights, Charlie's gang, the "Leather Jackets," would go downtown, hoping for a showdown with another gang across town called the "Levi Jackets." They never stirred up any real trouble—just hung out under the street lamps calling each other names and daring each other to cross the street and start something.

Eventually, when they became bored with taunting each other, both gangs would go over to the Acme Chili Parlor in downtown Lincoln and order chili and malts. Sometimes the gangs would meet at Capitol Beach, an amusement park, and play "chicken-out," a game in which two cars would speed toward each other. The driver who swerved to avoid a crash would be the one to "chicken-out." Charlie was master of the game.

Bob and Charlie bought a 1941 Ford together and would cross the state line into Kansas, where they would buy 3.2 beer and sell it to friends in Lincoln. Sometimes Charlie would strip down cars they initially swiped for joyrides, using the parts for his own car or selling them. One time Charlie stole a gray 1946 Chevy sedan from the parking lot at the northwest corner of 16th and Vine and took it down to Bob's where he junked the car by cutting it up with a hacksaw. Bob kept the radio and tires. Charlie gave Bob the five dollars he made selling the junk. What he couldn't sell was hauled away in his brother Rodney's garbage truck.

While in Everett Junior High, Charlie started seeing a girl in his class. A few years later, while he was on death row, she explained incredulously, "I met him after he was kicked out of Irving. Nobody would accept him. We went to the movies together and spent a lot of evenings at home studying. In all the time I knew him I never once heard him swear, and he never smoked or drank. He never even tried to put his arm around me. He went to some of my church affairs with me and even ran errands for my mother. I thought he was one of the finest boys I've ever known."

"I can't believe he's done this. Maybe he's changed a lot in the last four years. Maybe I shouldn't pity him but I think more people should have given him a chance."

Charlie quit school at the age of sixteen and got a job at the Western Newspaper Union located at 2005 O Street in Lincoln. He started on October 5, 1955, and got paid 85 cents an hour baling paper.

"At the Newspaper Union the people was always watchin' me. They had me numbered for the bottom....I tried to do work good as anybody; even done things by myself that two of us should 'a done....I used to think: now, no more hate'n, no more fight'n....I've done what is right....then something would happen to take it all out of me. I used to wonder why 'no goods' like some I knowed was get'n praised for doin' what they done. Guess it's cause they talked better'n I did and 'cause they had better places to sleep in at night."

Charlie often complained that he had to train college kids at work, but that they got all the praise and raises while he got nothing.

"They made me hate. Then they couldn't a made me like them without their changin' and they wasn't goin' to change."

Charlie was seventeen when he developed an obsession with a recurring delusion that death had him "marked." He confessed to James Reinhardt that the thought gave him a strange bewildering delight. "She comed in a dream....she tolded me... don't be in no hurry. I won't let you forget....One time, Death comed to me with a coffin and tolded me to get in...then the coffin sailed away with me in it till it comed to a big fire...the coffin sort of melted, I guess. I was down there on a street with great flames of fire on each side of me. But it wasn't hot like I'd always thought hell would be...It was more like beautiful flames of gold...then I woke up."

Charlie admitted to Reinhardt that Death not only came to him in dreams, "she comed when I was awake, too." Sometimes Death came outside a small window in his bedroom right before dawn and while he was asleep.

"I don't know how it was...but I would always wake up and see her standing there in the window....and all I could see would be the part from the waist up. It was kind of half human and half bear...only it didn't have no neck. It just tapered off from a big chest to a small pointed head....It didn't have no arms and no ears."

Death also appeared to Charlie in another way—through the sound of a whistle. "It was close and loud at first, but it got further and further away and the sound became mournful and sad until I couldn't hear it no more....For about a minute or two, I couldn't move my legs or arms."

Charlie professed to Reinhardt that he had no fear of death because he knew "the world on the other side couldn't be as bad as this one." He said he knew so because of "the coffin dream." "Besides, nobody has to tell me what a mean world this is."

22

Charlie thought the world was so mean because he had been denied the better things in life. "I haven't ever eaten in a high-class restaurant, never seen the New York Yankees play, or been to Los Angeles or New York City, or other places that books and magazines say are wonderful places to be at. There hadn't been a chance for me to have the opportunity, or privilege, for the best things in life."

Charlie also developed an unconscious search for disaster. He loved hot rods because they gave him assurance that "Death was close by." He would speed in his hot rod on hazardous road strips, one time thinking that he would help Death along by steering into a gorge. "But, I guess if Death had wanted any help she'd a tolded me."

The only thing Charlie seemed proud of was his skill with a gun. Aside from hot rods and his family, he admitted that firearms "have been my ruling passion, but between the firearms, and the automobiles, I'd rather hear the crack of a firearm than have or drive the finest car in the whole wide world. I love the smell of guns. I love to take a gun apart and put it together again. A gun gave me a feeling of power that nothing else could match...I remember once thinking that if the devil comed at me I would shoot him with a gun."

Rodney, Charlie's brother, once admitted to his wife Barbara that, while hunting, Charlie could not quit shooting once he pulled the trigger of his semi-automatic rifle. He shot "crazy-like" and emptied the gun at no target at all.

CHAPTER 3

It was a cold Saturday night in mid-November for everybody else in Lincoln, but not at the Bartlett residence. That night, Barb, Caril, and Betty Jean were far off in a make-believe world—on a warm, sandy Hawaii beach, where they were drinking out of coconut shells. Barb and Caril cut up the *Lincoln Journal* newspaper into long strips and made a hula skirt for Betty Jean by tying a belt around the strips to hold them to her waist. They hung clothespins on the ends of the strips and sang while Betty Jean danced the hula.

"Now twirl around," they said as the skirt would sway this way and that way.

"Oh," the older sisters cried, "Look at the hula dancer!"

Velda shook her head, laughing while little Betty Jean grinned from ear to ear.

Just then, they heard a knock on the front door. Barb shot a furtive look at Caril and her mother and went to answer the door. It was Barb's boyfriend, Bob Von Busch, and a friend. Caril was pleased to see Bob as much as Barb was. Bob and Barb almost always took Caril out with them. One time they went swimming at the municipal park and some smart aleck scooped up Caril and swam with her to the deep end. Despite Caril's screaming that she couldn't swim, he dropped her into the deep water and Caril went down twice. It was Bob who jumped in and saved her from drowning. Caril owed him her life.

Bob introduced his friend to Caril and said his name was Charlie Starkweather. Charlie was about 5'5" and had the reddest head of hair Caril had ever seen and the prettiest green eyes.

"We thought we'd go to the Runza, Mrs. Bartlett." Runza was the name of a local fast-food drive-through where sandwiches were made with bread dough stuffed with ground beef, cabbage, and onions. "Is it alright if Caril comes along?" Bob asked.

Although the family had eaten dinner and the girls couldn't possibly be hungry, there was always room for a Runza.

"Yes, I guess it's okay," Mrs. Bartlett said, "but I don't want the girls to get home too late."

The foursome drove over to the Runza in Bob's car. Caril and Charlie sat in the backseat. Charlie was quiet.

To break the ice, Caril asked, "Are you any relation to Robert Starkweather—he's a boy in my class at school."

"Robert is my younger brother," Charlie said. "I'm eighteen."

Wow, thought Caril, an older boy!

Charlie and Caril liked each other right away. Charlie couldn't take his eyes off Caril's beautiful blue eyes, and Caril couldn't stop laughing at the things Charlie would say and the way he could mimic people. And he looked so cool in his black leather jacket, blue jeans, and cowboy boots, with a cigarette always dangling out of the corner of his mouth. It always seemed ready to fall out of his mouth, but never did. A real James Dean in the flesh.

"Do you work somewhere here in town?" Caril asked Charlie.

"Yeah. I'm a foreman over a bunch of guys at the Western Newspaper Union."

Later that night when Caril and Barb were getting ready for bed, Caril told her sister that she thought Charlie Starkweather was really cool and hoped she got to see him again. Barb said she thought that could be arranged, and she thought to herself: mission accomplished!

She and her boyfriend Bob wouldn't feel bad anymore about her dropping Charlie for Bob. From that night forward, the four of them went everywhere together. They went to the movies at the Nebraska Theater on O Street, to the Runza, and to the car races at Capitol Beach. At the time, Capitol Beach was called the "Coney Island of the West"; it featured a saltwater swimming pool, dance hall, and amusement park.

Marion protested to Velda that Caril Ann was much too young to date. Velda told him not to worry so much; Caril and Charlie never went out alone; they had two chaperones with them at all times. Besides, Charlie seemed like a very nice young man. He would have to be if he was a friend of Bob's.

Charlie was the king of the demolition derby, and Caril thrilled at watching his bravery. He drove his own car in the derby. Caril would scream in excitement when Charlie won at "chicken-out." He was by far one of the most exciting things that had ever happened to her. And as for Charlie, he had really fallen for Caril. He placed her high on a pedestal, something he had never done with anyone before.

Caril developed a great tenderness for Charlie. She fussed over him like a mother hen after his accident with the paper baler at the Western Union Newspaper, where he worked. The baler was a large piece of machinery that compressed and bound paper into solid bales; Charlie was injured when he was hit in the head by a piece of moving equipment. The injury caused recurring headaches. Caril had worried about him ever since the accident. Early on in their relationship, she noted he did not feel good about himself, and it saddened her when he would put himself down. He was a loner and would sometimes get into melancholy moods and complain about how short he was, how he had bowlegs and a speech impediment, and had hair as red as Bozo the Clown's. Caril would laugh at him and tell him that he was just the right height for her; that she loved his legs and the more bowed they were the better she liked them. As for his hair, Caril would pull a strand out of his head and say she loved every hair on his head.

Charlie bought Caril little trinkets and started spending all his money on her. Caril never asked Charlie for anything. She said she was born poor and that things didn't matter to her, only love mattered to her. She told Charlie she didn't want him to spend his money on her. She just wanted him to love her. Charlie's love made her feel special and worthwhile. She knew her family had to love her, but she now had earned the love of an older boy for no other reason than just by being herself. In a way, Charlie's love for Caril made up for the neglect she felt from her birth father, who dropped out of her life when her parents divorced. For Caril, having an older boyfriend gave her a sense of power; she could wrap him around her little finger.

Even though he was an older boy, Charlie never went any further with Caril than "first base," or French kissing. According to Bob Von Busch, "These weren't hot dates at all. It was more like a bunch of kids just piling in the car and looking for a good time. Charlie was pretty young for his age. He wasn't much for making out at all. To tell the truth, I don't think he knew what to do. He talked about it a lot, but when it came down to doing anything I think he just got too excited. And Caril was awfully young, too—she didn't know her way around nearly as well as people thought." All the time Charlie dated Caril, he never once mentioned his fascination with death to her. Nor did he ever reveal to her his obsession with guns and knives.

Charlie's family didn't like the fact that he seemed to spend every spare minute of his time with Caril and seemed to forget about his brothers and the rest of the family. Nothing else seemed to matter to him but Caril Ann. But, although he loved Caril, loving her never caused him to stop hating the rest of the world.

On February 14, 1957, Caril's sister, Barb, married Bob Von Busch in Council Bluffs, Iowa. Both being sixteen, they were too young to get married in Nebraska. Velda and Marion weren't thrilled about their daughter marrying at such a young age, but she was adamant and Bob Von Busch was a nice young man with a steady job as a garbage collector. After their marriage, the newlyweds moved into the tenement house run by Mae Holley.

Caril took over Barb's babysitting job for the five children down the street. Every day after school, between 4:00 and 9:00 P.M., Caril watched five children ranging in ages from six months to eight years old. Their mother, Virginia, worked at the Tastee-Inn at nights and their father, Sonny, drove a cement truck. Caril would change the baby's diapers, feed her, and rock her to sleep. She baked cakes for the older children, cooked their dinner, bathed the younger ones, and got them ready for bed. It was a lot of responsibility for a thirteen-year-old girl.

After Barb left home and Caril finally got an empty bed to herself, Betty Jean insisted on sleeping with her big sister. One night Caril woke up to find Betty Jean tugging at her breast and smacking her lips in her sleep! Shocked, Caril picked up the half-asleep little girl, took her to her mother's bedroom, and said "Mom, Betty Jean wants something I can't give to her. You take her!"

Charlie started teaching Caril how to drive a car. They practiced out in the country in his 1941 blue Ford. Caril felt very grown up at learning to drive at thirteen. None of the other girls in her class had an older boyfriend who was teaching them how to drive. Charlie also took Caril hunting outside the nearby community of Bennet. Although she never met the kind farmer who allowed Charlie and his friends to hunt on his property, she knew he was elderly and his name was August Meyer. Charlie and Caril hunted on his land twice, but they never went alone. Barb and Bob accompanied them, along with Rodney Starkweather and his wife, Barbara.

In the late spring, Caril's sister Barb found out she was going to be a mother! They were all hoping for a girl, especially Velda. She was always talking about her future little granddaughter and how nice it would be to have another little girl in the family. Velda, Barb, and Caril would dream about the baby-girl-to-be and plan what little dresses they would buy her and what color ribbons they would tie in her hair.

Charlie was laughing his head off. Caril had just told him the story about Marion's garden. Marion was always growing a summer garden, and he kept bees, too. He had just dug a garden and was planting seeds. Betty Jean was following her father around, and as soon as Marion planted a seed Betty Jean would pick it up. She thought her father had dropped it by mistake. Marion thought he planted a whole garden until he turned around and Betty Jean handed him all the seeds he thought were planted.

What an idiot, Charlie thought. He was glad Marion had to do it all over again. Charlie and Marion didn't like each other and neither one of them could keep his feelings hidden from the other. Marion thought Charlie was too old for Caril and that she shouldn't be spending so much time with him. Why, she still read comic books and went roller skating. Marion also didn't like the fact that Barb had gotten married at such a young age and now was going to have a baby. He didn't want to see Caril follow in her sister's footsteps. He was encouraging Caril to get an education and become a nurse as she always wanted to. And there was something about Charlie he just didn't like but couldn't put his finger on.

There was also that one incident Caril told him about when she came home from school and found her mother cleaning and bandaging up a knife wound on Charlie's face. How in the hell did he get that if he wasn't out fighting with some hooligans! Marion would have had a lot more to worry about if he only knew about Charlie's beer-joint visits, his obsession with guns, and his visits with Death.

One evening when Charlie arrived at Caril's house, he appeared sad, but within a few minutes of being with Caril he was grinning from ear to ear. She had that effect on him. It seemed only Caril could take the look of despair off his face and make him enjoy life for a little while. Without Caril, life wasn't worth living for Charlie. He was mad at the whole world. At work, upper management had hired some college boys for the summer. Those good-for-nothings had already gotten promotions while Charlie, who trained them, got nothing—just because they go to college and talk better and sleep in better places than he did.

He wondered, how come I always get left at the bottom? What kind of future do I have at this place anyhow? I'll never make enough money to take care of Caril the way I want to. I'll never get promoted because I come from a poor neighborhood. This job is taking me nowhere fast. It's been like this for me ever since kindergarten, always getting the raw end of the deal!

Over the past few weeks, Caril had begun to worry about Charlie. He was always telling tall tales about being a sheriff in Texas and how many Indians he had caught. At first his stories were entertaining and obviously made up to make her laugh. But now, sometimes it seemed as though Charlie really believed them. And why was he so keen about making a lot of money? She told him from the beginning that all she really wanted from him was for him to love her.

In July, Charlie quit his job at the Western Newspaper Union. Marion was not happy—now the guy doesn't even have a job, he thought. Now he'll probably be over here even more. Maybe he'll move in next. He might as well. It seemed like every time Marion looked up, that Starkweather clown was there. Doesn't he have anything else to do? At least Caril has other interests, thought Marion. Taking care of five children every night, looking out for Betty Jean during the day, and helping her mother with the household work. The only time Caril seemed to disappear was after a chicken was killed and it came time to pluck it.

As for Caril, she had never been happier in her life. She had friends in school and in the neighborhood; she doted on Betty Jean and just about spent all her babysitting money on the little girl. Caril adored her mother and older sister and was planning for her baby niece that winter. And she had a stepfather who finally provided all the things for her family that her real father never did. Never once did Caril worry about coming home from school to find her mother packing boxes because they were being evicted. Never once did Caril and her family go without a warm coat or worry about when their next meal would be.

Marion Bartlett gave her a sense of stability that her natural father never did. And Marion loved Caril and Barb just as much as he loved Betty Jean, whom he had fathered. He never bought Betty Jean a treat without buying something for Barb and Caril. Even though Barb was married and planning a family of her own, she still came to see her mother almost every day. Barb often came over to help Velda and Caril with the washing. Soon, Marion hoped to buy Velda a washing machine. Maybe for a Christmas present.

Another school year began and Caril was now in the eighth grade at Whittier Junior High School. Charlie was now working with his brother Rodney as a garbage collector for Harry Niederhaus.

On weekdays, Caril could take the bus to school with her friend and neighbor, Bonnie Gardner. Every morning, Bonnie would walk to Caril's house to pick her up and both girls would then walk together down the road to catch the bus. After school, Caril would drive Charlie's car home, which he'd leave parked across the street from Caril's school and get a buddy to drive him home.

Charlie sold his '41 Ford, and his father, Guy, cosigned a loan for $150.00 for Charlie to buy a newer car—a 1949 blue Ford with a backseat. Both Guy and Charlie were responsible for maintaining the car insurance. Guy never liked the idea that his son allowed Caril to drive the car and warned him to stop this practice.

At first, driving Charlie's car home from school was a blast. Caril would get behind the school bus and honk the horn, thinking, Look at me everybody! I'm driving a car and you're in a dumb old school bus. One afternoon she pulled out from a parking space in front of an oncoming car. The car hit her and forced her to hit another car. Her girlfriend from school jumped out, and Caril waited alone for the police to arrive. The cops took down her name and address. When they asked for her phone number, Caril replied that her family didn't have a phone.

Caril started to walk home, crying. Fortunately, Bob Von Busch, her sister's husband, spotted her and picked her up. Caril explained what had happened and told him she was afraid to tell her father. Bob told her to wait in the car and he would go inside first and explain the situation to Marion. She just knew she was in for it this time. However, Marion came out of the house, took Caril in his arms, and asked her if she was hurt. Caril, crying, said, "No," and promised her stepfather she would never drive again. For this infraction, Caril was ordered by a judge to write an essay on the hazards of underage driving.

Charlie fared much worse. His dad, Guy, became so angry that he threw Charlie out of the house, literally—out the window! Charlie went to stay with Caril's sister, Barb, and her husband, Bob, at Mae Holley's tenement house; he would stay there until an elderly tenant moved out and a room became available.

When Charlie explained to Caril about how angry his father was with both of them, she wondered why his dad should be mad at her. It was Charlie's idea for her to drive the car, not hers. In fact, he was adamant about her driving.

Caril had noticed a gradual change in Charlie. He was becoming jealous, even possessive of her. He was always questioning her about her every move, accusing her of talking to other boys in class. He had long tried to get her to quit her job babysitting so they could spend more time together. He kept telling Caril that he could take care of her. One day Charlie brought over a signature card from First National Bank for Caril to sign. It was a savings account Charlie had opened. He told Caril that if he ever got killed while running around with his gang, he wanted her to have his money.

Caril couldn't seem to get away from him. He even lived in the same building now with her sister and grandmother. Whenever she would visit one of them, Charlie turned up like radar. When she was alone with Charlie, he would tell her that he was going to quit his job as a garbage man and move back to Texas where he could resume his duties as a sheriff and catch Indians. He was going to make a lot of money and take her away where they could be alone together, just the two of them in their own little world where nobody else would bother them. Caril wondered whether Charlie was actually starting to believe his own crazy stories.

In the middle of the night, Charlie suddenly awoke from another dream. In this dream, he was in his car that was swerving to the sound of bullets whizzing by and the frenzied laughter of Caril, who was clinging to his arm. He realized that he only lived for Caril, that she was the only thing on earth that would never fade from his sight. She would go with him along the road to the next world. But, he wondered what he would do if her parents threatened to kill him if he didn't leave her alone? He'd just have to get her away and let her see that he'd kill for her. Soon, he thought, I'll be buried with the dead. Better to be left to rot on some high hill behind a rock, and be remembered, than to be buried alive in some stinkin' place, and go to bed smelly like a garbage can every night.

As he lay staring up at the ceiling, he thought of the people he hated whose garbage he picked up. He had to look polite while he was heaving up their garbage, but at the same time, he just wanted to explode and throw garbage in some bitch's face! Look around this place. How long can I live here like this? Forty years? That's too long. Ten years? Too long. Better a week with Caril who loves me for what I am. Lying in her white arms makes me feel like an infant for a little while. Other girls want a guy for a steady job and a paycheck, and that's all.

For the life I live, the job I have, the place I live in, that kind of girl wouldn't have no excitement. Just stay in one place and go nowhere. I must get money for Caril and get us the hell out of here! I know the end is coming near. She's the only thing that will go with me along the road to the next world, where we'll have a little world all our own. Me and Caril. Alone. A girl to go with me to the end. And the trail must end in a blaze of glory.

He drifted off to sleep for a little while. He woke up clutching an imaginary gun. He was dreaming of death again. Death had come and talked to Charlie again. This time he found himself in a coffin surrounded by beautiful flames. But the flames didn't burn; it was just like being surrounded by beautiful gold. Soon, soon it would be here, and he knew he wasn't afraid.

Suddenly, he was awakened by the voice of his brother Rodney, who was telling him it was time to go to work. More garbage to pick up. Charlie dragged himself out of bed, filled with hate and dread about the new day.

Caril quit her job babysitting the five children without any warning. When Virginia, the children's mother, drove over to Caril's house to find out why, Caril explained that Sonny, Virginia's husband, smirked at her and told her she looked pregnant! Caril was so offended that she refused to be in the same house with that man again. She explained to Virginia that if she wanted her to watch her children, that from now on she would have to drop them off at Caril's house. But Virginia found another babysitter, and Caril's evenings were now free. Charlie was glad about this and no doubt thought that they would be able to spend more time together. All he wanted was to be alone with Caril. He barely saw his family anymore and didn't spend much time with Rodney after work. He spent all his money on gifts for Caril and sometimes couldn't afford to pay his rent. When that happened, Mae Holley, the landlady, would lock him out of his room. Charlie had no choice but to sleep in his car at the Crest Service filling station on Cornhusker Highway.

Sometimes Charlie would stop by the Western Newspaper Union to chat with some former work buddies after his garbage rounds. One day he came in and announced that he and Caril had just gotten married. Donald Gillham, one of the employees who heard this announcement, met Caril just once when he dropped Charlie off at her house on Belmont to work on his car that had broken down. He asked Charlie who signed for him and Caril to get married. He knew that Nebraska required you to be at least twenty-one years of age to get married without a parent's consent. Charlie said nobody did, and Gillham really didn't feel like making an issue out of it. About one week later, Charlie stopped by and announced that he was going to be a father! Gillham didn't know whether to believe Charlie or not. He was always joking around and nobody really took him seriously.

Over the past several months, Charlie had made friends with a graveyard shift attendant at the Crest Service Station. Robert McClung worked at the station from 11:00 P.M. until 7:00 A.M. He felt sorry for Charlie and let him sleep in his car in the parking lot whenever he got into a fight with his father and, after he left home, whenever he'd get locked out of his apartment for not paying rent. Charlie used the station's restroom to wash up. McClung thought of this man as a waif who used the service station as his home away from home. But he also thought Charlie was a bit strange and wanted to keep his distance, so he never even asked Charlie his name.

Charlie would read comic books in the station and talk about hunting and cars. One time, in the middle of a story,

Charlie fell asleep. He never seemed to have any money, and McClung once gave him a dollar to wash his car and was always floating Charlie for cigarettes and soda pop. Charlie was eager to help McClung out on the job and would often wipe windshields when McClung got too busy. McClung saw the strange redhead as a very lonely young man.

Cecil Bowlin, the other attendant at the Crest Service Station, didn't have as much patience with Charlie. Bowlin didn't like the unusual interest Charlie showed when cash was counted at the change of shifts every night at 11:00 P.M. He even told his boss, Vernon Dopp, about this. Dopp told Bowlin that whenever he was in charge of the station and saw people hanging around, which he objected to, that he should run 'em off.

CHAPTER 4

Early morning, December 2, 1957

On December 2, 1957, the readers of the early-morning *Lincoln Journal* saw the front-page headline proclaiming, "Lincolnite Slain! Theft Motive Seen!" Under the headline was a photograph of the victim; it showed a smiling, pleasant-faced young man by the name of Robert George Colvert. Described as a "victim on lonely road," Colvert was found dead on a gravel road north of Lincoln; he had been killed by a shotgun blast fired at close range to the back of his head. Colvert, recently discharged from the Navy, was a twenty-one-year-old expectant father. He had replaced the previous night attendant at the Crest Service Station about a month earlier.

Wilbur Stalons, operator of the Nebraska Detective Agency of Lincoln, found Colvert's body at 5:15 early Sunday morning while making his rounds of businesses on Cornhusker Highway.

Lancaster County Sheriff Merle Karnopp reported that his men and members of the Safety Patrol checked out the entire area on foot for clues but no sign of a murder weapon was found. He stated, "There is no question but that robbery was the motive" in the slaying. Karnopp opined that an unknown person or persons came into the station between 11:00 P.M. Saturday and 4:00 A.M. Sunday, robbed Colvert of his night's receipts, and drove him to 30th and Superior Avenue where he shot him in the back of his head with a shotgun. Crest Service Station operator Vernon Dopp estimated that about $160.00 was taken from the till and about $66.00 off Colvert's person.

Dopp also stated that Colvert did not know the combination to the safe that was mounted in concrete under a counter. The safe indicated no signs of an attempted forced entry. C. B. Hermance, a farmer who lived on the corner of 27th and Superior, about a quarter mile away from the murder scene, reported hearing nothing unusual during the night.

December 2, 1957, 10:00 A.M.

Mrs. Katherine Kamp, owner of a used-clothing consignment store and gift shop on North 12th Street, felt something just wasn't right. A regular customer of hers was acting odd. A young man, no more than 5'6" with fiery red hair and what she could only describe as "cat's eyes" was picking out merchandise and laying it down on the counter without looking at any of the prices. Usually, this man took his time checking out the prices on the pin tickets and never spent more than two dollars at a time—a few shirts for a quarter apiece and a pair of underwear. But today he was on a veritable shopping spree. Overshorts, a jacket, shoes, four or five shirts, several undershirts, and some jockey shorts. He'd never bought this much stuff before.

When it came time to pay, the man asked Mrs. Kamp if he could pay in change. Mrs. Kamp, who needed the change, said yes. But, she didn't think he would pay it *all* in change. First, he counted out silver dollars, then quarters, nickels, and dimes. The bill came to $9.55. He even threw down too much money; Mrs. Kamp had to call him back and give him his change. As the man left the store, Mrs. Kamp thought to herself that he must have gotten lucky at a craps game last night.

Later on, while listening to the noon news, Mrs. Kamp heard about last night's slaying of Robert Colvert. The news mentioned that a robbery had also taken place. Becoming suspicious, Mrs. Kamp called the police station which sent over a police detective to take her statement.

Mrs. Kamp asked Detective Davis, "What kind of denominations were stolen from the Crest Service Station?"

"Everything," he answered.

Mrs. Kamp described what had occurred just two hours ago when a regular customer of two years came in and bought a lot of merchandise with all silver. She gave a detailed description of the man, right down to the blotchy freckles on his face and the broken horn-rimmed glasses patched up on the left side with adhesive tape. She described his eyes being betwixt and between green and blue and that he was a "fooler," meaning his age could be anywhere between twenty and twenty-six.

Later that day, the detective came back with four pictures of various suspects to show Mrs. Kamp, but none of them were of the young red-haired man who had shopped in the store earlier. She was unable to assist the Lincoln police with their ongoing investigation of the homicide they had on their hands.

The next day, Charlie paid his landlady, Mae Holley, the back rent he owed. Mae and her husband, Orlin, noticed that he was wearing new clothes and asked him how he suddenly became so rich. Charlie explained that he took money out of his savings account. He then drove over to his parents' house and visited with his mom and dad. His mother, Helen, was especially happy to see him. Ever since Charlie had started dating Caril Fugate he was home less and less. His family didn't seem to exist for him anymore. He used to be so close with his brothers.

Now all that mattered to him was Caril. She seemed to have a hold on him nobody else ever did. Helen knew he spent all his money on her. When Charlie was living at home, as soon as he got home from work, he would change clothes and immediately leave the house to be with Caril. Helen hardly ever saw him back then, and she saw her son even less since Guy threw him out of the house after Caril had that car accident with his blue Ford. Helen was worried about her son. She wondered if he still got those terrible headaches that plagued him ever since his accident with the paper baler at work. Before Charlie left he told his folks his eyes were bothering him, and Guy told him that there was some aspirin in the medicine chest.

Caril was looking forward to Christmas. She knew that Marion was getting Velda a washing machine, and she couldn't wait to see the expression on her mother's face when she saw it. No more bending over a bucket for me either, thought Caril. She was also excited about giving her mother a music box with a little poodle on top. Betty Jean would be getting some play dishes from her. But the most exciting event to look forward to was a brand new baby girl she was sure her older sister Barb would add to the family this holiday season.

Charlie's head was killing him again—the headaches from his accident with the paper baler were recurring. Still, Charlie was intent on changing the tires of his 1949 Ford and painting the exterior black. He also removed the grille and used red paint to cover the space where the grille had been. When some buddies asked him the reason for the new paint job, Charlie told them some young drunks had smudged his car with paint. Little did they know that Charlie's real purpose was to paint the car a different color in case anyone had spotted his blue Ford at the Crest Gas station, where Robert Colvert had been murdered a week ealier.

The guys at the Western Newspaper Union were on their afternoon break, joking around with each other and chitchatting about their Christmas plans when Charlie Starkweather walked in. The mood was jovial, and every one of these guys knew how to take a ribbing. Donald Gillham even asked Charlie what he was going to do with all that money he got from robbing the filling station attendant at the Crest Service Station. Charlie answered that there were lots of things he could spend it on, and everybody started to laugh, including Charlie.

Christmas came and went too fast for Caril. There was a lot of excitement this year when she exchanged gifts with her family. The new washing machine almost did Velda in; she declared that for the first time in her life, she couldn't wait to wash a load of laundry. It was the first Christmas Barb spent with her family as a married woman. A pang of sadness came over Caril when she watched her older sister put on her coat to leave for her own house with her husband. Caril was closer to Barb than anyone else on earth. She missed the old days when they were small children sleeping in the same bed, sharing each other's secrets, dreams, and fears. Then she remembered how much different and better their lives were now. She had a real father now, a beautiful baby sister, and a very happy mother with a brand-new washing machine. As Barb kissed her mother good-bye, Velda told her that the next time they saw each other Barb would be holding her new daughter in her arms.

But it was little Bobbie Von Busch, a boy, who was welcomed into the world on December 30, 1957. When Velda first laid her eyes on her new grandson in the hospital, Barb asked her whether she was disappointed that he wasn't a girl. Velda assured her daughter that she was thrilled with little Bobbie, and that she couldn't take her eyes off of him. When Velda got back home, she decided to prove her unconditional acceptance of little Bobbie into the family by writing a poem:

Now that he has arrived
I hope you are satisfied.
It makes no difference to me.
Because I'm the grandmother, you see.

Caril kissed Charlie in the front seat of his '49 Ford, got out of the car, and walked up the double row of one-foot-by-twelve-foot planks that served as a sidewalk from the driveway to her front door. She waved good-night to him from the doorstep. They had made the rounds that night at the tenement house where Charlie lived at 425 North 10th. She and Charlie had visited her sister Barb, her grandmother, Pansy, and their landlady, Mae Holley. Mae's husband, Orlin, even took a picture of what he referred to as "the happy couple," Caril and Charlie, sitting on their living room love seat.

Orlin's expression, "the happy couple," troubled Caril. Tonight in Charlie's apartment, he started up with his crap again about moving back to Texas and resuming his duties as sheriff. He said he was tired of Lincoln and tired of all the people whose garbage he had to heave and was tired of the hole he had to live in because he only made forty-two dollars a week.

"It will be just you and me together, Caril. Where nobody will get in our way. When we get to Texas, we'll be rich and we can do whatever the hell we want to do." That's what Charlie kept saying as he repeatedly threw his knife against the wall.

Thank God Barb and Pansy lived in the same building as he did so he would have to shut up whenever they were around other people.

Caril had loved Charlie from the very beginning. She felt sorry for him and tried to build him up and make him like himself more, but he had been smothering her lately and talking crazy about making all this money which she knew he never could. He was always talking about buying her this and buying her that and how he wanted to be with her only—that nobody else mattered to him in this lousy world but Caril and only Caril.

Charlie was always demanding that she tell him everything she did every minute of the day—what other boys she talked to in school and what she told them that she didn't tell him. It was getting on her nerves. Caril felt trapped. All she wanted in life was to get an education so she could become a nurse one day. She needed time to accomplish this, and here's Charlie pressuring her to leave her family and move to Texas with him. I'm not ready for this, she told herself. Why can't he just slow down?

As Charlie watched Caril walk away from his car he thought about tomorrow and another day of garbage hauling before he would see her again, and he was hating it. Funny how loving Caril never made him love anybody else. He always heard how loving a girl makes a man love everybody else. But Charlie never tried to love anybody else; he got a thrill out of telling the world to go to hell. In fact, he didn't know how he could want to live at all, even with Caril, if he had to quit hating other people.

He knew that the world had given them each other and that they were going to make the world leave them alone. Everything turned on his wanting to be with Caril. To live with Caril and die with Caril. A girl to go all the way to the end with him. Before he met Caril he used to ask himself what is there in the world that would make him happy. Caril changed that. Caril gave him something new; she took away the dread. She made time pass fast. The end didn't even matter. People didn't bother him as much anymore, but he still hated them. Sometimes, lying in bed, Charlie would say to himself that Caril was thinking of him at that moment. She was thinking if there was anything worth saving in him, worth standing by, and whether he would fight for her if the chips were down. What would he do if her parents threatened to kill him if he wouldn't let her alone? Then he knew that he had to get Caril away from them. He had to let her see that he would even kill for her.

Charlie's boss Harry Niederhaus decided he'd had enough of this clown. Charlie was lazy and mouthed off to people driving behind the garbage truck most of the time he was on duty. Charlie's brother, Rodney Starkweather, was a great worker, and he was the only reason Harry gave Charlie a job in the first place. If it weren't for Rodney, Harry wouldn't have kept that good-for-nothing on his payroll for as long as he did. But today was the last straw. Charlie had told a customer of Harry's to go to hell. Rodney or no Rodney, that foul-mouthed redhead was history!

"Who gives a shit?" thought Charlie when Harry fired him. He knew that a man could get money without hauling garbage, that money was just lying around somewhere if he would just pick it up. He also knew how to shoot a gun—and he knew what it felt like to kill a man.

Sunday evening, January 19, 1958

Caril was helping her mother with the dishes when Charlie came over. She wasn't feeling very well that night and had to get ready for school the next morning. She could see that Charlie was in a foul mood, and she didn't feel like coaxing him out of it. He started accusing her of talking to some boy for a long time at school. He said she was going out on him and that he wasn't going to stand for it. Caril snapped back that she wasn't going out with anybody and that she was sick and tired of him always saying so. Even if she were going out with somebody else, what was it to him anyway? They weren't married or engaged.

Caril told Charlie, "If you're going to be in such a bad mood, just get out and go home." "I'm not going anywhere. I'm staying right here," he said. He was getting on her nerves for the last time. "I want you to get out and not come back anymore. I don't want to see you ever again."

Velda told Charlie to go home because he was upsetting Caril and she didn't want any kind of scene there tonight.

Before leaving, Charlie looked at Caril and asked, "Are you serious about never seeing me anymore?"

"Yes," Caril said. She began to cry and ran out of the kitchen.

Tuesday morning, January 21, 1958

Tuesday morning for Velda Bartlett began the same as every other morning. She woke up at 6:00 A.M., lit a cigarette, made coffee and toast, sat down at the kitchen table, and opened the *Lincoln Journal,* the city's morning edition. The headlines that morning read "President Denies U.S. Weak." President Eisenhower had advised 5,000 diners at a $100.00-a-plate GOP rally not to pay any attention to those pessimists who said NATO bases could be wiped out by Soviet missiles! The nation's defenses were strong.

Velda also read that the famous soprano Roberta Peters was in town and would perform tonight with the Lincoln Symphony. Scanning the ads, she saw that Lincoln local dairies would reduce the price of home-delivered milk by one cent. Every penny saved helps, she thought.

Caril and Betty Jean joined her at the table. Caril put Betty Jean in her high chair and sat a glass of milk in front of her. Caril poured her mom another cup of coffee, got a cup for herself, and popped some bread into the toaster. Velda continued reading about how Johnny's Dairy Sweet over on 64th and Havelock was running a special introductory offer of one-half chicken dinner for 85 cents on Tuesdays and Wednesdays only.

Johnny was touting a new device to cook chicken: a "Pride & Joy—A Brand Spankin' New Broaster" that in just six minutes would give you the "best eatin' chicken you ever ate!"

"Honey, do you know where I can get a Broaster to cook chicken with?" Velda asked Caril jokingly.

"Try *Queen for a Day*," Caril kiddingly retorted as she left the table to get ready for school. The popular afternoon television program featured women who were down on their luck, and one of them would be chosen as "queen" for that day. She could win such things as cash prizes and a new washer and dryer. Maybe a new gas stove.

Evenings at the Bartlett home always included several hours of television. Tuesday evenings at 7:00, it was always a toss-up between the *Phil Silvers Show* and *Burns and Allen*. At 7:30, it was always *Eve Arden*. At 8:00, *To Tell the Truth*, and at 8:30 *Bob Cummings*. At 9:00, they watched *Don Ameche*. Velda liked comedies.

Marion had joined the family for breakfast. Velda got up to answer a knock at the front door. It was Caril's friend and neighbor Bonnie Gardner, who met Caril every morning to walk the few blocks to the bus that took them to Whittier Junior High School. Today Bonnie brought a sweater to loan Caril that would match her new black-and-white dress. Caril put the sweater on and kissed her mom, little sister, and dad good-bye.

As the two girls walked out the door, Caril heard her mother tell her dad, "Honey, milk goes down one cent tomorrow." Little did Caril realize that those words would be the last she would ever hear her mother speak.

When the school bell rang that morning, Caril's day began just the same as all the others: first period, English; second period, American History; third period, Mathematics. At 11:00 A.M. when the lunch bell rang, Caril walked to the drugstore across the street from her school and bought a bottle of pop, potato chips, and Ho-Hos.

At the same time Caril was eating lunch, Marion, Velda, and Betty Jean were visiting Velda's mother, Pansy Street, on North 10th Street. They were planning a family get-together at the

Bartletts on Saturday night. Pansy was bringing the hamburgers, which she would get from the restaurant where she worked as a fry cook. It was 11:15 A.M. and Pansy had to get ready to go to work. The Bartletts walked down the hall to Barb's apartment, where they chatted and admired the new baby.

It was 12:00 noon and Charlie and his brother Rodney had just quit their garbage rounds for Harry Niederhaus. Charlie had volunteered to help his brother on his garbage rounds this morning even though he had been fired recently for cussing at people. Charlie asked Rodney if he could borrow his .22 rifle; he said he was going hunting with Marion Bartlett that afternoon. Rodney drove Charlie over to his apartment, picked up his .22, and dropped Charlie off in front of his tenement building on North 10th.

It was about 12:30 when Marion, Velda, and Betty Jean left Barb's. Marion had to work that night and wanted to catch a few hours of sleep before starting his 5:00 P.M. shift at Watson Brothers Trucking as a night watchman. Barb carried her baby, Bobbie, in her arms and walked her family out the door into the hall. Barb couldn't wait to show off little Bobbie to everyone on Saturday night at the Bartletts. He had been sick ever since he was born and was just now feeling well enough to attend his first family outing.

Barb picked up his little hand and made him wave "bye-bye" to her family as Velda kissed her little grandson on the cheek and promised her eldest daughter that she'd have the pictures she took of the baby developed by Saturday night. When she returned to her apartment door, Barb was surprised to see Charlie carrying a rifle and standing outside his room which had been locked by Mae Holley—he'd failed to pay his rent again.

Charlie turned to Barb and started to say something to her, then stopped and walked away.

Virginia Robson's lunch hour was between 1:00 and 2:00 P.M. every day. She worked as a receptionist and filer at Watson Brothers Trucking. Today she decided to use her lunch hour to do some grocery shopping. She drove about one mile to the Safeway Store on North 27th and there she ran into one of her coworkers, Marion Bartlett. Virginia liked Mr. Bartlett; he was very friendly and nice. After exchanging pleasantries, Virginia went back to her shopping. It was about 1:20. At 2:00 when Virginia returned back to work, her replacement handed her a message she had taken from some man who phoned to say that Marion Bartlett was sick and wouldn't be coming into work for a few days. That's odd, thought Virginia. She had just seen Mr. Bartlett, and he seemed just fine to her.

It was a quarter to 2:00 and Caril was just finishing her project in art class. She was disappointed that Robert Starkweather wasn't in class today; she wanted to ask him to tell his brother Charlie to stop by the house sometime. She missed Charlie and was having second thoughts about breaking up with him. Then the bell rang; the school day would end after just one more period.

The last period of the day was homeroom. Today, the class was meeting in the gym because they were learning how to square-dance. Four couples made a square. First, they honored their partners, and then honored their corners. The giggling started after they dosey-doed and changed partners. It was hard for the teacher to keep discipline when most of the boys, out of embarrassment, made raspberries at their change of partners.

"Settle down or there won't be any music!" the teacher hollered.

They settled down.

The teacher put "The Turkey in the Straw" on the record player, and the pandemonium started up again. The music was loud and fast as dancers changed partners. During a break, Caril sat down on the lower bleachers for a minute to rest. She was out of breath.

Across town, Charlie was out of breath, too, as he stood in the Barletts' kitchen. But he wouldn't stop to take a rest. He had a lot of work to do before Caril came home. He cursed when he found he couldn't drag a heavy bundle through the back door. He walked into Marion's workroom, found a screwdriver, and proceeded to remove the back screen door.

CHAPTER 5

Tuesday afternoon, January 21, 1958

The school bell rang at 3:15. Caril met up with Bonnie, and both girls took the bus back home. As they stopped outside Caril's house, she took off the sweater she borrowed from Bonnie that morning and walked up to the house. Caril's dog was waiting by the front door.

She opened the screen door, let the dog inside, and the front door flew shut behind her. Caril turned around to find Charlie pointing a .22 rifle at her face.

"Sit down," he ordered.

Caril, her heart in her mouth, stared at Charlie, dumb-founded. She couldn't move.

"Sit down, I said!" Charlie bellowed as he pushed her down into the rocking chair.

Caril stood up. "Charlie, put down that gun and stop acting so silly!"

Starkweather shoved her back down again.

Angry now, Caril got up again, but this time Starkweather slapped her across the face so hard she fell back down. She started to cry.

He continued to aim his rifle at her while he began screaming something about her parents and Betty Jean. "They ain't here." Did she know that old lady who let him use her garage to work on his hot rod? Well, her folks were there. They're over there because they know too much. He asked them if they would go peacefully, and they said they would go peacefully, and he took 'em out to the old lady's house because they can't be here. They've been taken hostage at the old lady's house. Charlie and his gang are robbing a bank and need a place to hide out so her folks couldn't be here, he explained. Furthermore, his gang was watching this house, and if Caril tried to escape he'd know about it because his gang would tell him. And it would be her fault. Everything would be her fault.

Caril stared at Charlie and thought the aliens had finally taken over. Here he was, scaring her half to death, smacking her around and rattling on about another one of his stupid-ass, crazy fairy tales about playing cops and robbers and cowboys and Indians and God knows what his twisted brain could come up with. She had had all she was going to take from this crackpot. "I don't believe a word you're saying, Charlie. You're crazy!"

"If you don't shut up and do everything I tell you, they're dead, you hear? I'll make one phone call and they'll be dead, and it will be your fault. And don't ever, ever call me crazy again or I will kill them!"

Caril thought Charlie had really gone over the edge this time, as if he thought she was so stupid to believe an incredible yarn like this. Bank robbers! Hostages! The whole story was ridiculous and a figment of his pea-brained imagination! She stared at a Charlie Starkweather she had never seen before and wondered if he now believed in his own fantasies. She looked around. Her family wasn't home. With her dad's car still parked in the driveway, she wondered where they were. She had never once returned home from school without her mother being there. It was also dark in the house. She noticed that the drapes were drawn.

Her anger turned to fear as she realized she was quite alone in the house with a man with a rifle sitting across his lap. He was rubbing the rifle with a rag while he stared into space, into something only he could see. It was as though Caril wasn't in the room. She started to cry and asked Charlie where her folks were. But he didn't answer. He just stared at the wall behind her, his mind a million miles away.

She needed to do something to pull Charlie out of his trance and hopefully send him home. "Can I get up?" she asked.

"No," he shouted.

"Can't I just go make some coffee?" Maybe a dose of caffeine will snap this loony tune out of his trance, she thought. Starkweather followed Caril into the kitchen and sat in Betty Jean's high chair. He still kept rubbing the rifle with a rag, almost as if he were caressing it.

It was then that Caril noticed her mother's pistol inserted inside his belt behind his buckle. He looked over at the kitchen window that faced the alley and told Caril his gang was watching her. From the kitchen window someone could see right into the living room.

When the coffee had percolated, Starkweather refused a cup. But Caril poured herself a large one, hoping the caffeine would wake her up out of a bad dream.

"Go and change your clothes," Starkweather ordered. "Go put on a shirt and jeans."

"No, Charlie. I don't want to," Caril replied.

"Either you change your goddam clothes or I'll change them for you!" he screamed. He followed Caril as she walked to her room, placed a chair by her open door, and sat down and watched her change her clothes as he continued to rub his rifle.

After she changed her clothes, Caril walked into the living room and sat on the sofa. She asked him when she could see her mother. She was worried about her and Betty Jean.

"If you do everything I tell you to, you can see them later. If you don't, they'll get hurt, and it will be your fault."

"My fault? Charlie, please, this whole thing is so fantastic, I just can't believe...." Suddenly, Starkweather threw his gun at Caril. "You don't believe me? Then shoot me! Go ahead. Just shoot me!" he hollered.

"Cut it out, Charlie! I'm not shooting you. Why are you acting this way? Why are you acting so crazy? Quit acting so crazy," she cried.

"Shut the hell up! And didn't I tell you don't ever call me crazy!" he screamed.

She sat there on the davenport all night, not saying a word. Just sat there listening with incredulity to Starkweather's rambling on and on about how if the cops caught him, tell them O'Brien killed that guy at the Crest Station. He had nothing to do with it. He threw her mother's black-handled kitchen knife at the wall while she just sat watching him. Starkweather turned on the television. While Caril tried to watch *Burns and Allen,* he kept throwing the knife at the living room wall. This went on for hours until Caril finally lay down on the daven-port and fell asleep. Starkweather crawled next to her, and she cried, "Get off," but he wouldn't budge.

Wednesday, January 22, 1958

Caril awakened to the sound of her dog barking inces-santly. He always did so whenever anybody was outside the house. Starkweather looked out the window and saw Bonnie Gardner, Caril's classmate, waiting on the sidewalk. She was afraid of the dog and wouldn't come right up to the door.

"Get rid of her," he told Caril. "Don't tell her anything, or I'll kill her."

Caril went to the door, opened it, and told Bonnie that she was sick and wouldn't be going to school that day.

Caril turned on the television and *Jimmy Dean* was playing. At 8:00 A.M., *Captain Kangaroo* came on—little Betty Jean's favorite show in the world. She wondered whether her baby sister was watching *Captain Kangaroo* at the old lady's house. Starting to cry, Caril wondered whether her folks were all right and what they could be doing. She knew something was terribly wrong, and she also knew that she would do anything to get them all back home safe and sound again. The whole hostage story still seemed fantastic to Caril, but she had no choice but to believe it.

Starkweather kept telling her that his gang was outside the house watching her. If she made one false move, the gang would know and her family would be killed. They would watch her from the kitchen window and know whether she went to the front door. They would know if she tried to escape. He told her if she didn't do everything he told her that he would make one phone call and have his gang kill her family. And it would be too bad for Caril. It would be all her fault. So Caril did whatever Starkweather told her to do. If he wanted eggs, Caril cooked him eggs. When he ordered her to go outside and get the mail, she did it. When he told her to go outside and feed the dog, she did that. When he made her follow him to the bathroom and sit on the bed so he could see her when he needed to take a pee, she did it. When he told her to shut up and quit asking him about her family, she shut up. If he had told her to swing like a monkey from the trees, she would have found a way to do that, too.

In the afternoon, Starkweather's brother Rodney came to the door. Starkweather looked out the window and told Caril to get rid of him and not to let him in the house or he would kill him. Caril said he'd never kill his own brother, but Starkweather said he would if he had to. Rodney asked if Charlie was there because he had Rodney's rifle and he wanted it back. Caril said no, she didn't know where Charlie was, that she never knew where he was. Rodney thought Caril looked sick.

Later on that afternoon, Starkweather told Caril he had to go out and that he was going to tie her up. He cut up a pair of her mother's dish towels into strips and tied her hands together, tied her feet together, and then tied her hands to her feet. He placed her on her side on the davenport and turned on the television and left the house. She lay that way for hours. Caril knew it was about three in the afternoon because *Queen for a Day* was on. Caril tried to get loose. The dish towels were tied tight, and she got all sweaty and out of breath just from trying to get her hands free of the dish towels.

When Starkweather came home and saw that she had tried to get loose, he shook her up good and said if she tried anything like that again he would make one phone call and her family would be history. *Sky King* was about to go off the air. Starkweather changed the channel to watch *Wagon Train*. He loved westerns. He untied Caril. She sat crying on the davenport with him until the television test pattern came on.

Thursday, January 23, and Friday, January 24, 1958

The days spent isolated in the Bartlett house with Starkweather were all running together and monotonous for Caril. She only knew the days of the week by what was on TV, which was on constantly. Starkweather never let her out of his sight, not even to use the bathroom. At first Caril was mortified to relieve herself in front of him, then she just became numb to the embarrassment. She felt as though she were a sleepwalker and that any moment she would awaken from this nightmare. Fear and worry made it impossible for her to eat anything.

Starkweather had brought back some Neapolitan ice cream, potato chips, and three bottles of Pepsi from Hutson's, a small grocery store near Caril's house—all her favorite things that Marion usually didn't allow her to eat. But she was barely able to look at the food without feeling sick.

When Starkweather ordered her to go outside for anything, such as the mail, he told her he would be watching her from inside and she better not think of running. After a while Caril never thought of running. She was certain now of his bank robbery story and was also certain that she had to do everything possible to save the lives of her family. She wouldn't have tried to escape now even if the Lone Ranger himself pulled up in her driveway and offered to ride her away to safety on Silver.

People came to the house that week at different times. Marion's boss and another young man who worked with him came to the house to inquire where her dad was.

Starkweather told her to get rid of them and make up a convincing story, so she told them her dad was sick and wouldn't be to work until Monday.

Mrs. Yordy, the landlady, came one evening hoping to buy eggs as usual. Caril told her there were no eggs that week because everybody was sick.

Keep people away from this house, Starkweather kept repeating. "You let anybody through that door and I'll blow them away!"

Caril was never more conflicted in her life. She wanted to get away from Starkweather but didn't dare leave the house. She believed that someone was watching the house because whenever Starkweather left, her dog barked. Starkweather must be lurking outside the house testing me, she thought. If I were really alone, the dog would shut up. Every time Starkweather left the house, he tied up Caril. He cut down the rope hanging in the living room on which Velda used to dry clothes and tied her up with it. Once he gagged her with a dish towel.

There were no conversations between them. Only the television audio cut through the deadly silence. Starkweather was in his own world and hardly responded to her questions about her family. It was as though he were in a constant daze. All he did was throw her mom's knife against the walls. That knife was never out of his hands. Neither was her mom's pistol, which was still tucked inside his belt.

Saturday, January 25, 1958

Caril dozed in the rocking chair and woke up only to find that Starkweather had sawed off her dad's .410 shotgun. He told her it would shoot better. Caril told him that her dad was really going to be mad at him when he found out about it. She thought it was strange Starkweather had been asking her whether her dad had a shotgun in the house. She knew her dad kept a shotgun in a cloth cover in her bedroom closet, but she had never seen the gun out of its cover and had never seen her dad ever take it out to use it.

At 4:30 that afternoon, Caril's worst fears came true, when, hearing the dog bark, she looked out the window to see her older sister, Barb, in the drizzling rain, walking up the sidewalk with her husband, Bob, behind her carrying little Bobbie in his arms. Oddly enough, Bob noticed that all the curtains were drawn, even the window shade in the front-door window. He thought nobody was home and told the cabbie to wait until his wife found out if her folks were home.

Starkweather, with the shotgun in his hands, ordered Caril to get rid of them and not say anything, because if she did he would shoot them all.

She opened the front door and stood between it and the screen door and hollered out, "Go away! Go away, Barb! Don't come any closer. Everybody is sick with the flu. So go away if you know what's good for you or mother will get hurt!"

The tone of Caril's voice and the look on her pale face stunned Barb so much that she stopped dead in her tracks. She turned to Bob and told him to take Bobbie back into the cab. Then she said to Caril that she wanted to see her mother.

Furiously, Caril turned on Barb and screamed for her not to come any closer if she didn't want to see their mother get hurt. "You don't want your baby to catch the flu, do you? Then go away now if you know what's good for you!"

Barb had never seen Caril act this way before or, worse, turn her away. Shocked, Barb walked back to the cab and got back inside. Starkweather told Caril she was a big blabbermouth and to go out to the cab and say something to make them think that nothing was wrong.

So Caril ran out to the cab, and Barb opened the window and noticed how frightened Caril was. Crying and grimacing at the same time, Caril told her, "I'm sorry to be so cranky but I have to, so just leave or mother will get hurt!" At this point, Caril feared more for her family than she did for herself. She turned and ran back into the house, crying.

Dumbfounded, Barb asked the driver to take them home.

Bob knew something was wrong in that house. At first, he thought nobody was home when he saw all the curtains drawn. But then Caril ran out of the house and started talking crazy. It wasn't like her to turn her own sister away, either. And Caril looked so different. Awfully run down and tired. Her face was pale and her hair all disheveled. She looked just plain rough, and that wasn't like his sister-in-law at all.

Shortly after Barb and her family arrived home, Rodney Starkweather, Charlie's brother, stopped by. Bob asked Rodney to go across the street with him to the police station. They met with the desk sergeant who sent them to talk to Captain Joe Harbaugh. Bob told Captain Harbaugh about the strange visit and what Caril said about her mother's life being in their hands and asked him to search the house.

Harbaugh said a search couldn't be done but that he would send two men to check out the situation. "Come back in about a half an hour," Captain Harbaugh told Bob and Rodney.

Captain Harbaugh sent two officers, Donald Kahler and Frank Soukup, out to check on the Barletts. They arrived at Belmont at 9:25 P.M. and parked their car on the street. They hesitated on the Bartletts' sidewalk when Caril's dog stood barking his head off at them. When they approached the house, Officer Soukup had to knock on the door about four times before anybody opened it. A young girl wearing a housecoat opened the door, and Soukup thought she looked as though she just woke up. He asked her what the trouble was here.

"There's no trouble here," the young girl answered.

Officer Soukup said, "We got a call that you were turning away people from this house and not allowing anybody inside."

Caril relayed the story about her family being sick with the flu and how she didn't want anybody else to catch it.

"What's your name?" the officer asked the girl.

"My name is Caril Fugate, but my mother's last name is Bartlett. She married a second time."

Officer Soukup responded, "It's funny your brother-in-law would call us down here just because you wouldn't let them in to try to keep them from getting the flu."

Caril explained that her brother-in-law didn't like her family and kept sticking his nose in everybody's business. He just called the police because he didn't get along with her family, that's all. At that moment, Caril's dog, his paws covered in mud, was jumping up and down on the officer's pants. Caril opened the screen door and the dog slipped on past the officers into the house. Convinced that nothing was amiss, the officers left and drove to Cornhusker where they stopped at a call box to relay that message to headquarters.

Bob had wanted to make sure Captain Harbaugh sent somebody out there, so he and Rodney had driven back out to the Bartlett house and parked Rodney's car about a half block away from the house. They watched the two police officers speak to Caril for about five minutes and then leave. Bob and Rodney followed the two policemen to Cornhusker and saw them stop at the call box.

After they trailed the police officers, Bob and Rodney drove back to the Bartletts' house. Caril opened the door and again stood between it and the screen door.

"I want to see your mother and pay her for doing my family's laundry," Bob told her. Caril once again told him that they were all asleep and for him not to bother anybody. Bob grabbed the screen door and said he was coming in anyway. As he grabbed the screen door, he noticed the front door move toward Caril.

"Please don't try to get in," she cried. "My mom's life will be in your hands if you try to get in!" Bob and Rodney left.

After Bob and Rodney left the house, Starkweather tied up Caril and left her sitting in the chair with the television on. She had no idea where he was going and didn't even want to know at that point. As she began to cry again, she wondered why the tear ducts in her eyes hadn't dried up yet.

When Rodney and Bob arrived back at Bob's apartment, Barb told them that Charlie had just called to tell them that he was at Tate's Conoco Station and for them to come and pick him up. Charlie said that he would be walking back from Tate's on Cornhusker. Rodney and Bob first stopped at police headquarters to find out what the officers discovered at the Bartlett house. Captain Harbaugh told them that the Bartletts were sick and under a doctor's care and for Bob to leave them alone.

Rodney and Bob then drove to Tate's to pick up Charlie, but they didn't see him on Cornhusker. They asked the station attendant and the waitress at the café adjoining Tate's if they had seen a red-headed man wearing glasses, but both said they hadn't seen anybody fitting that description.

Approximately fifteen minutes after Rodney and Bob left for Tate's, Starkweather called Barb again and said that her mom, dad, and baby all had the flu and advised her not to go over to the house. He said he went to the store and got groceries for them and now he was back at Tate's and asked to have Bob come and get him.

When Bob arrived home that evening, he told Barb that Starkweather was nowhere to be found and that the cops weren't doing anything. He decided there was nothing more he could do that night, either.

Caril was kicking herself for those nasty things she had told the police about her brother-in-law, Bob. Part of her hoped the cops would repeat to Bob the lies she told about him, and then he would know something was wrong at her home, because she had never said nasty things about Bob before. On the other hand, what if the cops tell him what I said and he tips them off that something is wrong at home and the cops come back after Charlie and they encounter his gang and then Starkweather makes that phone call like he's been threatening to do and her family gets killed? Me and my big, fat mouth! She was totally alone for the first time in her life and wondered if she was doing the right thing. She kept telling herself that if she saved her family's lives then by all means she was doing things right. No matter what she had to do to save them, she would do it.

That evening Starkweather told Caril to go to her room, change into a nightgown, and get into bed. He also told her that he had just talked to her folks at the old lady's house, and they told him to be sure to tell Caril that she was to do anything he told her to do. Anything. Caril, mortified, stood with her back to Starkweather while she undressed. He was hollering at her to hurry up, but her hands shook so much she could barely unbutton her shirt. Once undressed and into one of her shorty nightgowns, she quickly jumped into her bed, pulled the covers over her head, and told Starkweather to get out.

But he kept standing over Caril's bed, looking at her. Then, he started to undress.

"What the hell are you doing? Get out of here!" she cried.

He pulled the covers down and lay next to her. He informed her again that her parents said for her to do anything he told her to do. He didn't seem to notice her sanitary napkin between her legs as he climbed on top of her and started touching her and kissing her and telling her how it was going to be one day with them. He said she was the only thing in the world he loved and he didn't need anybody else in the world but her. It's just you and me in our own little world. My own girl to go all the way to the end with me.

She turned her head to the side and prayed she might pass out, but she didn't pass out. She just lay there, helpless and awake, while Starkweather groaned softly and tried to enter her. No! She just couldn't do this, not this, she thought! During the entire time she had dated Charlie, they never did anything more than French kiss. Now she found herself naked in bed with him, and he was suddenly furious with her. He stopped whatever he was trying, then roughly rolled her over onto her stomach while he rubbed his penis between her two cheeks over and over and over again, all the time cussing and swearing and calling her filthy names. At just fourteen, Caril was not aware of just how the sex act was performed. In her innocence, she did not realize Starkweather was unable to get an erection.

Too frustrated to even speak, Starkweather rolled out of bed and cursed her out while he put his clothes back on. He turned on the television. Caril could hear the theme song from the TV western *Gunsmoke*, as she felt a wave of nausea come over her. She was glad she had an empty stomach so she couldn't vomit.

Sunday, January 26, 1958

Starkweather's sister, Laveda, came out to the Bartletts' house twice, once in the morning of January 26 and once in the evening. Caril whispered to her that Charlie was going to rob a bank with his gang and that her family was being held hostage.

Laveda couldn't really hear Caril well and was fed up with standing outside in the cold. She looked at Caril like she was just plain crazy and left.

Starkweather had enough of people coming up to the door. He told Caril to write a note and leave it on the front door to keep people away. Caril found a yellow permit to build that Marion had lying around in the dining room and wrote the following on it: "Stay away. Everybody is Sick with The Flu. Miss Bartlett." "Miss Bartlett" was underlined. There, she thought. If the "Miss Bartlett" doesn't give them all a clue that something's wrong here, nothing will. The only Miss Bartlett in this house is barely three years old and can't write.

CHAPTER 6

Monday, January 27, 1958

Once again, Caril's schoolmate, Bonnie Gardner, stopped at Caril's house before catching the bus for school. As she approached the Bartletts', Caril opened the door and Bonnie noticed the yellow note on the door that warned everybody about the flu, so she started to walk away when Caril called out to her. Caril asked Bonnie if she would turn her books in for her and bring her back her notebooks after school; it was the end of the semester and time to turn in books. Bonnie agreed.

Pansy Street had been disappointed but not worried when her daughter Lola had told her on Saturday that she didn't need to get the hamburgers because Velda, Marion, and Betty Jean were all sick with the flu and couldn't have the family over that night for their get-together. Lola told her mother that Barb and Bobbie had already been out to the house that day and Caril wouldn't let them in the house. However, something was nagging at Pansy now, and she decided she'd better get out to Belmont and investigate the matter herself. She had never gone this long without seeing her daughter, Velda, before.

Pansy took a cab out to Belmont and told the driver to wait. It was around 8:30 in the morning. When she got up to the front door, she found it open and saw Caril standing in the middle of the dining room.

Caril looked awfully white and was wearing a housecoat. She was staring terribly hard at her grandmother and began to shout, "Go away, Grandma! Go home, Grandmom, Oh, Granny, go away! Mama's life's in danger if you don't go away!" As she spoke, Starkweather, hidden, held a gun on her. But she feared more for her family's safety than she did for her own. Then, she backed away from the door, holding her left hand over her mouth and pointing over her shoulder. Pansy did not see that she was pointing to Charlie Starkweather.

Pansy shouted, "Velda, Velda, if you can't come to the door, at least come to where I can see you!"

But Velda never came to the door. And, oddly enough, little Betty Jean didn't make a sound.

Pansy became angry and hollered out to Caril, "Well, if you won't let me in here I'm going to town and get a search warrant. I will get in there!"

As soon as Pansy had left the Bartlett house, Starkweather said to Caril, "Get your coat. We're getting out of here."

Caril begged him to leave her home, but he spat back that the only place her grandmother could get a search warrant was at the police station.

He told her they were going to get his car at the Griggs, then he wrapped her dad's .410 shotgun he had sawed off in a blue blanket and carried it along with Velda's knife and pistol. Starkweather had already dropped off Rodney's .22 rifle one of the nights he left Caril tied up at the house.

Caril was wearing her black jeans, blue coat, white boots, and red scarf. It only took a short time to walk to the Griggs.

On the way over, Starkweather warned Caril that if she said anything, somebody would get hurt. When they arrived at the Griggs both of them went inside and Starkweather got his car keys. When he got to his car he noticed that the tire on the driver's side was flat, so he ordered Caril to go inside and get a screwdriver while he started to take off the wheel. He warned her again not to say anything because he would be watching, so she stood by the screen door and asked for a screwdriver. Once the tire was changed, they drove away. Starkweather drove to the Crest Service Station on Cornhusker and had his tank filled up and bought a map of Nebraska and neighboring states. He was waited on by Cecil Bowlin, the other attendant at the station where Robert Colvert had been robbed and then murdered on December 1, 1957.

61

Starkweather told Caril that he was driving over to the old lady's house where her family was being held hostage and when they got there she was to stay in the car because his gang would be watching her. The "old lady's house" to which he referred was owned by the Southworths, a kindly couple on his garbage route who allowed him to rent a space in one of their garages for him to work on his hot rod. Caril remained in the car while Starkweather went inside the garage and came back out with some wheels. She was crying because she was so close to her family but couldn't do anything about it.

The owner of Dale's Champion Service Station, Dale Smallcomb, and his employee, Lee Lamson, had just finished waxing the floor of their office when they saw a '49 black Ford pull up into the station, in front of the grease rack. Dale watched Starkweather get out of his car and hoped to himself that the man wouldn't step on his newly waxed floor, but the man walked into the office and asked if he could get his transmission checked.

Starkweather went back to the car, and Lee Lamson guided the car onto the rack. Starkweather bought two bottles of pop at the machine in the grease room and gave one of them to a young girl sitting in the front passenger's seat. The girl stayed in the car as it was lifted about eight feet up on the rack. Lamson noticed that the window on her side of the car was partially opened. Lamson checked the transmission, noticed that it was about a quart and a half low, and filled it up.

While hoisted up in the air, Caril tore a white piece of paper off the inside of the windshield, got a pencil from the glove compartment, and wrote, "Help. Police. Don't ignore," and stuck it inside of her right coat pocket. Now is my chance, she thought as she held the note in her right hand and lowered the window, even though the heat was turned off in the car and it was freezing outside. She didn't see Charlie anywhere around at the moment. "I'll slip this note to the attendant working on the transmission, and oh…I just can't do it. What if Charlie sees me do it? What if the attendant reads it and starts asking questions and Charlie is tipped off? So she put the note back inside her coat pocket, and the car was lowered to the floor of the service station.

Dale Smallcomb didn't like the looks of the redhead in the cowboy hat and tight Levis—the man looked nervous, just didn't appear right. Smallcomb was in the grease room but kept his eye on the redhead while he was at the cash register; he also noticed that the man kept looking out the office window. Smallcomb was concerned that he just might get robbed.

Starkweather came out of the office and bought another bottle of pop from the machine just as his car was being lowered to the ground. He then used the restroom and came back to the office and asked Smallcomb how much he owed. Smallcomb said he owed $1.20. When Starkweather asked if he could change a $20.00 bill, Smallcomb said no. A regular customer walked into the office and asked Smallcomb if he could cash a $10.00 check. Smallcomb said no. Starkweather dug into his pockets and found enough change to pay Smallcomb. When Starkweather left the office, Smallcomb cashed $10.00 for the man he had just refused a few minutes earlier.

Starkweather drove south on Highway 77, heading for the town of Bennet. He told Caril he was meeting his gang at his friend August Meyer's farm where they would finalize their plans to rob a bank. He stopped at Homer Tate's Conoco Station about eight miles south of Lincoln. The same building housed Brickey's Café, a popular stop between Lincoln and points south. At Tate's were two islands with two pumps at each; one island was directly in front of Tate's whereas the other one was in front of Brickey's. Starkweather pulled up to the island directly in front of Brickey's.

Martin Kruger, the station attendant, asked Starkweather what he needed.

"Fill 'er up," Starkweather answered.

Kruger approached the driver's side to wipe off the window, and Starkweather told him it wasn't necessary, that the windows were clean. Kruger noticed that the tank only took 45 cents to fill it up—it was almost full. Starkweather got out of the car and brought a tire out of the backseat, saying he wanted to fill it with air because it was leaking. Starkweather filled the tire and then wondered out loud whether the tire had a hole in it.

Homer Tate, the station's owner, said he would blow it up a little more to find out and that he would fix it. While Tate took the tire into the garage, he saw a young girl get out of the passenger's seat and heard her ask Starkweather what he wanted from Brickey's.

Starkweather said he'd have whatever she wanted.

"You sell .32s?" Starkweather asked the attendant, referring to bullets.

"No, we don't."

Then Starkweather asked Kruger whether they had any ammunition for a .22 rifle and a .410 shotgun. Starkweather bought one box of short .22 caliber rifle bullets; one box of long, hollow-nose .22s; and one box of .410 shotgun-gauge shells, size seven. Then he asked for a pair of work gloves and maps of Kansas, Missouri, and Nebraska. He paid for everything and left the garage for Brickey's.

About fifteen minutes earlier, Juanita Bell, the waitress at Brickey's, was cutting pies when she noticed a young girl walking rather rapidly toward the café. There were about three or four other customers already in the café when Caril walked over to the counter and ordered four hamburgers to go.

Juanita walked to the kitchen door and gave Mr. Brickey Caril's order and resumed cutting pies. Juanita was keenly aware that the young girl was staring holes into her; in fact, she never took her eyes off Juanita the whole time she sat at the counter. Juanita also noticed that the girl's right hand was draped over the counter while her left hand was in her coat pocket.

Caril thought to herself, if the waitress gets a little closer I'll pass her this note. Caril was pleading with her eyes to the waitress to please come a little closer. Please take this note I have and give it to the police. Please help me. I'm going somewhere I don't know. My family is being held hostage, and I don't know what to do. If you'll only just come a little closer, she thought.

It took about ten minutes or so to cook the hamburgers. Juanita wrapped them up, put them in a bag, and brought them over to Caril. By now, a young man had entered the café and gave the girl a $10.00 bill to pay for the hamburgers. Juanita went to the cash register, got change, and gave it to the girl. The girl turned around and bumped into the man and said something to him Juanita couldn't hear. She then saw the girl give the man a shove and watched them leave. As she left the café, the young girl kept staring at Juanita through the windows as she followed the man out to the car.

After being turned away by Caril at the Bartlett house, Pansy had climbed into the backseat of the cab, declaring that she had never been so angry in her life. "I am going to get into the Bartlett house and find out just what is the matter with my daughter if it is the last thing I ever do!"

After the cab dropped her off in front of the police station on 10th Street, Pansy stomped over to the front desk and told the sergeant sitting on the other side that she wanted somebody to go out with her to the Bartletts' house. "Something was very, very wrong over there," she said.

Just then, the telephone rang and the sergeant answered it. He listened and repeated back, "a gun, and a carton of cigarettes. Charles Starkweather."

"That's Caril's boyfriend," Pansy said.

The call was actually from Charlie's father, Guy Stark-weather, who phoned to tell the police that Charlie had just been to the Griggs' house, the neighbors who lived a couple of blocks from Caril's, and left. Guy wanted his son picked up by the police after hearing what his daughter Laveda repeated from her visit to Caril—that is, that Charlie was inside the Bartlett house with a gun and that he was going to rob a bank.

Two plain-clothes officers, Hansen and Fisher, got into a police car with Pansy and drove out to the Bartlett house around 10:00 A.M. After finding both doors locked, they raised the window in Velda's bedroom and entered the house. They unlocked the front door for Pansy to go in and look around. Pansy ran past the two officers and checked out every room in search of her daughter, even looking under the beds. But Velda's bed was perfectly made. The bed had clean sheets and pillowcases and a clean, pink coverlet. Velda's new drapes hung on the bedroom window, and the entire room looked too clean to have had three sick people in it, as Caril had said. In fact, nothing in the house caught Pansy's attention except that it was empty, and she was worried sick about her daughter and family.

Despite the fact that there was a sawed-off barrel of a .410 shotgun lying on top of the piano in plain sight, Officers Hansen and Fisher agreed with Pansy that nothing in the house looked amiss. Pansy didn't notice the shotgun; after all, she was looking for her daughter and nothing else.

Apparently, the officers didn't notice it either. Perhaps it was because they didn't take Pansy seriously. In fact, they advised Pansy to go home and not stick her nose into her married kids' affairs if they didn't want her around.

When Pansy got home, she and Barbara went to a neighbor's house to use her telephone to call all the hospitals in the area to see if maybe her daughter had been admitted to one of them. They got nowhere.

Pansy said to her granddaughter, "Barbara, it's now 11:00, Granny will have to go to work, but when Bobbie gets home, you tell Bobbie that Granny's not satisfied."

When Pansy arrived at the diner where she worked as a fry cook, she asked Al, her boss, if she could have the radio on in the kitchen because she was expecting to hear troubling news.

Bob Von Busch, husband to Caril's sister, Barb, had just quit his route for the day as a refuse hauler. He went straight back to Captain Harbaugh and asked him whether anything more was discovered with respect to the Bartlett family. Harbaugh told Bob that he thought the family went on vacation and left their young daughter at home and that she probably has her boyfriend staying with her in the house and didn't want anybody to know about it.

"Marion don't go away and leave his car, and he don't leave no fourteen-year-old-girl out there in the house alone. She goes everyplace they go," Bob said, at the end of his rope.

"Leave them alone," Harbaugh said to Bob. "You don't want to go stirring up trouble."

When Bob got home, he found Charlie's brother, Rodney, waiting for him. "Can you drive me back to the Bartlett home?" "Sure," Rodney replied.

When they arrived there, Bob noticed the card on the front door telling everybody to stay away. He tried to open the doors and the windows, but they all were locked. Marion's car was still in the driveway. He asked Rodney to drive around back to the alley.

It was 4:00 when Bob looked on the back porch and tried to open the door. Finding that door locked as well, he walked over to the chicken house and looked in. "Oh, my God," he said.

PART II

STARKWEATHER'S
Rampage

CHAPTER 7

The morning of January 28, 1958, the readers of *The Lincoln Star's* morning edition were shocked with the following headline: "BELMONT FAMILY SLAIN: Tot and Parents Found Dead in Apparent Murder."

The article went on to say that three members of the Marion Bartlett family, apparently the victims of a triple murder, were found dead about 4:30 P.M. Monday in two sheds behind their home at 924 Belmont. Dead were: Marion Bartlett, 57; his wife, Velda, 37; and their daughter, Betty Jean, who would have been three years old on February 11.

Lancaster County attorney Elmer Scheele said a preliminary autopsy report showed the parents died as the result of small-caliber bullet wounds in the head. There were also cuts "about their bodies" which "may have been made by a knife," Scheele said.

The little girl apparently died of a skull fracture, it was reported. She had no bullet wounds.

Scheele said no one had been taken into custody in connection with the crime, but added that authorities were seeking Mrs. Bartlett's daughter by a previous marriage and her boyfriend for questioning. He identified them as Caril Fugate, fourteen, and Charles R. Starkweather, nineteen. Fugate reportedly lived with her mother and stepfather at 924 Belmont. An address for Starkweather was not immediately available.

"Police in six states are seeking the pair, who reportedly were last seen about 5:30 P.M. southbound from Lincoln," Scheele said. "They may be armed," he added, but he declined to elaborate.

THE LINCOLN STAR

Fire 2-2232   Telephone 2-1234   Police 2-3641

FIFTY-SIXTH YEAR   No. 98   LINCOLN, NEB., TUESDAY MORNING, JANUARY 28, 1958   SEVEN CENTS

BELMONT FAMILY SLAIN

Congress

Atomic Gifts Asked

Power Is Urged To Give Allies A-Secrets

Tot And Parents Found Dead In Apparent Murder

Daughter, Boyfriend Sought For Questioning; Couple Shot, Child Had Skull Fracture

By DEL HARDING
Star Staff Writer

Authorities eye scene where bodies found. Two bodies were found in the shed at the left and one in the shed at right. The box in which one of the victims was located is in front of investigators. (Star Photo).

Navy Try At Space Given Up

Starkweather murdered Marion, Velda, and Betty Jean Bartlett on January 21st. Their bodies were not discovered until January 27th. Mr. and Mrs. Bartlett had been shot to death; the toddler died from a blow to the head.

Authorities reported the bodies of the Bartletts were found by Robert Von Busch, nineteen, a son-in-law of Mrs. Bartlett, and Rodney Starkweather, twenty-one, brother of Charles.

Von Busch and Rodney Starkweather had reportedly gone to see if anything was wrong after Velda Bartlett's mother, Pansy Street of Lincoln, had been refused admittance to the home by Caril Fugate about 9:00 A.M. Monday.

Mrs. Street reportedly then returned to the home about 10:00 A.M. with two police detectives, but found Caril had gone. The police entered the home through a window and, finding nothing apparently wrong, they left. They did not check the two sheds at the rear of the house, which later yielded the bodies.

Mr. Bartlett's body was found wrapped in rags and discarded quilts in a chicken house, and the bodies of Mrs. Bartlett and young Betty Jean were found in an abandoned outhouse. Scheele said the bodies were not dismembered.

A handwritten note on the home's front door had this warning: "Stay away. Everybody is Sick with The Flu." It was signed "Miss Bartlett."

Frank McKay, manager of Watson Brothers Trucking's Lincoln office, where Bartlett was employed, said Bartlett had not been to work for more than a week. "Someone had called in and reported him sick," he added, "and Bartlett had no phone so nobody called him to see what happened."

The county attorney said it had not yet been determined how long the Bartletts had been dead before their bodies were found.

The car Charles Starkweather reportedly was driving was described as a 1949 black Ford, 1957 license number 2-15628. The car had its grille missing and had no hubcaps, police said.

The *Lincoln Star* article concluded, suggesting that the murders may be linked to the recent murder of Robert Colvert of Lincoln, a twenty-one-year-old service station attendant, who was also shot in the head. He died from a shotgun blast early the morning of December 1, after apparently being robbed at the Crest Service Station at 1545 Cornhusker, which is only about a mile from the Bartlett home.

The *Lincoln Journal* offered a similar suggestion:

The deaths of a Lincoln couple and their child recalled the unsolved, nearly two-month-old Robert Colvert murder case.

Colvert, a night attendant at the Crest Service Station on Cornhusker Highway, apparently was robbed at the station early Dec. 1, then driven to a county road north of Lincoln where he was shot in the head with a shotgun.

So far, authorities have failed to solve the case.

On January 28, 1958, in the neighboring state of Wyoming, the *Casper Tribune-Herald* ran a headline article titled "Three Found Murdered in Lincoln; Daughter Hunted." The article mentioned that Marion and Velda had been shot in the head and that their child died of a skull fracture. It then went on to say that a general alarm was out for Caril Fugate, Velda's child by a prior marriage, and her boyfriend, Charles Starkweather.

CHAPTER 8

Monday, January 27, 1958

On January 27, Starkweather had driven away from the city limits of Lincoln, heading onto a two-lane country road. He was heading to the farm of August Meyer, who lived two miles east of the small town of Bennet, not far from Lincoln. Caril had been to the Meyer farm a couple of times with Starkweather, Barb, and Bob. While the others would hunt, Caril would shoot at tin cans. She had never actually met Mr. Meyer, but she knew he was a friend of Charlie's who let him hunt on his property whenever Starkweather wanted. A mailbox bullet-marked by hunters stood by the entrance to his two-story white farmhouse accessed by an unpaved road.

As Starkweather turned into Meyer's drive, he got stuck in the snow. Trying to drive out of it, he tore out his reverse shift and cursed that he could kill that old man for not having his driveway cleaned off! Caril was beside herself with worry, she had hardly eaten anything for days, and now she was freezing to death. Starkweather told her to get out of the car to help him push it free. But push as hard as they tried, they couldn't move the Ford. Twenty yards from where the car got stuck was what remained of the old District 79 schoolhouse—a foundation and a storm cellar locally referred to as "the cave." Starkweather told Caril they could warm up in the cave. He grabbed a battery light, his knife, and both guns, the .32 and .410; together they lifted the heavy wooden door, which was coming off its hinges, that covered the cave and walked down the cement steps into what looked like a dark hole.

74

Inside the cave were some old wooden school desks. Starkweather hung his lantern up on the ceiling because it was dark. Caril sat down and tried to get warm but couldn't. She was watching him as he got some bullets out of his pocket and began to load her father's .410 shotgun. He told her they were going up to August Meyer's to get his horses to pull the Ford out of the snow.

The distance from the cave to August Meyer's was close to a half mile long. At first it ran steep downhill then started up again. In the cold and the freezing wind, it was a miserable journey. Starkweather carried both guns and the knife while Caril followed meekly behind him. When they made it to one of the barns, a dog started barking. Starkweather turned to Caril and told her to shut up and not say anything and to do exactly what he said or she knew what would happen— one phone call and your family is dead. At the sound of the dog barking, August Meyer came out of the house and up to Starkweather, who told him their car was stuck and he needed some of Meyer's horses to pull them out of the driveway and back toward the county road.

August Meyer said of course Starkweather could use the horses but that he needed to go back to the house for something first. He turned and started for the house while Starkweather followed behind him. Caril saw Mr. Meyer climb the stairs to his porch and approach his kitchen door. She then saw Starkweather running to catch up to him. Then, Starkweather stopped and raised her father's shotgun, aiming directly at Meyer's back. And then, he did it. He pulled the trigger! She first saw the hole in the kitchen door window made by the blast and then heard the thud of Mr. Meyer falling to the floor.

Now, Meyer's dog was growling at Starkweather, so he took the barrel of the .410 and hit the dog with the handle. As the dog ran off yelping, Starkweather tried to shoot it, but the gun wouldn't fire. "Damn gun's jammed," he muttered.

Suddenly, Caril felt as if she were "outside her own body," watching herself as an onlooker. It was as if she saw herself screaming, but she couldn't hear the scream. She wanted to run but couldn't move her feet. In stunned disbelief, she watched as Starkweather lifted Mr. Meyer's feet and dragged him about fifty feet to an outbuilding with a chimney, where he left that poor man's body.

"Get his hat," Starkweather told Caril.

Obeying silently, she picked up Mr. Meyer's hat that had fallen on the porch and threw it on the floor of the outbuilding.

"Now, get in the house," Starkweather ordered.

"I don't want to go inside the house," Caril cried.

"Get in the house or you'll get it like the old man did," he threatened.

Trembling, Caril obeyed without speaking.

They entered the house from the kitchen door, and she heard Starkweather say he had to look for some money, about $500.00 that the old lady gave to Meyer. He also said Meyer had bought some new clothes he wanted to look for as well. He grabbed her by the arm and led her upstairs.

Caril couldn't seem to put up any fight; she went with him just like his shadow. As she watched, Starkweather went into every room upstairs, pulling things out of drawers and scattering everything on the floor, leaving a mess. Then they went back downstairs and he did the same thing, opening drawers and closets looking for who knows what.

Caril found herself sitting by a stove in the kitchen. She could look out the window. She could also see into an adjoining room which had an overturned mattress on the floor and what looked to be her father's gun lying on it. She saw Starkweather walk into the kitchen with two very big guns. Neither one was a .410 like her dad's.

Now Starkweather was sitting in the room where the mattress was, taking off his boots and socks and putting on a new gray pair of Meyer's socks. "Here," he said, as he threw Caril another new pair of socks, "put these on."

She stared at the socks on the floor, seemingly unable to move.

Back in the kitchen with a brown pouch in his hand, Starkweather pulled out some bills and put them into his billfold. He gave Caril the loose change, which she put into her coat pocket. He opened a closet and brought to the table some cookies and got Jell-O. He put his finger in the Jell-O. "It's good. Wouldn't you like some?"

"I want to get out of here!" Caril screamed. Mr. Meyer was dead, and the idea of a dead body nearby frightened her. "Let's get out of here, Charlie," she pleaded. "I'm afraid. I'm afraid. I'm afraid."

He kept telling her to shut up, that they would leave now. But first, he had to find that dog. He gave Caril her father's .410 to carry. He would get it fixed later. Starkweather was carrying another two rifles along with the small .32 pistol and knife. They left the house and found the dog lying by a brook. Starkweather shot the dog with the rifle he took from Meyer. He said they were going back to the car and to keep her mouth shut about what happened or else her family would be killed just like Meyer.

As she followed him meekly back to the car, Caril kept saying to herself that she saw Charlie shoot Mr. Meyer. He had his back to Charlie and was just going back inside his house for something. What made him shoot Mr. Meyer? What did Mr. Meyer do to deserve to be shot? Charlie just killed a man for no reason. Why?

When they were back in the car, Starkweather put the rifles and pistol in the backseat but kept the knife. He jacked up the car and with Caril's help was able to get it out of the snow. He then told Caril to help him push the front end of the car so he could get it back onto the gravel road.

Just then, a neighboring farmer, Howard Genuchi, pulled up to the young couple as they were trying to push their car out of August Meyer's driveway. He stopped and got out to ask if he could be of some help. Maybe if they had a chain or rope he might be able to pull their car back onto the road. Genuchi watched the young man open his trunk with a knife and heard him tell the young woman to get inside the car in order to steer it. Starkweather pulled a cable out of the trunk and proceeded to attach each end to both rear bumpers. Without saying a word, Caril got inside the car behind the wheel to steer while Genuchi tried to pull the car out. Caril was startled when she heard a loud snap. The cable had broken. The farmer fixed the cable and tried again. This time he pulled the car out of the ditch and onto the road. The young man asked Genuchi what he owed him.

"Ah, you don't owe me anything," the farmer said.

Saying nothing, Starkweather gave him two one-dollar bills and watched as Genuchi drove away.

Starkweather drove to a back road, which led to August Meyer's place from a different direction. He made Caril get out of the car to open up two wooden gates, and as she walked ahead he followed her in the car. He stopped and got out to look inside the outbuilding where he left Mr. Meyer's body. After peering through the window, he ran back to the car. He told Caril somebody must have been there because the white dish towel he covered the old man's face with was no longer there but was lying on the floor.

Caril thought that August Meyer's ghost had removed it, and she started screaming again. "Let's get the hell out of here!" She thought that because Meyer was murdered his spirit would come out of his body and he would be waiting for them. She was terrified. She must have spooked Starkweather, too, because he turned the car around and tore out of there.

They arrived back at Tate's Service Station around 5:30 P.M. Marvin Kruger was still on duty and waited on Starkweather at the gas pumps.

"Fill it up," Starkweather said.

Kruger filled the tank. "That comes to $1.40," he said.

Starkweather handed him a dollar bill and some change and then asked for a Kansas road map; he also asked for some rifle shells for a .22 long rifle.

Kruger went inside the station and came back out with the map and the shells.

Starkweather said, "I wanted the hollow head, but I'll take these."

Kruger looked into the backseat and noticed several tires, wheels, and a shotgun. In the front seat he saw a rifle pointing at a young girl's left side. His suspicions being aroused, Kruger wondered what these two were up to—maybe they had been out stealing cars. As the pair drove away, Kruger took down the license number and later called the information in to the police.

It was starting to get dark, and Starkweather and Caril needed a place to stay for the night. Starkweather headed back to August Meyer's farm, but when he drove into the driveway Caril became hysterical again. She started complaining about Meyer's ghost being there because he'd been shot.

"All right, all right, goddamn it," Starkweather yelled as he stepped on the gas pedal and got his tires stuck again in the mud. Now what in the hell was he supposed to do? "Get out of the car," he screamed.

She got out of the car carrying her father's .410 shotgun while Starkweather carried the rifles. He had hold of her arm and dragged her along while they walked for about a mile in the freezing cold.

It was very dark, and the only things Caril could see were snow-covered embankments and lights glowing in a few houses in the distance. Suddenly, headlights approached, and Starkweather told her he was going to flag that car down and for her not to open her big, fat mouth or she would get what was coming to her.

The car stopped, and a person on the passenger's side rolled down the window. Caril couldn't see who was driving because Starkweather stood between her and the car, but she heard a man's voice ask what the matter was. The voice was that of seventeen-year-old Robert Jensen, who was on a date with his sixteen-year-old girlfriend, Carol King, both of Bennet, Nebraska.

"Damn car got stuck in the mud down the road," Starkweather explained. "Can you give us a lift into Bennet so that I can make a phone call?"

The fact that Starkweather and Caril were carrying rifles were of little concern to the young couple because it was common in rural areas like Bennet for people to be carrying guns. Most people hunted.

"Sure. Hop in," Jensen said.

Starkweather opened the back door and told Caril to get in first on the passenger's side. He then climbed over her to sit behind the driver. A girl was sitting in the front seat in front of Caril. Starkweather took the .410 out of Caril's hands and laid it over his lap with the barrel on her stomach.

When they arrived in Bennet, Jensen said that the telephone booth he was driving them to didn't always work and, on second thought, maybe he should drive them somewhere else.

Starkweather picked up the .22 and poked the barrel into the back of the young man's head. "Keep on driving. Do like I say or I'll blow your brains out," Starkweather warned.

Jensen remarked he didn't believe it.

"Do you want to find out, buddy?" Starkweather asked.

The young man was silent.

"Do you know where the old schoolhouse is?" Starkweather asked.

"Yes, I do," Jensen said, his voice now sounding wary.

"Well, drive there. I'm going to leave you down in the cellar and take your car. You got any money?" Starkweather asked.

"I've got about four dollars."

"Well, I want that, too."

"You can have anything you want as long as nobody gets hurt."

"Didn't I just say I was gonna put you down in the cellar? Somebody will find you, OK? Didn't I just say that to you?" Starkweather yelled.

Caril barely recognized Charlie, so angry and yelling. And his face, flushed and drawn, looked like he had just come out of a fight.

"Give me your billfold," Starkweather told the young man.

Jensen handed his billfold to Starkweather and turned around to look at him.

"Turn around. Keep your eyes on the road," Starkweather ordered. He took out his own billfold and handed both of them to Caril. He told her to take Jensen's money and put it into his billfold. She didn't move. As Starkweather started cussing at her, Jensen pleaded with her to just do what he said so nobody would get hurt. So, Caril did what she was told, taking Jensen's money and putting it into Starkweather's billfold. She then handed the man's billfold back to him.

"Thank you," he said.

They pulled into a driveway at the old school, and Jensen stopped the car.

Starkweather got out of the car. "Okay, get out now, both of you."

Only the teenage boy stepped out of the car as Starkweather held the rifle on him. The girl was frozen to her seat. She couldn't move. Starkweather told Caril to hold the .410 on the girl and tell her to get out of the car.

If I do as he says maybe nobody gets hurt, Caril thought. So she held the gun on the girl and whispered to her to please get out of the car.

Starkweather ordered Caril to get in the front seat. Caril waited until she saw Starkweather walk away with the boy and girl, noticing how small the girl was and that the young man was rather big. She never saw their faces. When she could no longer see them, Caril climbed over the back of the front seat and into the passenger's seat as Starkweather had ordered. She was too afraid to open the door to change seats for fear that Starkweather would shoot her for trying to escape.

Caril sat for quite a long while until the heat that was left in the front seat finally gave out. She was cold and started to ask herself whether she was just dreaming everything that happened because things like this never happened.

Then she heard them. Gunshots. And she knew what Starkweather had done. He lied! He lied! He lied! Oh, dear God in heaven, why did he lie? Sobbing uncontrollably, she rocked herself back and forth until the front door was opened and the ceiling light turned on. She saw the barrel of the rifle staring at her and knew she was next. But Starkweather threw the gun in the backseat. He was in a rage and cussing and screaming about how the boy had given him a lot of trouble. He grabbed hold of the steering wheel and just sat there.

"Why, Charlie? Why did you kill them? You said you wouldn't harm them. Why did you kill them, why did you lie, Charlie?"

But Starkweather wasn't answering. He just stared straight ahead into the blackness of the night as if he were in a trance. The Charlie she knew was no longer with her. He had become something else—a raging shell of a man who was off in his own world—unreachable. So they sat in the car for several minutes until Starkweather snapped out of his trance. Then, in a kind voice, he said, "I will take you home now because you've seen enough and heard enough." Charlie was being nice to her. He acted as though nothing had happened back at the cellar. "Yes, I'll take you back home now."

It's over, Caril thought. The nightmare is finally over, and I can go home. Sadly, unbeknownst to Caril, the nightmare was far from over.

All Caril could think about was going home and getting away from him. She looked in the backseat and told Charlie there were some schoolbooks there that ought to be thrown out. She was thinking that the books might be found and leave a trail leading to the young couple who had met such a violent end. When Starkweather agreed that they should dump the books, Caril bent over the back of her seat and dropped one book at a time out the window.

They drove back to Lincoln and slowed down as they approached Belmont and could see Caril's house. The lights were all turned on, and police cars were parked in the driveway. So Starkweather drove on. He said the cops found out about the bank robbery they were planning and that's why they're at Caril's house. "Besides," he said, "I can't leave you off. You might tell the cops what I done." He had the radio in the car turned on, and she heard something about three bodies being found when he suddenly turned the radio off. She assumed that August Meyer and the young couple had been found already. Starkweather drove out of Lincoln for about an hour and then told her they were going back.

She kept thinking he lied. He lied again. He's not taking me home. He said he would, but he isn't taking me home. He is a liar. A liar. What else has he lied to me about? Then, she turned her mind off. She really didn't want to know what else he lied about.

Starkweather was driving through the Country Club section of Lincoln, where all the rich people lived on his former garbage route. The old lady lived around here. Where her mother was. Before Caril drifted off to sleep, her thoughts were of her mother.

CHAPTER 9

Tuesday, January 28, 1958

Caril woke up to find that Starkweather had parked the car in front of a big, beautiful white house on some street in Lincoln. She watched a car exit the driveway and heard Starkweather say, "There he goes." Caril watched the man drive away from the white house. Starkweather started his car and drove it into the man's driveway in front of the left garage where it wouldn't be visible from the street. He got out of the car with the .22 rifle, the knife, and the pistol. He told Caril to wait in the car until he motioned for her to come in. When he motioned her, she was to bring his jacket and the other gun with her. Starkweather entered the house through the garage door. She could see him through the window in the door that led from the garage into the house. A few minutes later, he came to the door and motioned for her to come inside. Like a zombie, she got his jacket and gun and went inside the house. Caril saw two women sitting at the kitchen table. One was Clara Ward, lady of the house, and the Ward's maid, Lilyan Fencl. Starkweather had the gun pointing at them, and they were silent.

Caril wandered into a room that must be a library—it had lots of books on shelves. Starkweather followed her with a cup of coffee in his hand and told her to drink it and then lie down on the davenport. She didn't want any coffee, but Starkweather said to drink it or he'd pour it down her throat. So Caril drank the coffee in front of him. When he left her for a moment, after warning her that he would be watching her, Caril tried to open the door but couldn't unlatch it. She went to lie down on the davenport and fell into a deep slumber for the first time since she opened the door on Belmont to find Starkweather's shotgun staring her in the face.

She awoke to find that Starkweather was in the library with her and eating pancakes that the lady of the house had brought in on a tray. Starkweather asked Caril if she wanted any pancakes. "No, I'm not hungry," she said. She watched Starkweather finish off the pancakes, then she took the tray back to the kitchen. She returned to the library and went back to sleep.

She woke up in the afternoon to find Starkweather holding a bloody knife. Her mother's knife. Starkweather told Caril that the lady was dead upstairs.

"How did you kill her?" Caril asked.

"Oh, I stabbed her in the throat." He handed Caril her mother's knife and told her to go wash it off.

Caril took her mother's knife and walked into the powder room and ran the knife under cold water just like he told her to.

"It stinks of blood up there," Starkweather said. "Go upstairs and throw some perfume around." So Caril walked up the stairs and into a room with a mirror over a dresser that had many perfume bottles on it, and she took one, uncapped it, and sprinkled perfume on the rug in the room and on a chair placed outside the door.

"Come here and hold the gun on the maid while I go turn the car around," Starkweather demanded. Caril obeyed. She held the gun on the maid. She tried to tell the maid that she wasn't going to hurt her, but the woman didn't seem to understand her, so Starkweather said to write the maid a note. So Caril wrote her a note telling her she wasn't going to hurt her and then, as Starkweather told her to do, she flushed the note in the toilet with other notes he said he had written to the maid.

"Come into the kitchen," Starkweather ordered.

Caril went into the kitchen and found him sitting at the breakfast table with a pair of scissors in his hand. He had begun cutting an article from the newspaper. He showed her the paper, and she saw the picture of the two of them taken at Mae Holley's the night Orlin called them "the happy couple." Starkweather was wearing his cowboy boots, and Caril held her purse in her hand. They were both smiling. He continued cutting the picture out of the paper.

"See," he said, "they're looking for you and me because they know about the robbery. Here, you cut the rest of it out."

Starkweather gave Caril the scissors, and she started to cut out the picture, but then he took the scissors and paper away from her and cut out the rest of the picture himself. Then he showed Caril some pictures of her mother, dad, and Betty Jean. Their pictures were in the paper, too, he said, because the cops were looking for them, too. Starkweather took the paper away from Caril and clipped out the photos of her family. "They're looking for all of us."

"Watch out the window for the man and let me know when he pulls up in the driveway," Starkweather said. So Caril looked out the window and when she saw a car approaching the driveway, she called out that the man was home. She ran into the powder room and shut the door, closed her eyes, and covered her face with her hands. She heard the running of footsteps, a gunshot, and a scream. Starkweather opened the powder room door and pulled her out, and she saw the man lying between her and the front door, groaning. Starkweather hollered at him to shut up!

"He grabbed at my gun," Starkweather explained. "I let go of it and the man fell down the cellar stairs so I ran down after him and he tried to go for my gun but I got it away from him. The man picked up an iron and swung at me and I held the gun on him and made him go back upstairs and he ran."

Caril tried not to look at the man lying on the floor, so she turned her head away and saw the maid sitting in the dining room chair. Starkweather told Caril to hold the gun on the maid while he searched the groaning man for money.

Starkweather, Caril, and the maid were climbing the stairs to the second floor. Starkweather held a .22, and Caril held a .22 and a flashlight that Starkweather had handed her. They went into one of the bedrooms, and Starkweather sat the maid in a chair and started to tear the bedsheets into strips. As he tied the maid's wrists together with the strips, Caril asked him why he didn't let her lie down on the bed because she would get tired sitting up all night. So, with the maid face up on the bed, Starkweather tied her legs together and tied her wrists to the back of the bed and her legs to the front. The maid was saying something that sounded like "light, light," but the maid was deaf and Caril couldn't understand what she was saying. Then, Starkweather lifted his knife and stabbed the maid over and over and over again. Caril heard the maid moan every time he brought the knife down on her, but she wasn't looking at what he was doing to the maid. Caril, with the flashlight shining on Starkweather, watched with incredulity at a face she had never seen before. It was a face filled with rage beyond all comprehension, a face with grimaced lips that kept screaming, "Die! Die! Die!" each time he raised the knife and plunged it into the helpless woman.

When the maid finally stopped groaning, Starkweather said, "I thought she would never die." He sat down in the chair and said no more. He just sat and stared ahead in the darkened room, looking into space.

He didn't respond when Caril screamed, "Why, why, why? Why did you kill her? What did she do that you had to kill her?"

But Starkweather wouldn't answer. He said nothing, so she shined the flashlight on his face and told him to answer her, but once again he wasn't there anymore—it was as though he wasn't even in the same room with her. He was frozen inside his own mind. Looking into his eyes, Caril saw nothing. No emotion. No feeling. His body was there, but his mind was somewhere else. She felt as if she had been left all alone in the room with a murdered woman's ghost.

"You're gone and you've left me alone with a dead woman, Charlie. Why do you leave me alone? Can you see me? Can you hear me? I'm frightened! Frightened! Why do you leave me alone?"

When Starkweather snapped out of his stupor, he walked

over to the bed and covered up the maid's body with a blanket. "Shine the flashlight on my arm." He saw blood on his shirtsleeve and cuff. "I'm going to need another shirt," he said. Caril wondered when he was going to kill her, too. Because she knew he was going to kill her. He had to. He killed everybody else, so why not her?

"Wash this knife off while I change my shirt," he told her. She found herself back downstairs in the powder room but didn't remember how she got there. She washed the knife off once again, and Starkweather told her to help him put black shoe polish in his hair, and she did that, too.

It was time to leave. Caril put on her blue coat and felt in her right pocket for the note that she wrote for the police and held onto it tightly. Starkweather held up a light suede jacket and told her to put it on instead. She insisted her own coat was warmer and that the suede jacket was too light for this weather, but Starkweather insisted she change into it. She lifted her right hand out of the blue coat pocket, holding onto the note, and changed into the suede jacket. She transferred the note into the right pocket of the suede jacket and walked out into the garage with Starkweather. Later, it would be discovered that Starkweather already had placed the newspaper clippings of the pictures of her family in this suede jacket. I can't go on, she thought. I can't go on. Why should I? she thought. He'll just kill me, too. Then she remembered why she had to go on. For them. To save her family. So she would do whatever else he told her to do. Whatever else she had to do to stay alive.

Over the week, Lincoln newspaper headlines about the series of murders grew more ugly and gruesome by the day. Media coverage had moved out of Lincoln and into Bennet, Nebraska, where the *Lincoln Journal* reported that "the county sheriff's office reported that Carol King, 16, and Robert Jensen, 17, who live in the Bennet area, have been missing overnight. Officers said that young Jensen had picked the King girl up at 6:00 P.M. Monday and they had not returned." The article continued:

A 1949 model automobile believed to have been used by two teenagers wanted for questioning in connection with an apparent triple murder in Lincoln has been located east of Bennet, the Nebraska Safety Patrol said shortly after noon.

The patrol said the car was apparently abandoned about 1 ½ miles east of the Lancaster County maintenance shops at Bennet.

—*Lincoln Journal,* Jan. 28, 1958

On January 28, at least twenty law enforcement officers and at least a couple dozen local residents gathered outside the house of August Meyer, a Bennet farmer. Authorities had discovered Starkweather's 1949 automobile on Meyer's property. A loudspeaker unit was brought up from Lincoln. Sheriff Karnopp took the loudspeaker and shouted into the house, where he suspected Starkweather and Fugate were, to come out peacefully. No response being given, the officers shot tear gas bombs into the house. However, when the officers entered the house, no one was found. Following a trail of blood in the snow leading to the stove house, officials found the body of August Meyer.

Everett Browning, a local farmer and neighbor of August Meyer's who was also at the scene, had more startling information. When he took the cover off the old school cellar, he discovered the bodies of Carol King and Robert Jensen. Carol King was found nearly nude and lying on top of Jensen at the bottom of the stairs. Browning, later quoted in the papers, admitted "(he) just happened to check that old storm cellar on a hunch."

January 29, 1958

The headlines in the *Lincoln Star* newspaper the next day read:

3 MORE BODIES FOUND—
Bennet Victims Bring Toll to 6
BENNET, Neb.—This village was an armed fortress Tuesday night, fearing another onslaught by the Lincoln couple believed to have been involved in the

slaying of three Bennet residents.

Hardware store operator Herbert Randall reported that the 400 town residents and surrounding farm
families "all have guns and won't mind using them."

Tuesday night a group of about 30 men armed
with shotguns and rifles stopped in the store for ammunition. They planned a search "foot-by-foot" of the
surrounding countryside for the slayers of two Bennet high school students who had been out on a date
when last seen.

Third of the senseless slayings was a 70-year-old
bachelor farmer, August Meyer, "a man who minded
his own business," according to R. E. Clark, Bennet,
the Lincoln Star editor.

—Lincoln Star, January 29, 1958

Other newspapers continued to report on the growing list
of victims, as well.

On January 29, 1958, in the morning edition of the *Laramie Daily Boomerang,* a Wyoming newspaper, bold headlines
proclaimed: "Nebraska Posse Hunts Killers of Six People." This
article reported the deaths of August Meyer, Robert Jensen, and
Carol King. It further mentioned that officials pointed out that
a .22 caliber rifle was stolen from Meyer's home and that the
subjects of the manhunt were Starkweather and Caril.

The morning edition of the *Lincoln Journal* reported:

While the search for the 14-year-old Caril Ann
Fugate and her boyfriend, 19-year-old Charles Starkweather, continued, Nebraskans were shocked as they
followed the trail of violence that first appeared Monday night in Lincoln.

The two, both charged with first degree murder,
are wanted for questioning in connection with the killing of a total of six known Lancaster County residents.

—Lincoln Journal, Jan. 29, 1958

The preliminary autopsies revealed that August Meyer
had died of a shotgun wound to the head, Robert Jensen

Panic began to spread throughout Lincoln and the surrounding area as the body count mounted. The story was making front-page headlines in newspapers across the country, including the *Los Angeles Times*.

died of multiple gunshot wounds to the head, and Carol King died of one gunshot wound. The autopsy report on Carol King also stated that she "was the victim of an unnatural sex attack." The coroner also noted that sticks and other debris were shoved into Carol King's vagina. This fact was never revealed to the public.

The three slayings stunned the town of Bennet so much that during the night men armed with shotguns and rifles drove up and down the streets in search for the killers. Houses were lit up, and a knock on any door was answered by a person with a shotgun in hand. With a killer on the loose, a person might very well shoot first and ask questions later.

Sheriff Karnopp was seen on television calling for a posse to find the killers. More than one hundred area residents turned up at the Lancaster County sheriff's office in Lincoln to volunteer.

Both the *Lincoln Journal* and the *Lincoln Star* newspapers had round-the-clock reporters covering police headquarters and the sheriff's office, instructing them to call in every fifteen minutes whether they had anything new to report or not. While staff in the newsroom monitored three police radio

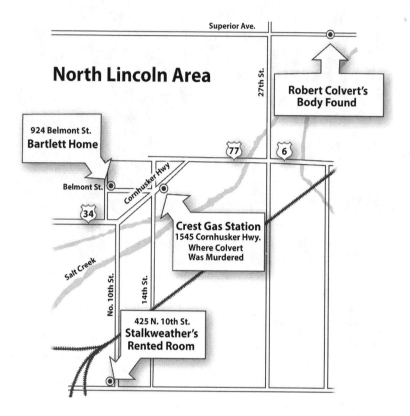

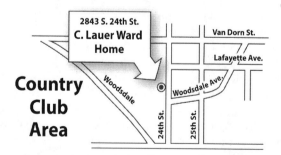

bands, others were assigned the task of scouting out the most reliable police reports on the search for the car Starkweather was driving.

At 12:30 P.M. on January 29th, a reporter called into the *Journal* the news that assistant police chief Eugene Masters had gone "somewhere in a helluva hurry." That somewhere turned out to be 2843 South 28th Street, the home of prominent industrialist and president of Capital Steel Co., C. Lauer Ward. Police found Robert Jensen's 1950 Ford parked in the Wards' driveway. Inside, they found three more bodies—those of Ward, his wife Clara, and their maid, Lilyan Fencl. This brought to nine the number of victims murdered in Lancaster County in the most shocking series of murders in Nebraska's history.

Police said a 1956 black Packard sedan, 1957 Nebraska license number 2-17415, was reported stolen from the Ward home. It was registered to the Capital Steel Co. Officers said it was believed to be driven by Starkweather and Fugate.

Later that day, the afternoon edition of the *Wyoming State Tribunal* contained another bold headline: "Search Spreads As Starkweather Eludes Officers." This article now updated the public about the murders of Mr. and Mrs. Ward and Lilyan Fencl. The police, finding the bodies, "said they brought to nine or more—the murders for which they sought Charles Starkweather, 19, and his 14-year-old girlfriend."

After the three slayings at the Ward home were discovered, hysteria took over Lincoln and its surrounding outskirts. Local hardware stores quickly sold off all the ammunition stocked on their shelves. Customers weren't being particular about what they bought—it was anything that could shoot. Businesses closed; meetings were canceled; phone lines were jammed; and cars driven by terrorized parents on their way to schools to pick up their children caused major traffic jams.

In Lincoln, Governor Victor E. Anderson, a personal friend of C. Lauer Ward, now ordered out the Nebraska National Guard to help hunt down and capture Starkweather and Fugate. The Guard was coordinated with Lincoln police, sheriff's officers, and the highway patrol. With weapons in hand, the Guard patrolled Lincoln streets in pairs.

All one had to do was look out a window and watch as a steady stream of cars drove by on the hunt for what the papers referred to as "a mad-dog killer." Residents were asked to stay off the streets and to leave their garage doors open in order to allow the authorities to search for Ward's car which Starkweather was said to be driving. Armed men stood in their front yards ready to defend their families. All roads leading out of the city were blocked. Authorities warned that Starkweather was still in Lincoln and could strike again. Nobody knew who was going to be next. Nobody was taking any chances.

PART III

THE ARRESTS

CHAPTER 10

Wednesday, January 29, 1958

Starkweather had decided they were going to Washington state where his brother Leonard lived. They were going to drive there in the Ward's car. He had gotten behind the wheel, dropped the dead man's keys on the floor, picked them up, and tried each key in the ignition until he got the right one and they drove away.

They had driven through the night and stopped a couple of times to get gas. Caril had a map in her hand and circled the towns as they passed them. She wanted people to know where they had been. Starkweather was at the wheel, talking to himself, or was he talking to her. She couldn't make him out anymore, and sometimes he seemed to be carrying on a conversation with a ghost. Somebody she couldn't see. He stopped the car and told Caril to change into another shirt he brought for her, so she climbed in the backseat and changed her shirt. She didn't even ask him why.

They were driving on Highway 20 through Wyoming for a while before Starkweather spotted a white Buick parked along the highway. He parked on the side of the road behind it, got out of the car, and walked up to the door on the passenger's side and said something. Then he aimed and fired the shotgun through the door.

Caril tried to start the Ward car to get away but didn't know how to drive an automatic. Starkweather was approaching her with the shotgun. He must have seen her trying to escape, and he was going to kill her.

"Get out of the car," he said to Caril, "and get in the Buick."

Caril saw the body of a man lying on the front seat of the Buick with his head in a puddle of blood. Starkweather moved the front seat forward and motioned for her to get in the backseat. He tried to release the emergency brake but couldn't start the car, so he yelled to the dead man, "Man, man, are you dead?"

Now, suddenly, another man, a big man, was approaching them on foot. He approached the car.

"You kids need some help?" he asked.

Caril wanted to warn him stay away, but no words came out of her mouth.

Starkweather pointed the .22 rifle at the man. "Help me release this brake or I will kill you!"

Keeping his cool, the big man reached down to pull on the brake lever, but instead grabbed the barrel of the rifle. All of a sudden, he and Starkweather were in the middle of the road in a deadly game of tug-of-war with the rifle.

Caril's mind was racing. This is it! Now's my chance to escape, she thought. I'll run, and if I get shot in the back that's just too damn bad. I just can't take this anymore. But by then, the big man had wrestled the rifle away from Starkweather.

During the commotion, two other vehicles had come up behind them and stopped on the country road. First, a car with a couple in it had rolled to a stop. A few moments later, a milk truck came to a halt behind them.

Wyoming's Natrona County deputy sheriff William Romer had been driving along Highway 20 on an assignment. He was proceeding between Glen Rock and Douglas and had been following the milk truck when it suddenly stopped at the top of a hill. Romer saw three cars parked, two men wrestling on the ground, and a young girl racing toward him. As Romer later told the press, "I stopped my car and a girl came running over. She was saying, 'He's going to kill me. He's crazy. He's just killed a man.' "

Caril had bolted from the car and raced toward him. She ran in a zigzag fashion, hoping to dodge any bullets Starkweather might manage to fire at her. She screamed as she ran, "He's going to kill my mother and father and little sister!

He's already killed other people!" The words spilled out of her mouth nonstop as she told Romer that she was being held hostage. "He killed an old farmer, two teenagers, and the people who lived in a big white house in Lincoln. And he's going to kill me, too. He's crazy. He's crazy. He's crazy."

Romer saw one of the men pull a rifle away from the smaller man. At that point, the smaller man—Starkweather—jumped into his car and sped off, heading toward the community of Douglas, Wyoming.

Deputy Romer opened his car door for the approaching girl, and she slid in. He told her she could stop crying, that she was safe. But she couldn't stop sobbing. Caril was still mumbling that he was going to kill her.

Romer interrupted her, "Who? Who is going to kill you?"

When he heard the name "Charles Starkweather," he could feel the adrenaline begin to pump into his bloodstream. He immediately radioed the highway patrol in Casper, Wyoming, telling them to call nearby Douglas lawmen and get a roadblock set up. "I've come upon Charles Starkweather," he said.

Colonel Stan Warne of the highway patrol, listening on the other end of the radio, heard Romer exclaim, "My God, it's Starkweather and all I've got is a little bit of a peashooter pistol!"

Warne got the location and headed out to Highway 20.

By now, Starkweather had taken off in the black Packard with Romer in pursuit. Romer followed Starkweather for about a mile. Looking up the side roads leading to the mountains and not seeing anything in front of him for about three miles, Romer radioed that he was going back to the crime scene, where he stayed with Caril.

Warne, already at the crime scene when Romer returned, witnessed a young girl sobbing in Romer's backseat and wondered how such a frightened little girl could have been involved in such havoc. She was so small, and her eyes were very red and very puffy. Warne thought to himself that she didn't get eyes like that from crying for the last twenty minutes; those eyes look like she has been crying for days. He tried to understand what she was saying, but she was babbling to the point that she was incoherent. Warne recognized that she was in such a state that there was nothing he could do to calm her down, so he just stood by, making sure she didn't harm herself. She said something like she gets to live until they get to Washington, and then he's going to kill her, too. Warne thought he heard her say that he killed her little brother. "He wouldn't kill my little brother, too, would he?" That's confusing, Warne thought. The papers didn't mention anything about Caril Fugate having a little brother.

Warne walked over to the Buick and saw a man's body lying on the floor by the passenger's side in the front seat. His name was Merle Collison. He was an area salesman who had made the innocent, but ill-fated mistake of pulling over to take a nap.

While Warne took photographs of the crime scene, Romer walked over to the big guy who had been wrestling with Starkweather. He was an area resident by the name of Joe Sprinkle. Romer said to him, "Do you have any idea who you were playing tug-of-war with? It was Charles Starkweather. Charles Starkweather, the man who killed all those people in Nebraska!" Sprinkle turned ashen.

Another Wyoming county sheriff, Earl Heflin, along with Douglas police chief, Robert Ainslie, captured Starkweather after a high-speed chase at 115 miles per hour right through the center of Douglas, Wyoming. Both Heflin and Ainslie shot at Starkweather's car, finally causing him to stop about fifteen miles east of Douglas.

"One of the shots shattered the front and rear windows of the car, and Starkweather was cut by the glass," Heflin told reporters. "It was his own blood that got him. He thought he was shot deader'n hell when he saw that blood. I guess he thought he was bleeding to death. That's the kind of yellow S.O.B he is."

After being captured, Starkweather remarked, "If I'd had a gun I'd have shot them." The .32 pistol recovered from his car was out of ammunition.

The radio in the squad car crackled to life with lawmen's voices and urgent commands. Caril pleaded with the men not to let Starkweather get loose. Don't let him get away or he'll kill my family. If I got away from him, he said he would kill my mother and father and little sister. Please don't let him get away!

One of the men exclaimed to her. "You can stop your crying now, okay? He's captured." Deputy Romer drove off with Caril, finally silent, in the backseat.

When the car stopped, Deputy Romer ushered Caril toward a house. He opened the door, and Caril saw a woman walking down the stairs. The woman was Hazel Heflin, the Sheriff's wife. She had a kind face and spoke sweetly to Caril, "Now, now dear. It's all over, don't be afraid anymore." The woman led Caril, still trembling, over to a sofa and had her sit down next to her. Caril continued to speak incoherently, and the kind woman shook her head. "Dear, I'm not able to understand what you're saying. Your story is all broken. You don't have to shake so, dear."

Caril heard the woman mention a doctor and saw a man with a black bag approaching her. The woman was kneeling in front of her and holding a cup of broth in her hands and telling Caril to drink some soup so she would feel better.

Caril screamed, "Don't let him near me," referring to Starkweather. "Please don't let him near me. Please don't leave me alone. I don't want to be alone."

"He would never get near you now, dear. You are safe. You won't have to see him again. Now, please take this pill the doctor has left. We'll go upstairs, and you can lie down. Won't that be nice? Here, let me take your jacket so you'll be more comfortable."

Caril cried for her mother and baby sister. "Why won't they call me?"

"The telephone lines are probably so busy at the moment that they couldn't get through anyway," Mrs. Heflin told her. Caril followed Mrs. Heflin to an upstairs bedroom. She took the pill and lay down on the bed.

While Mrs. Heflin was attending to Caril, Sheriff Heflin was searching the jacket she was wearing when she fled from Starkweather. When Hazel returned to her husband, she remarked, "I don't think she knows her mother is dead."

Thursday morning, January 30, 1958

When Caril woke up the next morning, January 30, after sleeping for seventeen hours, she didn't realize where she was until she saw Mrs. Heflin smiling at her and offering to help her wash her face and hands.

"I stayed with you all night, dear. You were too afraid to be left alone. Now have a little bit of breakfast. It will make you feel better. And take this sedative the doctor left for you."

A few hours later Mrs. Heflin asked, "Wouldn't you like a nice, warm bath, dear? Now, now, it's just us girls here and I can tell you're having your period, but you don't want other people to know that, do you dear? I went out this morning and got you a nice change of clothes, and I'll help you get undressed and into the tub."

"No. I don't want a bath!" Caril hollered. "I can't take off my clothes. I'm safe with my clothes on. He might see me, and I can't let him see me with my clothes off. Besides, I have to be ready to go when my mother comes for me. I can't take off my clothes," Caril wailed.

"My, my," the kind woman said, biting her lip. "Caril, why don't you take a pill the doctor left for you and try to rest."

Within hours of Starkweather's capture, newsmen from all major newspapers in the Rocky Mountain area descended on the town of Douglas, Wyoming, population 2,500.

Sheriff Earl Heflin described the chaos on the radar units upon Starkweather's escape after Collison's murder was discovered as follows: "You couldn't understand anything, Casper was on the air, Romer was on the air, and I believe every police officer up there was on."

Headlines over the next few days told the story of Starkweather's capture. In a newspaper article printed by the *Casper Tribune-Herald* on January 30, 1958, one day after Starkweather was captured, Deputy Romer was quoted as saying "I stopped my car and a girl came running over, yelling, 'He's going to kill me. He's crazy. He's just killed a man.'"

Douglas, Wyoming: Site of Starkweather's Capture

The map above shows the route police took from Douglas to Lincoln, Nebraska.

After the capture of Starkweather, Romer made several statements to the press. Although he acknowledged that Caril's "talk was confused and incoherent," he nevertheless assured the press that "he was able to piece together" the information he relayed for the headlines. Romer said he was able to decipher some of Caril's jabbering, and he talked about Caril telling him about Starkweather's gang wanting to rob a bank and that a boy by the name of O'Brien killed the filling station operator last December. These were lies told to Caril by Starkweather. She also mentioned $500.00 in connection with August Meyer's farm, but Romer got it wrong when he was quoted as saying Starkweather paid Mr. Meyer $500.00 for the use of his farm as a hideout. However, Starkweather had searched Meyer's house for $500.00 after he killed the farmer.

On January 31, 1958, the *Laramie Boomerang* quoted Romer: "She kept saying, 'I've seen nine people killed. My mother and my father and my sister are dead.'" In reality, Caril did not tell Romer that Starkweather had killed her family. In her jabbering, Romer had misunderstood her. She had told Romer that Starkweather would kill her family because she had escaped from him.

The front-page headline of the January 31, 1958, *Casper Tribune-Herald* proclaimed: "Starkweather Now Admits 11 Slayings." In Lincoln, Lancaster County sheriff Merle Karnopp said that while riding from Douglas, Wyoming, back to Gering Thursday night, Starkweather admitted the eleven killings, ten in Nebraska and one in Wyoming, where he was captured Wednesday.

"I always wanted to be an outlaw," Starkweather said to Karnopp during the trip from Douglas.

Karnopp also related that Starkweather, speaking freely and without a sign of remorse, told him: "I always wanted to be a criminal, but not this big a one. I didn't mean for it to be this bad. I wanted to be somebody. I wasn't mad at anybody."

The Sheriff said, "He told me that he just had a hatred that built up in himself and that since he was a kid he wanted to be an outlaw. I have never seen a more vicious mad killer who could talk so cool and collected."

After Starkweather's capture by the authorities in Wyoming, the citizens of Lincoln, after undergoing a literal siege of terror, began asking why law enforcement didn't catch the killer sooner. There was such hostility directed at the local authorities that the Lincoln City Council and the Lancaster County Board of Commissioners had no choice but to authorize an "impartial" inquiry into the conduct of the Starkweather investigation by Harold G. Robinson, former FBI Special Agent and member of the California Bureau of Criminal Investigation.

However, Robinson soon exonerated all local authorities of any incompetence, and in his opinion, "the law enforcement agencies participating in the investigation subsequent to 4:30 P.M. January 27, 1958, did a remarkable job in coping with a situation which greatly exceeded the available manpower and taxed the experience and training of the available personnel to the utmost."

Despite the fact that the local law enforcement authorities received praise from Robinson, the citizens of Lincoln continued to heap criticism upon them. The fact was that the police department had basically ignored the phone calls and requests for help from Caril's grandmother and brother-in-law. Now, the citizens were left with only one way to strike back at the two young people who had apparently heaped such tragedies on area communities. That would be in the court of law.

CHAPTER 11

Late Thursday, January 30, 1958

Caril woke up feeling groggy. It was hard to get alert. She was startled when she heard a man's loud voice, "She's awake, she's up now." It took a moment for her to remember where she was, and she wanted the kind woman to come back and talk to her, but the woman wasn't around.

"Are you ready to talk to us now?" one of the men asked her. "Can you tell us what happened?"

She found herself sitting in a kitchen and surrounded by so many faces she had never seen before, all men's faces who kept telling her she had to come back with them to Nebraska and tell them what happened because she was the only person who knew how all these people were killed.

"You want to tell your story, don't you? You want to help us put Starkweather away, don't you?"

She heard the words "trial" and "witness" and "governor of Wyoming" and pieced together that somehow these faces needed her help. They needed her to come back to Lincoln with them and help them take care of Starkweather.

"Look," they showed Caril a telegram from her sister, Barbara. "The telegram says 'Tell them everything you know'— and you trust your sister, don't you, Caril?"

"What should I do?" she asked one of the faces.

"Your sister gives you good advice," a face told her. "You should cooperate. You know that this is a terrible mess, a very serious situation, don't you? You do want to tell us everything you know, don't you?"

"Yes," Caril said. She would help. She would go back to Lincoln with them and tell them everything she knew.

They kept jabbering at her about things she didn't understand and then gave her a piece of paper and told her to sign her name to it and as soon as she did they would take her back home.

"Is my family dead? Are they dead? If I sign this paper how long until I can go back to see my family?"

The faces told her if she signed that piece of paper she could leave right now. After she signed the paper, the trip back to Nebraska was a blur.

"Where are we going?" Caril, asked, sitting in the backseat of a car next to a strange man.

"We are taking you to the jail in Gering, Nebraska."

Mrs. Heflin was sitting in the front seat next to the driver. "Here dear, take another tranquilizer the doctor left for you."

Caril took the pill and swallowed it with a sip from the bottle of soda pop they had given her. She looked out the window in the dark of night and softly cried.

Early morning, Friday, January 31, 1958

The cars left Douglas, Wyoming, a small town in eastern Wyoming, at about 6:00 P.M. and arrived in Gering, Nebraska about two hours later. It was dark. as Caril crawled out of the backseat, she was blinded by the flashbulbs of cameras surrounding her.

Cameramen yelled, "Look over here, Caril. Turn around and give us a smile, why don't you, Caril."

She was taken inside what looked like a jail.

Mrs. Heflin told her, "Mrs. Warrick, the sheriff's wife, will take care of you now."

Caril heard Mrs. Heflin remark to Mrs. Warrick, "The poor thing. She's been through so much."

Caril's mind was spinning. I'm all confused about things, she thought. What am I doing here? I thought I was going home. But she was in a jail cell.

Then a man told her that he was sorry about her family.

"Why?" Caril asked with questioning eyes.

Just then, someone else said, "My God, girl. Don't you know they're all dead?"

Caril thought that woman was nuts. She asked again, "When can I see my mother?"

The faces kept staring at her.

Caril screamed and cussed. "You're all crazy! How could my family be dead when I did everything Starkweather told me to do?" As far as she was concerned, her family was still at the old lady's house. They'd been at the old lady's house this whole time, or she never would have left with Starkweather. She never would have done what she did with him if her family wasn't still at the old lady's house. "Dirty liars!" She screamed over and over again.

Then, a doctor approached and stuck a hypodermic needle in her arm. She felt limp and went to sleep.

She passed in and out of a deep sleep. She wondered why people were lying to her about her family being dead. Was it a big sick joke? She just knew they couldn't be dead. Maybe if she could wake up out of this fog she would be in a different place and things would be all right. Because this was just all wrong. She saw a pretty young girl looking at her through the bars in her cell, and the girl looked sad for Caril. Then the young girl was called away, and a strange man tried to talk to Caril about her family.

Caril not only told him where he could go, but what he could do to himself once he got there! The shocked look on his face made her laugh. She hadn't laughed in a long time and now found that she couldn't stop laughing. She was laughing at all of them because they were a bunch of stupid liars telling her that her mother was dead. They must think I'm pretty stupid to believe that lie when I was with Starkweather the whole time, and I know he never made that phone call.

It was time to go again. A woman took her by the arm and ushered her into a car. She was a tall woman and wore glasses. Her name was Gertrude Karnopp; she was the wife of Lancaster County Sheriff Merle Karnopp from Lincoln. The Karnopps were among those who had made the drive to Wyoming to take Caril and Starkweather back to Lincoln.

"You can call me Mrs. Karnopp. I will be riding back to Lincoln with you. You and I are going to be seeing a lot of each other."

For a long time Caril didn't talk. She cried and Mrs. Karnopp gave her several tissues to dry her eyes. But Caril used the tissues instead to make little paper dolls she would give to Betty Jean when she saw her. Her baby sister loved tissue dolls. But, wait a minute. Didn't some fool tell her that Betty Jean was dead?

"Are my folks dead?" Caril asked Mrs. Karnopp.

Mrs. Karnopp looked at her and didn't answer.

"Who killed them?" Caril heard herself asking.

"Don't you know, Caril?" answered Mrs. Karnopp. Then, Mrs. Karnopp asked her what she was doing with the tissues, and Caril said she was making dolls for her little sister.

"But, Caril," Mrs. Karnopp said, "they're all dead."

Caril looked at Mrs. Karnopp and started to cry. She felt strange, confused. It's all those pills and the needles they gave me that is making me cloudy, all confused, she thought. Once I get home and see my mother, everything will be all right. Because she's alive. She's alive because I did everything he told me to do. I know it. This other stuff is all a dream. A very bad dream.

Lancaster County sheriff Merle Karnopp drove a second car, transporting Starkweather back to Lincoln. Lancaster County attorney Elmer Scheele accompanied them. During the drive back, Starkweather confessed to the murder of Robert Colvert when he robbed the Crest Service Station back in December in Lincoln. Starkweather revealed that on the night of the murder and robbery, he tried to disguise his appearance by wearing a red hunting cap and a bandana covering his face. He also told the two men that he tried to avoid detection afterwards by changing the tires on his car and painting his car black.

As both cars entered the Lincoln city limits, Caril heard the man driving the car tell her, "We're stopping at the penitentiary to drop off Starkweather, and then we're taking you to see the judge."

Why should I have to see a judge? Caril thought.

After they had arrived in Lincoln, they were soon in somebody's office, and a man who they said was a judge looked like he didn't want to be there this late at night. He looked annoyed and shook his head and asked, "What are we going to do with you, young lady?"

Caril just sat down on a hard chair and stared at the wall.

When the judge was finished talking, they all went back to the car, and she heard someone say they were taking her to a hospital. Caril did not realize she was being taken to a mental institution in Lincoln.

She was in a receiving room now, and two nurses were helping her take off her jacket and walking her over to a large scale and telling her to stand on it and hold still. "Ninety-eight pounds," she heard, then they started taking her clothes off.

Caril protested mildly, but it was all in vain because there were so many of them and only one of her. They put her into a tub filled with tepid water. She was cold and felt rough hands on her body and a hose rinsing her hair; the nurses told her if she did everything she was told to do they would get along just fine.

"Lift your arms," one of the nurses told Caril.

She obeyed because the nurse was talking to her in such a mean tone.

"You don't shave your underarms, do you?"

Caril shook her head no, and the nurse lifted her left arm and in a flash shaved it with a razor blade. "Lift the other arm."

Caril was afraid not to.

They dried her off and made her put on a big housedress. Then she was ushered between two nurses into a room.

"Where am I?" Caril asked.

But nobody would tell her anything.

"I want to see my mother. I want to see my sister. When can I get out of here? Why won't anybody tell me anything?" she screamed

Still, no one would answer her questions. They just told her that they were in charge and she had to do what she was told. Then they turned off the lights and told her to stay in bed, leaving her with wet hair and still cold from the bath.

Saturday, February 1, 1958

The next morning it was very noisy in the corridor. Caril looked around her room and tried to remember where she was. Sitting up in bed, she could see a chair facing the door to the corridor. A nurse came in, got her out of bed, and walked her across the hall to the washroom and toilet; she stood by while Caril washed her face and hands.

Then another nurse walked her down the hall to a big room with tables and chairs.

"You'll sit down here to eat your breakfast. Do not to talk to the other patients at the table."

Caril thought, other patients? Why did they put me in a hospital? Am I supposed to be sick or something? With the nurse standing right behind her, Caril looked down at her plate and ate some of the cold scrambled eggs and drank some milk. She was still cold and would have preferred a cup of coffee but didn't think she dare ask for a cup.

After she had finished breakfast, the nurse ushered her back to her room.

"You are to sit in this chair and not lie down on the bed during the day until we tell you it's time for rest period," the nurse said matter-of-factly.

"What am I doing in here? When can I go home?"

The nurse answered her only with a warning, "You are never to leave this room unattended. Do we understand each other?"

Caril smiled weakly and shook her head yes and didn't ask the nurse any more questions.

Caril sat in her chair and stared into an empty room directly across the hall from hers. She could see a bed and a wood box lying on top of a table next to it. Then, she saw men in hospital uniforms heading toward the empty room as they tried to restrain a woman in a straightjacket. The men had quite a hard time getting her into the bed. She was fighting and crying out incoherently. Her face was beet red.

The men took leather belts and used them to tie the woman down to the bed while she kept fighting with them and hollering, "No, no, no!"

A doctor and a nurse went into the room, and the doctor took some wires out of the wooden box on the table and attached them to the woman's head while she kept screaming and crying in terror. The doctor turned the knobs on the wooden box, and the woman jerked a few times and then went limp. They left her alone in the bed and when she awoke, Caril heard her say, "Water, water."

At that moment, Caril knew where she was and why she was here. She was in a mental institution and had been committed because she kept hearing voices that told her that her mother was dead. She sobbed and sobbed.

Later that morning, she was ushered into a larger room with a table and chairs and a davenport. Again, she was surrounded by unfamiliar faces staring at her. She did recognize Mrs. Karnopp and one of the men she had seen last night.

A dark-haired man wearing a suit told her his name was Dale Fahrnbruch. He was the deputy county attorney for Lancaster County. "I want to ask you some questions," he said. He introduced Caril to two more men, one of whom mumbled something about representing the public and making sure she was treated right.

Fahrnbruch told her that all he wanted was the truth and the reason he was there was to find out what had happened these last few days. He started asking her questions about what she and Starkweather did at Belmont, where her family lived. He asked questions about the retired farmer and the teenagers Robert Jensen and Carol King, but Caril didn't recognize their names.

He skipped around to different topics; he wanted to know about the gun she carried and whether it was loaded.

All Caril could think about was the shock treatments she had just witnessed and was afraid that if she didn't answer this man's questions the people at the hospital would give her shock treatments, too.

When she started to answer a question, sometimes Fahrnbruch would interrupt her and ask, "Now are you sure it happened this way? Didn't it really happen another way?"

Caril was afraid to disagree with him and repeated back to him some of the things he told her. Over and over again, he asked the same questions. He kept asking her whether she knew these things were wrong when they were happening. Caril would answer "Yes." Then, as she folded her arms across her chest she told him she was very cold. Someone left the room and brought a sweater back to her. The questions finally ended.

After lunch, Caril was taken back to her room. She wanted to lie down because she was so tired. But the nurses wouldn't let her rest; she had to go back downstairs with them that afternoon. When they got downstairs, there was Fahrnbruch, again, waiting for her.

There was another man with Fahrnbruch this time. "My name is Elmer Scheele." He was the Lancaster County prosecutor from Lincoln. He was neatly dressed in a business suit, and Caril noticed he had a very pronounced widow's peak. "We met at the jail in Wyoming. Do you remember me?"

When he said his name was Elmer, all Caril could think of was the cartoon character Elmer Fudd; she felt like calling him Elmer Fudd.

He told her that Starkweather was telling a different story than she was. "Which story is the truth? Are you sure it didn't happen this way?" he would ask.

Caril said, "No, it happened the way I told it."

He said something about sexual relations between her and Starkweather.

Puzzled, Caril just looked at him, knowing it didn't happen that way.

Scheele told her that she had sexual intercourse with Starkweather. He told her that Starkweather had stuck his penis inside of her; in fact, he stuck it in both places, didn't he?

Embarrassed as hell, Caril squeaked out that he tried but couldn't do anything and he got mad and turned her over and rubbed himself between her cheeks.

But Scheele kept insisting that what Starkweather did to her was have sex. That if he did what she said he did, that was having sex and that she should say so. In fact, he put it in your mouth, too, didn't he? You had it in your mouth.

113

Caril called him a filthy man and told him she never wanted to speak with him again, that she hated him and he could go straight to hell.

But the questions kept coming, often the same ones, over and over again. Fahrnbruch asked her to tell them what happened with the teenagers.

Caril told them about getting stuck in the mud and walking in the cold dark night until a car pulled up. She told him that Starkweather had told her to not say anything to anybody or he would have her family killed. She said she got into the backseat of the car first and Starkweather made her sit on the passenger's side and, yes, she was holding a shotgun because he made her do it.

She said she also pointed the shotgun at the girl and told her to get out of the car because Starkweather told her to. She told them about climbing over the seat to get in front because he told her to and that it was so cold. She talked about hearing gunshots and crying because she knew what Charlie had done. She knew he killed those people even though he said he wasn't going to hurt them. When he got in the car, she thought he was going to kill her, too. But, he didn't. He just sat there staring at the steering wheel and not responding to anything she said or asked him.

But the men said don't tell us about that, just tell us whether the gun you held was loaded and whether you knew Starkweather was going to take the boy's car.

The questions continued until Caril wanted to collapse. She would answer Fahrnbruch's questions, and then he would leave the room, and when he returned he would say to her that it really didn't happen the way she told it, did it? "Didn't it really happen this way?"

Caril became angry and shouted, "You all seem to know more about this than I do!" Under the relentless questioning, Caril grew tired, confused, and scared that if she didn't tell them what they wanted to hear that they would give her shock treatments, like the lady across the hall from her room.

Sunday, February 2, 1958

On Sunday morning, February 2, Caril was back in the reception room with Sheriff Karnopp, Mrs. Karnopp, a nurse, and Dr. Coats, the man in charge of the hospital.

Sheriff Karnopp asked her whether she might like to see Starkweather. "He's been asking about you every time I meet with him. How about it?"

Caril said, "I am scared to death of him and don't want to ever see him again."

"Well, Starkweather might not believe that if I tell him so, why don't you write to him and tell him you don't want to see him, and I'll give him the note later on," the Sheriff said. He gave Caril a piece of paper and pencil.

She wrote, "Charlie I don't want to see you. I'm afraid of what I might do." She handed the note to Sheriff Karnopp.

He smiled at her, said, "Thank you," and left.

Someone told Caril that she had visitors, and they ushered in her sister, Barb, her birth father, Bill Fugate, and his wife, Dot. But Caril wasn't allowed to be alone with them.

Her father told her to cooperate with the authorities and to tell them everything she could because this was such a serious matter.

Caril asked Barb whether it was true that he really killed the family, and Barb said yes, they were all dead.

Caril asked her how they were killed, and Barb said she didn't know. And it was only then that the full realization hit her. That the people who told her that her family was dead were telling her the truth all along. She thought they were crazy, and she didn't believe them, but she knew her sister would never lie to her. Never. And the only thing Caril said was that she wished he had killed her, too, so she could be with her mother.

In that moment, Caril didn't feel like crying. She didn't feel angry or sad or afraid. She didn't feel anything. She was numb. She didn't care what happened to her. She was a failure. Nothing mattered. Everything she did to save her family from being killed was for nothing. They were already dead all along. She felt stupid. Stupid to believe Starkweather's lies.

115

Starkweather did nothing but lie to her the whole time. Why couldn't she tell he was lying to her? All those times he told her he had just talked with them on the phone, and they said for her to do everything he said. All those times he got her to do whatever he wanted because he held that threat of making one phone call and they would all die. All lies from the beginning. Everything she did was for nothing. She could never have saved her family because they were already dead.

It was 8:00 that evening when Caril was taken to the admissions building at the Nebraska State Hospital to meet with Fahrnbruch again. Dr. Coats and Mrs. Karnopp were also there, along with another woman Caril had never seen before. This woman was already seated at a table with a pen and paper notepad in front of her.

"Caril, this is Miss Wheeler, a court reporter, and you know Mrs. Karnopp and Dr. Coats?" asked Fahrnbruch.

"Yes," Caril answered, zombie-like.

"Caril, you and I have talked a couple of times here, and you and I and your father talked this afternoon, is that right, Caril"? Fahrnbruch said pleasantly.

"Yes," she repeated.

"Will you speak up, Caril, when you answer my questions?"

"Yes."

"We discussed at that time, and talked over about taking this statement from you with the court reporter present, is that correct, Caril?"

"Yes."

"And you told me at that time that you would be willing to do that?"

"Yes."

"You also asked me at that time if there would be a trial?"

"Yes."

"And go to court, and I told you there would be?"

"Yes."

"And you understand that this can be used in court, this statement that we are taking? You understand that?"

"Yes."

"Now, have I made any threats or promises to you to get you to make this statement?"

"No."

"You are making it freely and voluntarily, is that correct?"

"Yes."

"And you want to tell me about the details of what happened, is that right?"

"Yes."

And so it began again. The same questions over and over again.

Caril knew the routine by now. She knew the answers they were looking for from her previous interviews, and she even repeated back information she learned from Fahrnbruch. For instance, when Fanrnbruch asked about the teenagers, she was now able to tell him that Starkweather did something to the girl down in the cellar besides kill her. She heard him tell that to one of the other men surrounding her since Wyoming.

Yes, yes, yes, she agreed that she held the gun on the girl. Yes, she knew the gun was loaded. Yes, she took money out of the teenage boy's billfold and put it into Starkweather's. Yes, she woke Starkweather up when the police came to her door and held the gun on the maid and held the flashlight for Starkweather when he was stabbing her. Yes, she looked out the window so she could let Starkweather know when Mr. Ward drove up to the house. She sprinkled perfume upstairs in Mrs. Ward's room. She watched television in the house and liked Abbott and Costello and enjoyed the comic book she went out to the mailbox to get.

Yes, I made Starkweather bacon and eggs. Yes, I cleaned off the bloody knife in the Wards' bathroom. Yes, I could have gotten away from him at times. She admitted everything. And, yes, she knew these things were wrong when they were being done. Yes, yes, yes to everything.

"Caril, are you getting a little tired now?" Fahrnbruch asked kindly.

"Yes."

"Would you like to stop now and have me come back later?"

"Yes."

"Is that what you would like to have me do?"

"Yes."

"All right, Caril, that's what we will do then."

"Yes."

"Have you been treated fairly here tonight?"

"Yes."

"Have I been courteous with you?"

"Yes."

"And have you answered these questions freely and voluntarily?"

"Yes."

"I haven't promised you anything or threatened you or anything, is that right?"

"Yes."

"And have you been answering these questions because you wanted to?"

"Yes."

"And you understand, Caril, these can be used in court in your trial? You understand that?"

"Yes."

"All right. That's all for now."

It was now 10:50 P.M. Caril had been interrogated on and off for over thirteen hours.

Monday, February 3, 1958

The next day, Monday, February 3, 1958, the interrogation resumed shortly after noon. After asking Caril whether she had a good night's sleep, Fahrnbruch started up again. This time he asked her about Starkweather's penis and whether he had it out of his trousers at any time and if he had put it into her sexual organs and her rear end and how far he stuck it in.

During this questioning, Caril said she acknowledged she knew how to load and shoot a gun. But no, she never told anybody at school that if her parents ever said she was pregnant, she would kill them.

When the session was coming to a close, Fahrnbruch told her that Miss Wheeler would type everything up and Caril would read and sign it later.

Caril said she would. It was now 1:25 P.M.

Then Fahrnbruch said, "Now Caril, the plans at this time are to take you to the courthouse this afternoon and there you will go to the county court to be arraigned in connection with the Jensen killing. Mr. Scheele has told me that this morning. We are asking that your father be there and that your sister be there, and you will be given an opportunity at that time to talk and consult with them. You talked with them for about an hour and a half yesterday, didn't you?"

"Yes."

"And they told you at that time to tell everything that you know, is that right?"

"Yes."

"And you have done that, is that right?"

"Everything I can remember."

"Now this charge, Caril, is a very serious one."

"I know that."

"And you knew at the time that these things were going on that they were wrong, didn't you?"

"Yes."

"And that is true in each case, the Meyer case?"

"But I didn't know he was going to kill them or I wouldn't have went."

"But you did know they were wrong at that time? And I have explained to you previously that when you participate in a case, that charges may be filed as if you had killed them yourself? You understand that?"

"Yes."

"And Caril, I told you that charges have been or will be charged on Robert Jensen against you, as Mr. Scheele told me?"

"That's what he (Starkweather) told me, yes."

"I beg pardon?"

"Never mind."

"Tell me what you were going to say," Fahrnbruch said to Caril.

"Charlie told me if I didn't do what he said my folks would be killed."

"And we are talking about this arraignment, and so forth, at the courthouse this afternoon, but I want to go over it with you now so you can be thinking about it. You will be taken to the county court after you have talked with your father and your sister, and then the charge will be read to you, and at that point the judge will ask you how you want to plead, and you have a choice, Caril."

"I'll plead guilty."

"Now Caril, I do not want you to plead guilty if you think you are not guilty."

"But I am. He (Starkweather) told me if I didn't go my folks would be killed."

"You make up your mind on how you want to plead, but if you feel yourself you are not guilty, then you should plead not guilty, you understand that?"

"Yes, but if I do plead not guilty....Well, I don't know, I can't explain it."

"Tell me what you mean, and I will try to explain it."

"If I plead not guilty, but yet they think I am, well, won't that just go bad against me?"

"Caril, a plea of not guilty cannot be used against you."

"Yes, but I have no proof from anybody that he threatened to kill my folks if I didn't do what he said. I have no proof."

"And Caril, the charge with which you are charged with is a very very serious one."

"I know it."

"It is murder in the first degree, and the charge will read that you did kill Robert Jensen of your own premeditated ..."

"What do you mean, I killed him?"

"...and deliberate malice," Farnburch added.

"I didn't hold the gun on him. I held the gun on the girl."

"In this state Caril, if you aid or abet, even though you do not pull the trigger yourself, then you are as guilty as the principal. And, as Mr. Scheele explained to you, and he did explain to you in Wyoming, did he not, that you could have a lawyer if you wanted one?"

"Yes."

"And you told him at that time you did not want a lawyer?"

"No, I never.... I didn't know what he meant at that time by that. I thought he meant by the district attorney."

"And were you aware at all times, Caril, that you could have a lawyer if you wanted one?"

"No, I wasn't."

"Did your father tell you that yesterday?"

"No, I don't think he did."

"Did you want a lawyer at that time?"

"Yes."

"And you want a lawyer now, is that right?"

"Yes, but who would take it?"

PART IV

The Trial of
CHARLES STARKWEATHER

CHAPTER 12

On February 3, 1958, Charles Starkweather and Caril Fugate were arraigned and charged with premeditated murder during the commission of a robbery of Robert Jensen, Jr. Each pleaded not guilty. On March 10, 1958, Judge Harry Spencer appointed T. Clement Gaughan and William T. Matschullat to represent Starkweather.

Before his trial even began, Starkweather told nine different versions of his killing spree and Caril's innocence or complicity in it.

Version 1. January 28, 1958—Written at Ward House

This was a letter written entirely in Starkweather's hand but was purporting to have been written by both him and Caril at the Wards' house. The letter was placed inside of a Lincoln Commerce Bank envelope and marked, "For the law only." It was taken from Starkweather's pocket upon his capture.

Caril supposedly wrote the letter and said that the Bartletts were dead because of "me and Charlie." She described Charlie as happy and full of jokes until her Mom, Velda, told him to get out, and Marion started hitting and pushing him all over the room. "Charlie shot Marion and mom grabbed a knife to cut Charlie. Then Velda got his gun, but Caril knocked the gun out of her hands and saved Charlie. Betty Jean was yelling so loud that Caril hit her ten times with the butt of the gun while Charlie threw his knife at her. The story ended with, "Charlie and I are sorry for what we did, but we know we are going to the end."

123

Version 2. *January 29, 1958*

After Starkweather was captured, William Dixon, county attorney in Douglas, Wyoming, took a transcribed confession from him on the evening of January 29, 1958, in the Wyoming jail. Betty Alberts, the official court reporter, transcribed Starkweather's statement.

Betty remembered the chaos and crowd on the front lawn of the jailhouse. Betty sat in front of the cell, which had a sink next to the bars. She remembers Starkweather being very polite and soft-spoken with the authorities. Starkweather admitted to all the killings and completely exonerated Caril, admitting she was his hostage the whole time. He also said killing all those people didn't make him feel any different than if he killed a rabbit. Starkweather went to the sink for a glass of water several times and, each time he did, Betty thought he was going to throw a glass of water at her through the bars.

Version 3. *January 29, 1958*

This was a confession written in longhand by Starkweather on January 29, 1958, in his Douglas, Wyoming, jail cell. In the letter, he says he killed the Bartletts before Caril came home from school. Mrs. Bartlett hit Charlie three times before Mr. Bartlett came into the room, hit Charlie again, picked up a hammer, and threatened him.

Starkweather said he shot Mr. Bartlett with a .22. Mrs. Bartlett brandished a knife, and he shot her, too. The toddler, Betty Jean, was screaming, so he hit her. Caril came home at 4:00. He said he told her a line that her family was somewhere. He wanted to tell Caril about her parents, but the days went by so quickly he never got around to it.

Version 4. *January 29, 1958*

In a letter to his parents, Starkweather said Caril helped him a lot but had "not a thing to do with the killing. All we wanted to do was get out of town."

Version 5. *January 31, 1958*

Written in pencil on his cell wall in Gering, Nebraska, "from L. NE they got us Jan. 29, 1958. 1958 kill 11 persons

(Charles kill 9) all men. (Caril kill 2) all girls." He also drew a heart with an arrow through it with "Charles S." and "Caril F." at the bottom of the message.

Version 6. February 1, 1958

This version came in the form of a formal statement taken by Elmer Scheele on February 1, 1958 in Lincoln, Nebraska.

In this statement, Starkweather stated he got to the Bartletts at 1:30 while Caril was in school. Mrs. Bartlett slapped him, and he hit her back. Mr. Bartlett came flying out and began hitting Starkweather. Mr. Bartlett ran into the kitchen and got a hammer and raised it, and Starkweather shot him. Mrs. Bartlett picked up the hammer and Starkweather shot her, too. She wasn't dead, so he hit her with the butt of his gun.

Betty Jean was hollering so loud that he threw his knife at her and hit her in the neck or head or chest. He also hit Betty Jean in the head with the butt of the gun. Right after he killed them, about 2:00, he went to Hutson's, a small grocery store down the street from Caril's house and called Watson Brothers to tell them Mr. Bartlett was sick and wouldn't be in to work. He returned to the house and cleaned up.

On February 2, 1958, Sheriff Karnopp asked Caril to write a letter to Starkweather. She told him she didn't want to see him and that she was afraid of what she might do to him. Sheriff Karnopp later testified that Elmer Scheele approved of him asking Caril to write this note.

It is likely that this letter helped turn Starkweather against her, and, as his next confession will show, made him implicate her further.

Note: After Starkweather received that note from Caril, he turned on her with a vengeance. It would appear that law enforcement's and the prosecution's motive was to do just that—turn Starkweather against Caril so that he would testify against her at her trial.

Scheele knew Caril was about to be arraigned the next day, February 3, before the county court. Once she pleaded not guilty, she would be bound over to district court where she would be appointed counsel to represent her as an indigent person with no money to hire an attorney. Interestingly, Scheele arranged to get Caril's note to Starkweather before she was appointed an attorney who would have not permitted her to communicate with Starkweather.

Further, it is grossly improper to sneak letters out of a jail. There is an established procedure for sending mail from jails. People in confinement have strict procedures as to the sending and receiving of mail. In order for attorneys to keep letters to their clients unopened before delivery, they must write "Attorney/Client Privileged" on each envelope. This was another rule that Sheriff Karnopp broke—he preemptively and deliberately circumvented the attorney-client relationships, not only of Caril and those people who would be appointed her attorneys, but also Starkweather and his future attorneys.

Version 7. February 27, 1958

A formal statement was taken by Lancaster County deputy attorney Dale Fahrnbruch on February 27, 1958. In this statement, Starkweather said he arrived at the Bartletts' house at 1:30. All three of the Bartletts were in the kitchen. Mrs. Bartlett told him that Mr. Bartlett was not going hunting and to leave. Starkweather told her to go to hell, so she hit him in the face. Starkweather left the house and drove around the block for about ten to fifteen minutes and returned to find out "what the hell was the matter." Mr. Bartlett kicked him out the door, so he drove to Hutson's and called Mr. Bartlett's employer to say Bartlett was sick and won't be in for work.

Starkweather drove back to the Bartletts around 3:00 and knocked on the door, but nobody answered. He drove to school to pick Caril up but had car trouble along the way, so he left the car at a neighbor's house and returned to the Bartletts.

He sat on the back porch and waited for Caril to get home. He heard Caril and her mother shouting at each other in Caril's room. Later, Mrs. Bartlett accused Starkweather of getting Caril pregnant and slapped him. Starkweather hit Mrs. Bartlett back, and Mr. Bartlett got into a fistfight with him. Then, both ran in different directions—Mr. Bartlett to his tool room, Starkweather into Caril's bedroom, where he'd left his .22. Mr. Bartlett came at him with a hammer, and Starkweather shot him.

Meanwhile, Mrs. Bartlett ran into the kitchen, where she got a knife and told Starkweather she was going to chop his head off. Caril jerked the .22 out of Starkweather's hands and told her mother she was going to blow her to hell. Mrs. Bartlett knocked Caril down while Starkweather grabbed back his .22, shot Mrs. Bartlett, and then hit her in the head with the butt of the gun a few times. He hit Betty Jean who was screaming, and Caril told her to shut up. Then he hit Betty Jean with the knife. Mr. Bartlett was still moving, so Starkweather hit him in the throat a few times.

Caril was just standing around and asked Starkweather what they were going to do with them. He asked her, "What do you think we ought to do?" But Caril said nothing and went into the living room, where she watched television on the couch while Starkweather cleaned up.

Version 8. March 28, 1958

In a letter to Elmer Scheele written on March 28, 1958, Starkweather states that Caril Fugate shot the teenage girl, Carol King, while he was trying to get Robert Jensen's car out of a ditch. Starkweather says Caril Fugate and Starkweather shot Merle Collison together.

Version 9. April 9, 1958

In a letter to Elmer Scheele written on April 9, 1958, Starkweather protested that he'll "be convicted for what I did and that's okay....But I'll be damned if I'll be sentenced for what I didn't do." He said that Caril Fugate was "the most trigger-happy person I ever saw." He also repeats that Caril Fugate killed Carol King and Merle Collison.

Starkweather's trial began on May 5, 1958, and ended May 22, 1958. This was the biggest murder case ever tried in Lincoln, Nebraska. At that time, cameras were barred in courtrooms. Outside the courthouse and inside the public corridors, the atmosphere was circus-like—filled with journalists from all over the world; they competed for space with the mobs of spectators in the hopes of catching a glimpse of the "mad-dog killer." Starkweather had gained notoriety as one of the nation's first spree killers.

As Starkweather sauntered into the courthouse, he grinned at the spectators and journalists as if he were walking on the red carpet at a movie premiere rather than being led in chains to his own murder trial. Journalists and photographers hollered, "Look over here, Charlie!" and "One for the camera, Charlie!" Starkweather seemed to eat up the attention. For the first time in his life, he was a "somebody," the famous criminal he had always yearned to become. It didn't bother him that his hands were shackled with handcuffs, locked to his belt as Sheriff Karnopp held on tightly to another chain clamped around the belt. When Starkweather entered the courtroom in handcuffs, shackles, and belt having been removed, the jury and spectators stared at him with looks ranging from fascination to horror. And through the huge pool of journalists there, the eyes of the rest of the world were inside that Lincoln, Nebraska courtroom.

The first action the defense counsel took was to change Starkweather's plea of "not guilty" to one of "not guilty by reason of insanity." The defense counsel alleged that Starkweather was suffering from a delusion and was legally insane at the time he killed Jensen.

Starkweather and his family were enraged by this change in plea and from that moment forward became enemies of his attorneys, who were trying to save him from the electric chair. The Starkweathers did not want the taint of insanity hanging over their family. Starkweather's mother, Helen, stared daggers at the defense counsel every time they brought up Starkweather's insanity as a defense for his senseless killings.

On May 15, 1958, Starkweather took the stand in his own defense and told the jury, "I killed them all in self-defense, the ones I killed."

Although Starkweather maintained that he killed in self-defense, his murders were premeditated and well planned. Starkweather loitered at the service station at night, exhibited an interest when cash was being counted and knew when sales were slow. He made Colvert turn out some lights so passing motorists could not see inside the station. He had borrowed a rifle, and wore a face mask when he robbed the station.

The Bartlett murders were also premeditated. The morning of the Bartlett murders, Starkweather volunteered to help his brother Rodney out on his garbage route, despite the fact that he had been recently fired from his job there. He needed to see Rodney to borrow his .22 rifle because he said he was going hunting with Marion Bartlett. Marion Bartlett and Starkweather disliked each other. Although Marion had a shotgun in the house, he never used it or took it out of its case and never went hunting, let alone with Starkweather.

Marion was seen at 1:20 that afternoon at a grocery store, but Marion's boss received a phone call prior to 2:00 saying Marion was sick and wouldn't be into work. Even though Starkweather later tried to convince Caril's jury that he killed the Bartletts after Caril returned home at 4:00, it is clear that he never would have made that phone call to Marion's boss shortly before 2:00 if Marion were not already dead.

Starkweather sawed off Marion's .410 shotgun while at the Bartletts' house. A sawed-off shotgun was not good for hunting, but it was good for shooting people at close range because the buckshot spray would cover a larger area. Starkweather was planning further murders.

August Meyer's death was also premeditated. Starkweather thought the farmer had a lot of cash, so he ransacked Meyer's home looking for it. Starkweather also purchased bullets for a .22 rifle after dropping his brother Rodney's .22 rifle off at the home of friends, the Griggs. Although at the time he no longer had Rodney's .22 rifle, he knew August Meyer had a .22 and planned to take it with him after shooting Meyer.

The murders of Robert Jensen, Jr. and Carol King were premeditated. Starkweather's car had gotten stuck in a ditch on August Meyer's farm. He needed another form of transportation to make his escape. When he saw Jensen's car approaching, he flagged it down, planning to steal it. When Jensen offered him a ride to a telephone booth, Starkweather first robbed him and later killed both teenagers.

The murders of the Wards and Lilyan Fencl were also premeditated. Starkweather knew the authorities were looking for him. He knew the basic layout of the Wards' house, and he realized that he could easily conceal Jensen's car from street view there. He also knew the Wards were wealthy and thought he could rob them for money.

Several psychiatrists and psychologists were called to the witness stand during Starkweather's trial. Dr. Nathan Greenbaum, a psychologist from Kansas City, testified for the defense. He claimed that a person "means no more to him (Starkweather) than a stick." Starkweather, he said, suffered from a severe mental illness and did not know the difference between right and wrong when he killed Jensen.

Dr. John O'Hearne, a psychiatrist also from Kansas City, also testifying for the defense, referred to Starkweather as a "wild animal" incapable of premeditation. O'Hearne stated that "pumping bullets into a human is no different to Starkweather than pumping bullets into a rabbit."

Dr. Robert Steinman, a psychologist, also testifying for the defense, told the jury that Starkweather sincerely believed he killed all of his victims in self-defense.

Another psychiatrist, Dr. Robert Stein, testifying for the prosecution, stated that even though Starkweather had a personality disorder, he was legally sane and was "not a fit person for confining to a mental hospital."

Yet another psychiatrist, Dr. Edwin Coats, acting superintendent of the Lincoln State Hospital, in testifying for the prosecution, described Starkweather as a "cooperative, pleasant young man who readily admits the crimes with which he is charged " and did not suffer from "delusions or hallucinations."

Dr. Charles Munson, a psychologist practicing at the Lincoln State Hospital, also testifying for the prosecution, offered his opinion that Starkweather was sane.

Deputy William Romer of Wyoming was called to testify for the prosecution about Starkweather's sanity. On the witness stand, Romer denied that Caril had called Starkweather crazy. To admit that Caril called Starkweather crazy would hurt the prosecution's contention that Starkweather was sane at the time he committed murder. And the State would not execute a defendant found not guilty by reason of insanity. Romer's testimony suggests that he forgot that on January 30, 1958, the *Casper Tribune-Herald* quoted Romer, describing what Caril screamed at him after her escape from Starkweather, "He's going to kill me....He's crazy. He just killed a man."

Starkweather's defense attorney T. Clement Gaug-han put a witness on the stand to refute Romer's testimony. That witness was Wendell Harding Jr., a reporter for the *Lincoln Star*. The reporter testified that he called Romer long distance on January 29, 1958. Describing their conversation, Harding testified that Romer stated that Caril Fugate said about Starkweather, "He's crazy."

The next two witnesses at Starkweather's trial were Sheriff Earl Heflin and the Lincoln assistant chief of police, Eugene Masters.

Under questioning by prosecuting attorney Elmer Scheele, Sheriff Heflin testified that after receiving an alert from Casper, Wyoming, a fellow officer picked him up, and they drove west to meet Starkweather's car. Five miles west of town they met up with the vehicle driven by Starkweather, turned around, and went after it.

With the siren on, they caught up with the car in town in Douglas, Wyoming, when Starkweather was stopped at a stoplight. They ran into the side of Starkweather's car and locked bumpers, at which time the bumper of Starkweather's car broke loose. Starkweather turned south with the Sheriff, following him out of town at 115 miles per hour. Heflin shot at the car with his .38 pistol and a 30-30 rifle. The shots struck the back window, and Starkweather stopped his car.

When Starkweather got out of his car, Heflin told him, "Put your hands up and come walking toward me, and lie down on the ground." He handcuffed Starkweather and took him to the jail.

Heflin went on to state that on January 29th, upon his capture, Starkweather gave a confession to the Converse county attorney and prosecutor William P. Dixon that was transcribed, and that Starkweather also wrote a letter to his parents while he was in jail. Heflin stated that he turned the letter over to the county attorney, who then turned it over to Lincoln assistant police chief Eugene Masters the following afternoon on January 30, 1958.

With Heflin on the witness stand, Scheele asked, "Did you, or Mr. Dixon in your presence, deliver anything else to Mr. Masters on the 30th of January, 1958?"

"There was a letter," Heflin replied.

Note: This letter to which Heflin is referring is Version No. 1—the letter written in Starkweather's hand at the Ward's house on January 28. It was one of the many versions of the story that Starkweather gave.

Scheele continued. "Where was that letter obtained, Sheriff?"

"My undersheriff obtained it from Charles Starkweather."

"To whom was the letter addressed?"

"To any officer."

"You gave that to Masters or the undersheriff?"

"That's right," Heflin responded.

Then, Starkweather's attorney, Clement Gaughan, questioned Heflin. "Now, this one letter that you got out of the car was addressed to an officer. Did you find the letter in Starkweather's pocket or in someone else's pocket that was addressed to an officer—law enforcement?"

"My undersheriff (in Wyoming)."

"What was that?" Gaughan questioned.

"My undersheriff. He searched (Starkweather) and found that letter."

"Who was that letter addressed to?"

"I never really read that letter. I turned it over to Eugene Masters" (the assistant police chief in Lincoln).

Note: The fact that Heflin stated he never read this letter will become critical during Caril's trial. It's important to also note that although Heflin must have seen the envelope which contained this note that was addressed "for the law only," he never actually read the note contained inside. When Heflin responded to Scheele's question, "To whom was the letter addressed?" with "To any officer," Helfin is talking about the envelope, not the letter.

Later, under direct examination by Scheele, Eugene Masters testified that on January 30, 1958, while in Douglas, Wyoming, he obtained three documents: a handwritten confession of Starkweather from county attorney Dixon (Version 3 of Starkweather's many versions of the killings); a handwritten letter Starkweather wrote to his parents, also from Dixon (Version 4); and a letter obtained by undersheriff J. C. Owens, "who took it from the person of Charles Starkweather" (Version 1).

Masters stated that Version 1 was contained inside an envelope marked "For the law only." The envelope had "National Bank of Commerce, Lincoln, Nebraska" printed on the front. The letter and envelope with "For the law only" on it were marked as Exhibit 30 and read into the record by Masters.

To summarize, Sheriff Heflin stated that he never read the letter taken from Starkweather by undersheriff Owens (Version 1). He simply took it from undersheriff Owens and turned it over to Eugene Masters, the assistant police chief from Lincoln. Masters testified that he received three letters in total from Douglas, Wyoming.

Note: At Caril's upcoming trial, Masters will testify that the Wyoming authorities only turned over one note to him; it was Version No. 1 marked, "For the law only." It was the note taken from Starkweather after his capture.

During his trial, Starkweather continually attacked Caril's character.

On May 15, 1958, during the trial, newspaper headlines read: "Starkweather Accuses Caril of King Murder." Clem Gaughan (Starkweather's attorney) referred to a portion of Starkweather's confession in which he said he got mad at Caril after the deaths of Jensen and the King girl. "What were you mad at Caril about?" Gaughan asked. "For what she did." "What did she do?" "She shot Carol King.'"

On May 16, 1958, headlines read: "Caril Fugate Accused of Stabbing Maid." The story said, "Caril Fugate, 14, knifed a woman to death as she lay on a bed with her hands and feet tied to a bedpost, according to a confession read at Charles Starkweather's murder trial today....Starkweather said flatly he did not stab Miss Fencl although he freely admitted the Ward slayings."

On May 18, 1958, headlines read: "Stunned Jury Hears Starkweather Testify." The article stated, "Starkweather's confession said his girlfriend rejoiced in the deaths of her mother, stepfather and baby half-sister, early victims in the marathon slayings. 'This is what we always wanted,' he quoted her as saying after the killings. Starkweather explained 'We had talked about leaving here and Caril said we would if we had to bump them off.' "

The trial of Charles Starkweather came to a close on May 22, 1958. The jury began deliberating Starkweather's fate at 5:25 P.M. that day. They deliberated for two hours and forty-five minutes before resuming deliberations the next morning at 9:07 A.M. They reached a verdict at 2:55 P.M. on May 23. They found Charles Starkweather guilty and determined that he should be sentenced to death.

As the sentence was announced, Starkweather stood emotionless. His mother's sobs were the only sound in the otherwise hushed courtroom.

On May 27, 1958, *United Press International* quoted Starkweather: "I will be glad to go to the chair if Caril will sit on my lap."

Charles Starkweather was executed in Nebraska's electric chair on June 25, 1959, approximately one year after being found guilty. But before meeting his death, Starkweather would do all that he could to take Caril down with him.

Upon learning of Starkweather's receiving the death penalty, Caril Fugate was devastated—he was the only other person who would ever be able to tell what really happened. She still had hope that someday he would.

Shortly before Starkweather's execution, Caril sent an impassioned telegram to President Eisenhower:

I am now fifteen years old. About a year and one half ago on a day when I was in public school, nineteen-year-old Charles Starkweather whom I had told several days before in front of my mother never to see me again, went into my home and killed my two-year-old baby sister, mother, and stepfather. Starkweather first confessed I had nothing to do with his murders—which is true. Later he changed his story and said I helped him do his murders, which is not true. He forced me to go with him when I got home from school against my will. Starkweather will be executed tomorrow. I have been denied by Governor Brooks a request to see him (Starkweather) and see if he will tell the truth in front of a minister or someone else who would be fair before he is executed. I know of no one else to turn to because all of my family I was living with he killed. I know you are very busy but please help in any way you can. Thank you.

The White House sent the following reply: "The Starkweather case is entirely a state matter. The President has no jurisdiction or authority to comply with your request."

Once Starkweather was executed, Caril would lose all hope of the truth ever being told.

PART V

THE TRIAL OF
Caril Fugate

CHAPTER 13

In October 1958, preparations were being made for the trial of Caril Fugate. She was accused of aiding and abetting Charles Starkweather in the murder of Robert Jensen, Jr. But Caril was convicted by public opinion long before she stood trial. Her character had been assailed in the press by Starkweather's boastful and untruthful accounts of his sexual relations with Caril. Even though he was impotent the one time he had attempted intercourse with Caril, he bragged about their sexual escapades, telling officers that they had sex every day at Caril's house and "twice on Sundays." In 1958, an unmarried girl who had sexual relations was considered a "tramp" and capable of anything. Lincoln was a small enough town that the rumor mill churned out seemingly endless claims, including that Caril had delivered Starkweather's child while waiting for trial.

Perhaps a letter sent to Caril's attorney, John McArthur, during her trial sums up what most of the public thought of Caril:

Sir,

Are you so bad off you must sear your soul and lie and cheat for a murderer and hoar [sic]? Supposing it was your son or daughter who had been so brutally butchered without cause. How would you like for some fat old lawyer to take the case of the criminal and raise heaven and hell to clear that brute? Why were you almost the only attorney in the city who was willing to defend such a horrible girl? For shame! How can you look yourself in the face? Be careful or the judgments of the Lord will fall on you and your loved ones for your dastardly actions. Let justice take its course and you keep your big mouth shut. How can any attorney like you escape the judgment? Better watch out!

Signed, Disgusted.

For months prior to her trial, local newspapers headlined Starkweather's accusations that Caril rejoiced in her family's deaths and that she killed Carol King, Lilyan Fencl, and Merle Collison. The press coverage about the "unnatural" sex attack on Carol King also loomed heavily over Caril's head. Was it possible for any potential juror not to have already been influenced by Caril's demonization in the media? Although Caril was being tried only for aiding and abetting Starkweather in the murder of Robert Jensen, Jr., the prosecutors would make certain to keep all the alleged but uncharged murders before the jury.

Note: Less than one week before being selected as a juror to decide Caril's fate, one juror made statements that should have resulted in his being disqualified as a juror. That juror, H.A. Wallenta, made a bet that Caril would get the death penalty. This fact came to light after Caril's trial. Her attorneys filed a motion for a mistrial, but the judge, Harry Spencer, did not declare one. While being questioned under oath during the voir dire part of trial—the part in which attorneys for both sides ask potential jurors whether they have formed any bias, prejudice, or opinion as to the guilt of the defendant on trial—Wallenta had sworn that he had no opinion as to the guilt or innocence of Caril. He also swore that he had never expressed any opinion as to her guilt or innocence; that he would keep in mind the presumption of innocence of an accused; and that he would be absolutely impartial if chosen to serve on the jury.

October 27, 1958

The trial of Caril Fugate began on October 27, 1958. Much like Starkweather's trial, the courthouse was packed.

The moment Caril entered the courthouse in the firm grip of Gertrude Karnopp, she was surrounded by a pack of journalists and photographers who worked for local, regional, national, and international news operations—newspapers, magazines, television, and radio. The coverage was worldwide and relentless.

How did this happen? Caril asked herself. Why am I here when all I did was tell them the truth? All these camera flashbulbs are blinding me, and all this hollering at me is making me insane. On trial for murder. Little soldier—that's what mom always told me to be. Remember Caril, even when you're afraid, don't show it. Always be a little soldier, honey, a little soldier. I'll be a little soldier for you, mom. I'll keep my head held high and pretend none of this is happening. I'll look straight ahead, and I won't look afraid, and I won't look sad because if I do I will fall apart. I am all alone. Nobody is in this place with me. I don't see anybody, and I don't hear anybody. This, too, shall pass, mother; this, too, shall pass.

Attorney John McArthur represented Caril Fugate in her murder trial. He told the court, "This girl was introduced into this horrible sequence of events by opening the door and having a gun stuck in her face. Hers was really a story of a child in fear for her life for eight terrifying days, a child who believed that not only her own life was in danger, but also the lives of her family. She did not know they were dead."

McArthur continued, "If people knew the truth, they would realize that Caril Fugate was no criminal. She was Starkweather's victim, as were all the other victims of Starkweather's madness. Must we condemn Caril for failing to do what no one else in Nebraska could do: Stop Starkweather? She was no accomplice. She was a captive."

The prosecution was the first to present its case. The first person the prosecuting attorney called to the witness stand was Robert Jensen, Sr., the father of the teenage victim Robert

E. Jensen, Jr. Mr. Jensen operated a general store in Bennet, Nebraska and identified his son, Robert, as the murder victim. In taking the witness stand, Mr. Jensen, once again, was forced to relive the nightmare of his son's violent death. The prosecution called him purportedly to identify his son as the deceased, despite the fact that there was no question as to the unfortunate young man's identity. In reality, Mr. Jensen was called to incite the jury against Caril. The fact that his son missed one year at school because of polio, that he liked helping his father at the store, that he was carrying American Legion literature to deliver to the home of the adjutant of the legion post were all offered for the strategic purpose of inflaming the jury against Caril.

Next to testify was Warren King, brother of Jensen's murdered girlfriend, Carol King. He told the jury that Carol King sang in the choir at the Bennet Community Church and was active in 4-H. He explained that his sister had been dating Robert, Jr. for six months and did so with her family's approval. He went on to say that earlier in the evening of the night she was murdered she discussed her report card of straight As and helped her mother with the dishes. Warren King's heart-wrenching testimony regarding the double funeral of these two very fine young people brought tears to the jurors' eyes—but all this had nothing to do with the case against Caril. Clearly, this testimony was meant to demonize Caril Fugate by contrasting her reputation as a tramp and possible killer with the flawless characters of Robert Jensen, Jr. and Carol King.

Dr. Edwin D. Zeman, the pathologist who performed the autopsy on Robert Jensen, was called next. Zeman described Jensen's body lying in the hospital cart, the clothes blood-stained, his face covered in clotted blood, dirt, and grime. Zeman showed that Jensen's violent death was as a result of traumatic multiple gunshot wounds to the head, producing lacerations to the large blood vessels in the brain. Zeman was also used by the prosecution to introduce two excessively inflammatory exhibits. He identified Exhibit 10, a photo of Jensen on an examination table, and Exhibit 11, a close-up photo taken of the right side of Jensen's head. Why would any judge allow more than one of these photos into evidence? No question, the jurors were already acutely aware that young Robert Jensen had been brutally murdered. John McArthur, Caril's attorney, made objections to the photos being shown. He said they were inflammatory and prejudicial and were clearly meant to sicken and inflame the jury. But the judge allowed the photos to be shown to the jury.

Deputy William Johnson was called next. He testified that when he arrived at the storm cellar other officers were there, and he observed the body of a boy and a girl laying at the bottom of the cellar, the girl partially up the steps. The bodies had been identified to him as Robert Jensen and Carol King. As was his duty, on January 28 he had taken photos at the cellar and of the surrounding evidence and the inside of the cellar. Johnson identified the photograph he took of the deceased Carol King. The photograph depicted the victim lying on her side with her shirt and jacket pulled up to expose her breasts and her pants pulled down around her ankles. Her buttocks and thighs were smeared with blood. Again, Caril's attorney objected to the photo being shown, but his objection was again overruled by the judge.

Caril Fugate was not charged with the murder of Carol King, but Starkweather's accusations that she did kill Carol King had been the subject of headlines in the local newspapers for weeks prior to her trial. This picture likely served its purpose to further inflame the jury. No doubt they would think that if a girl could possibly commit such a heinous act, she was capable of much worse. Caril Fugate never saw this photograph, but she remembers a look of total disgust on a female juror's face while looking at her after being shown this picture. After being released from prison, Caril saw the photograph of Robert E. Jensen, Jr. lying on his stomach in the cellar. She never saw or wanted to see the photo of Carol King, but she did have to listen to testimony of the knife wounds that tore through the teenage girl's vagina and into her rectum.

Note: Caril's attorney stated that Caril was never charged with the murder of Carol King. The prosecutors should not have been allowed to bring anything up about Carol King. Photos of the murdered teenage girl should never have been allowed in court. This is an example of what is legally referred to as "uncharged misconduct"—evidence that is prohibited from being used in a criminal trial. It is negative-character evidence used to improperly influence a jury to consider the defendant's bad character. A jury hearing about this bad character cannot help but draw conclusions that if the defendant did something bad before, such as killing and mutilating Carol King—if they believed Starkweather's claim—she was also capable of willingly participating in the killing of young Jensen.

Again, Caril's attorney John McArthur objected to the photo being shown, but the judge again allowed it in.

The court recessed at noon on October 30 and reconvened at 9:15 A.M. on Friday, October 31, 1958—Halloween. This Halloween in Lincoln, Nebraska, was different from past Halloweens in Lincoln, a town where free-spirited children, outfitted in masks and costumes, made their way down the tree-lined streets, filling their bags with candy. Until Starkweather's rampage, Lincoln had been considered an ideal place to raise children. This Halloween, parents would accompany their children with a flashlight. Starkweather was in prison and condemned to death, but the taint of the terror he had left had not yet subsided from this previously idyllic community.

After the prosecution had called the relatives of Carol King and Robert Jensen, Jr. and had shown the jury violent photos of both teenagers in death, the prosecution began to try to prove their case against Caril. They had to prove three crucial elements before Caril could be convicted. First, that she was not a hostage and that she had accompanied Starkweather as his willing participant. Second, that she gave her incriminating statement after being fully aware that she was charged with murder and was aware of the penalty. And third, that Caril knew she had the right to counsel during her interrogations, but that she willingly and voluntarily waived her right.

Deputy William Romer, of Natrona County, Wyoming, the man to whom Caril ran screaming after running away from Starkweather, served as a major witness for the prosecution. In his testimony there is a glowing discrepancy between what he told Wyoming reporters after Starkweather was captured and what he was now saying on the witness stand.

In an interview to *The Laramie Boomerang* that was printed on January 31, 1958, Romer had said, "She (Caril) kept saying, 'I've seen nine people killed. My mother and my father and my sister are dead.'" Although Romer first told the media that Caril told him she had seen Starkweather kill nine people, he later changed his statement at her trial and testified that she told him she had seen Starkweather kill ten people.

On January 30, 1958, the *Lincoln Evening Journal* had reported:

At speeds over 100 miles per hour, Caril Ann Fugate, 14, watched the last free moments of her boyfriend Charles Starkweather.

Natrona County deputy sheriff Bill Romer, one of the few people who talked to the girl before she became "too hysterical to understand," told the story:

"When I came on the scene where the young geologist (Joe Sprinkle) and Caril were, she immediately jumped out of the Packard and ran in beside me in the front seat."

She told the deputy that Starkweather, who had left the scene at a high rate of speed a few minutes before, had "just killed a man."

Also one of the last persons who talked to the girl before she was locked in Converse County Jail, Romer said the girl looked tired and hungry and "downright afraid."

"She just sat there in a high state of excitement as I radioed ahead to try and stop him. She told me that she had seen all nine murders in Nebraska." Romer said the girl "finally wound down and became unintelligible."

"I couldn't tell for sure what she was saying sometimes. Her memory seemed to become progressively worse as we got her near the jail."

Even though Romer was quoted in the newspaper as saying that when Caril first ran toward him, she told him she saw Starkweather kill *nine* people, but that her speech was unintelligible and that he couldn't tell what she was saying sometimes, at her trial, he would change his testimony. When questioned by prosecutor Scheele as to what Caril told him after she ran to him, Romer responded that "she told me that she had seen Mr. Starkweather kill ten people....she said she had seen him kill her mother, her stepfather, her baby sister, a boy and a girl, a farmhand, and three other people."

Romer continued, stating that "Caril said that her mother had slapped Starkweather, and he started to hit her when the stepfather interfered, and at that time Starkweather killed her stepfather and then killed her mother and killed her sister. She said that the baby was crying and that Starkweather took the barrel of the gun and pushed it in the throat of the baby."

During Romer's testimony, Caril's mind was racing. No, no, no! I never said that! You let him get away, and he was going to kill my family. Don't you see? I escaped from him! I was screaming at you not to let him get away! Then we heard on the radio that he was caught. When the other man in the car kept saying I could stop my crying now because he was caught, I was relieved. My family was safe from him, I thought. I saved their lives, I saved them. So help me God, I thought I had saved them.

Note: Colonel Stan Warne, who was never called as a witness, was present on the scene shortly after Caril ran to Romer, and Warne observed her condition firsthand. Warne had stated that he couldn't make out anything Caril said, that she was hysterical, that there was nothing he could do to help her, so he just made sure she didn't hurt herself. To show how confused she was, Warne remembers Caril saying, "He wouldn't kill my little brother, would he?"—but Warne hadn't read anything in the papers about Fugate having a little brother.

If Caril was this hysterical, how could Romer purport to hear her make such specific, incriminating remarks?

On cross-examination Caril's attorney John McArthur asked Romer if, before he happened upon the Collison crime scene, he had already heard about somebody by the name of Starkweather and his crimes.

"Yes," Romer responded.

146

"It was pretty much in the news there for a period of time there before, was it not?" McArthur asked.

"No, sir, it was not."

"Well, how had you heard it then?"

"I read it in the newspaper that morning, that was the first time it had appeared."

"Well, there was a rather detailed account of a trail of violence, wasn't there?"

"No, sir, there was not; there was a picture in there with a little title underneath the picture."

"That was all you knew about it?"

"Yes, sir."

"And this was on what day?"

"January 29."

However, as previously shown, the headlines in the Wyoming newspapers had been detailing Starkweather's murder spree since January 28, 1958. Furthermore, despite the fact that an all-points bulletin had been radioed over police radar units alerting authorities to the manhunt in more than eight states, including Wyoming, Romer stated that he had just learned of the spree killings the very morning of Starkweather's capture through a small blurb in the morning newspaper. By stating such, Romer gave the jury the impression that he first learned of there being ten murders when Caril ran to him. By Romer stating that Caril had told him she had seen ten murders committed, it meant she would have had to have been present when her family was murdered. Therefore, her contention that she went along with Starkweather as his hostage in order to save the lives of her family was being contradicted by Romer, a law enforcement officer.

Romer further contradicted himself about not hearing much about Starkweather's rampage when he answered more questions from the defense attorney, as follows:

"Did you tell Joe Sprinkle [the man who wrestled the rifle away from Starkweather)] who it was that he was fighting with?" asked defense attorney McArthur.

"Yes, I did."

"Tell the court and jury about that."

"Mr. Sprinkle handed me the gun, and I asked him if he knew who he had been fighting with, and he said no, and I

147

told him it was Charles Starkweather, the man who had killed all those people in Nebraska; and Mr. Sprinkle turned white."

Hazel Heflin, the wife of Sheriff Heflin, contradicted Deputy Romer's testimony. Testifying for the defense, Mrs. Heflin said that when she first saw Caril, "Caril was very nervous and upset, and in shock and she shook. She was very, very upset. We sat in the living room and I talked to her a little, but she was so upset her story was very broken. She was talking, but I couldn't understand her. She could hardly talk; it was more mumbling than anything." According to Mrs. Heflin, Caril was in such a state of shock and hysteria that Heflin called a doctor who, immediately upon arrival, administered a potent sedative. Heflin said Caril slept from 4:00 P.M. until 9:00 A.M. the next day, January 30—a total of seventeen hours.

Mrs. Heflin also testified that Caril was so afraid of Starkweather that she (Heflin) never left her alone and stayed up all night watching over her. Mrs. Heflin further testified that— "Caril cried and screamed for her mother and little half-sister and wondered why they didn't call, and I said the phones are so busy right now they couldn't call anyway."

Mrs. Heflin had first seen Caril around 2:00 P.M., less than one half hour after she ran to Romer; she also confirmed that she couldn't understand anything Caril was mumbling because she was in shock and hysterical.

Even though Colonel Warne and Mrs. Heflin stated that they were unable to understand what Caril was saying, Deputy Romer assured the court that Caril told him she saw ten people killed, including her own family, and added the information about her mother slapping Starkweather. Contrast his testimony with that of Mrs. Heflin, who stated that Caril screamed and cried for her mother. If she knew they were dead, why would she scream and cry for her mother and ask why she didn't call her?

Mrs. Heflin also testified that the doctor came back twice more to check on Caril. He gave Mrs. Heflin four more sedatives, telling her to give Caril a sedative every four hours to relieve her tension. Sheriff and Mrs. Heflin left Douglas for Gering, Nebraska, at 8:00 P.M., so Caril would have received the last sedative on the way. Mrs. Heflin made no mention of any conversation taking place with Caril on the drive to Gering.

The Bartlett house at 924 Belmont, where Caril lived with her mother, stepfather, and half-sister, three-year-old Betty Jean. The house was in a section of town also called Belmont. *The Fox Collection. Ralph C. Fox and Barbara Rehberg Fox.*

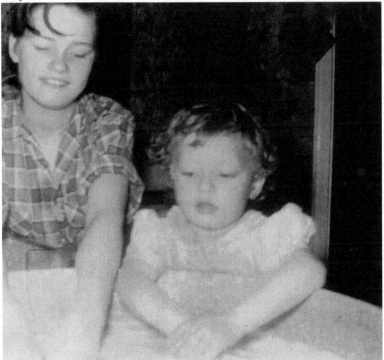

This photo of Caril with her baby half-sister, Betty Jean, was taken from Caril's wallet after her arrest. Caril spent most of her babysitting money on gifts for Betty Jean, shown here at age two. *Nebraska State Historical Society.*

Caril's little sister, Betty Jean, nearly three, opening a set of toy dishes—a Christmas gift from Caril. The coroner ruled that the toddler died of a blow to the head. Starkweather later claimed that Caril participated in the murders of her mother, stepfather, and little sister. *Nebraska State Historical Society.*

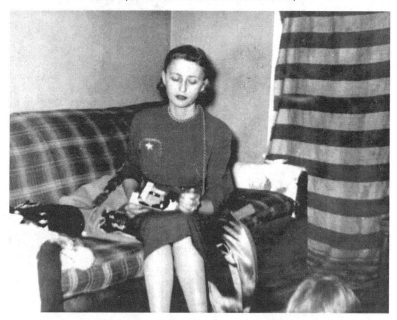

Caril's mother, Velda Bartlett, opens Christmas gifts in December 1957, just weeks before she was murdered. *Lincoln Journal Star.*

Caril Fugate and Charles Starkweather a few months before the murder spree. This photo was taken by the husband of woman who owned the rooming house where Starkweather lived. She would lock the door to his room when he was late paying his rent. *Lincoln Journal Star.*

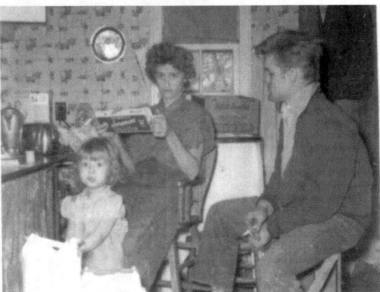

Caril's mother, Velda, baby sister Betty Jean, and Charles Starkweather, in the Fugate's kitchen in January 1958, just days before he murdered them. *Maria L. Diaz..*

The chicken coop in the Bartlett's backyard where Marion Bartlett's body was found. The bodies of Velda and Betty Jean were discovered in a nearby outhouse. *The Fox Collection. Ralph C. Fox and Barbara Rehberg Fox.*

After the body of farmer August Meyer was discovered, law enforcement officers moved in, preparing to lob tear gas bombs into the house in case the perpetrator was still inside. *Reprinted with permission by the Omaha World-Herald.*

When Starkweather's car got stuck at the August Meyer farm, he and Caril took off down a country road on foot. That's when two teens from Bennet, Nebraska, stopped to offer help. Starkweather murdered them both and stole their car. *Reprinted with permission by the Omaha World-Herald.*

The entrance to the storm cellar, where the bodies of Bennet teenagers, Robert Jensen and Carol King were discovered near Bennet, Nebraska. Starkweather had ordered Caril to hold the shotgun on Jensen while he robbed him. *Reprinted with permission by the Omaha World-Herald.*

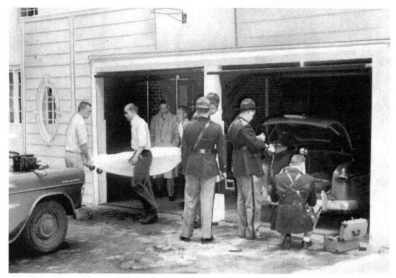

The bodies of three murder victims were removed from the home of Lincoln industrialist C. Lauer Ward. His wife, Clara, and their maid, Lilyan Fencl, were stabbed to death. Mr. Ward was killed when Starkweather shot him as the two struggled when Mr. Ward returned home. *Reprinted with permission by the Omaha World-Herald.*

After the bodies were discovered at the Ward home, panic spread throughout the city of Lincoln. Knowing a "mad dog" killer was at large prompted the governor to call out the National Guard to patrol the city streets. *Photo courtesy of Paul Shada.*

Douglas, Wyoming authorities fired at the car Starkweather was driving when he fled and a high-speed chase ensued. Starkweather surrendered after a bullet nicked his ear. Douglas police chief Robert Ainslie points to one of the bullet holes. The local sheriff said, "He turned yellow when he saw his own blood being spilled."
Chuck Morrison Collection, Casper College Western History Center.

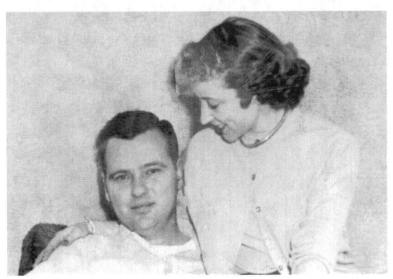

Wyoming resident Joe Sprinkle shown with his wife Pat, had stopped along the highway to offer help to Starkweather, whom he thought had car trouble. When Starkweather pulled out a rifle, Sprinkle was able to wrestle the gun away from Starkweather, who then sped off in the car he had stolen at the Ward house.
Reprinted with permission by the Omaha World-Herald.

Starkweather is booked into the Gering, Nebraska jail for the night, as authorities escort him back to Lincoln. Quite by chance, a Wyoming deputy sheriff had come upon Starkweather and Joe Sprinkle as they struggled over a rifle in the middle of the road. That's when Starkweather fled, and a brief high-speed chase followed. *Reprinted with permission by the Omaha World-Herald.*

Accompanied by Hazel Heflin, Caril Fugate is also booked into the county jail in Gering, Nebraska, for the night. As Starkweather fled, Caril ran toward the deputy sheriff, screaming for help. The deputy later reported that she "finally wound down and became unintelligible." *Reprinted with permission by the Omaha World-Herald.*

Deputy sheriff Bill Romer, left, the officer who came upon Starkweather and Sprinkle, speaks with Converse County sheriff Earl Heflin. Romer later misrepresented what the frantic Caril Fugate said to him when she first ran to him when Starkweather fled from authorities. *Chuck Morrison Collection, Casper College Western History Center.*

Deputy sheriff Bill Romer, carrying weapons confiscated from Starkweather, escorts Caril to the Converse County jail in Douglas Wyoming, a small town about an hour from the Nebraska border. *Chuck Morrison Collection, Casper College Western History Center.*

Caril sobs in the Converse County sheriff's office at the end of her eight-day ordeal with Starkweather. She was not expecting any charges to be filed against her. *Chuck Morrison Collection, Casper College Western History Center.*

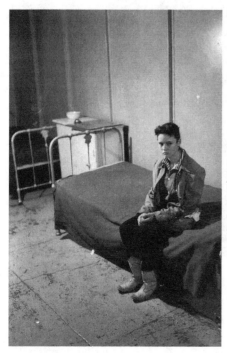

After being booked into the Gering, Nebraska jail, Caril sits alone in a cell. She was heavily sedated after becoming hysterical when someone said to her about her family, "My God girl, don't you know they're all dead?" *Reprinted with permission by the Omaha World-Herald.*

Hazel Heflin, wife of the Wyoming sheriff Earl Heflin, accompanied Caril back to Gering Nebraska, from Douglas, Wyoming. After meeting Caril, Mrs. Heflin remarked, "I don't think she knows her family is dead." Mrs. Heflin later served as a witness for the defense during Caril's trial. *Lincoln Journal Star.*

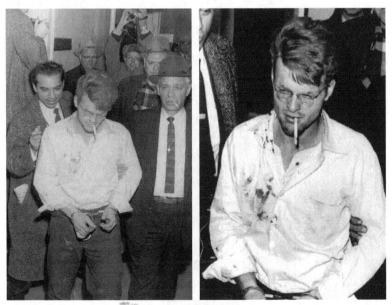

Starkweather, who always wanted to be a criminal, arrives in Lincoln. He is escorted by Lancaster County Sheriff Merle Karnopp. Still blood on his shirt from a bullet nicking his ear, Starkweather is surrounded by reporters. *The Fox Collection. Ralph C. and Barbara Rehberg Fox.*

Cleaned up and wearing a shirt and tie, Stark-weather on his way to a court appearance. Before he testified against Caril at her trial, he had provided nine different versions of how the murders occurred. *The Fox Collection. Ralph C. and Barbara Rehberg Fox.*

Escorted by Gertrude Karnopp, wife of Lan-caster County Sheriff Merle Karnopp, Caril is on her way to a court appearance. Her trial lasted nearly three weeks, from October 27, 1958, to November 21, 1958. *The Fox Collection. Ralph C. Fox and Barbara Rehberg Fox.*

Always in the firm grip of Gertrude Karnopp, Caril once again heads to the courtroom. Onlookers criticized Caril, saying she came across as cold and calm, rather than shy and tearful. *The Fox Collection. Ralph C. Fox and Barbara Rehberg Fox.*

At the time, Caril was the youngest person ever charged with first-degree murder in the United States. She's shown here, with her father, William Fugate and his wife, Dot. *Lincoln Journal Star.*

Starkweather's parents Guy and Helen, and his brother Rodney. The family opposed Starkweather's lawyers' change of plea from "not guilty" to "not guilty by reason of insanity." They did not want the taint of insanity hanging over their family even as Starkweather's lawyers tried to save him from the electric chair. *Lincoln Journal Star.*

Caril kisses her older sister Barbara during a brief family visit. She finally believed that her family was murdered only after asking her sister, Barbara, who confirmed the horrible news. *The Fox Collection. Ralph C. and Barbara Rehberg Fox.*

Lancaster deputy county attorney Dale Fahrnbruch, left, and county attorney Elmer Scheele, the prosecution team, who did all they could to ensure that Caril would be found guilty. *The Fox Collection. Ralph C. and Barbara Rehberg Fox.*

Starkweather leaves the courtroom, after lying about Caril during her trial. Upon his capture, he had claimed Caril was not involved in any of the murders. Only after the sheriff delivered a note from Caril saying she never wanted to see him again, did he turn on Caril with a vengeance. *Reprinted with permission by the Omaha World-Herald.*

Caril's trial started in October 1958 and lasted three weeks. At fifteen, she was the youngest girl in the United States to be tried for first degree murder. *Sally Raglin.*

Caril holds the arm of her attorney Merril Reller, as Charles Starkweather, the prosecution's lead witness, testifies against her. *Sally Raglin.*

Caril surrounded by her attorneys during her preliminary hearing. Left to right are Elmer Scheele, Merill Reller, Caril Fugate, and Sally Hays. *Sally Raglin.*

In the courtroom, attorney John McArthur, attorney Merrill Reller, and Caril are are seated at the defense table. *Sally Raglin.*

Caril's father William Fugate, his wife Dot, and Caril's sister Barbara at Caril's trial. *Sally Raglin.*

The jurors in Caril's trial found her guilty of being an accessory to first degree murder. On November 21, 1958, she was sentenced to life in prison. *Sally Raglin.*

Caril in April 1975, on the grounds of the Nebraska Correctional Center for Women, in York, Nebraska, where she spent eighteen years. Paroled in June 1976, she moved to Michigan, where she worked as a hospital orderly and as a nanny for two children. *Jim Furguson.*

During her years at the women's prison, Caril was described as a model prisoner. She participated in a work release program—working as a geriatric aide in a nursing home outside the prison grounds. She was driven to and from the job daily. *Jim Furguson.*

Having been granted parole, Caril's last day at the York Women's Correctional Center was June 8, 1976. She was thirty-two, having served eighteen years. *Photo by Bob Starck.*

On May 6, 1993, Caril made a rare appearance at a news conference, where she reacted to the release of the TV movie, *Murder in the Heartland*. She told reporters that she had passed seven polygraph tests and that she would be happy if people would say maybe, just maybe, they were too quick to judge her. *Lincoln Journal Star.*

Caril attended a March 2008 meeting with her attorney John Stevens Berry in Lincoln; she is shown here with Berry's wife, Margaret Berry.

In fact, when law enforcement authorities arrived with Caril at the Gering, Nebraska, jail at 4:00 am., Caril had asked for her mother. Mrs. Warrick, the sheriff's wife, told her, "My God, girl. Don't you know they're all dead?" Upon hearing this Caril became hysterical, and a doctor was called. When he arrived, he administered a sedative by injection and, once again, Caril dropped off to sleep. At 9:00 A.M., less than five hours after she was given the sedative, Caril left for Lincoln sitting in the backseat of a car with Gertrude Karnopp.

Prosecutor Scheele called Sheriff Heflin to the stand to describe the car chase and capture of Starkweather in Wyoming.

Note: None of this information about the capture was relevant to whether Caril aided and assisted Starkweather in the murder and robbery of Robert Jensen. So, why was Scheele asking how Heflin hooked bumpers with the car Starkweather was driving? What was the point in asking how Heflin chased Starkweather at more than 100 miles per hour for three and a half miles? What was the relevance to the case against Caril of Heflin shooting through the back windshield with his .38 pistol and describing how, when Starkweather exited his car, Heflin fired a shot between his legs and made him lie down on the ground?

Even more irrelevant testimony was provided to the jury when Scheele inquired about what ammunition Heflin found in searching Starkweather's car. To prove chain of custody, Heflin testified that he gave this ammunition to Lincoln assistant police chief Eugene Masters on January 30, 1958, in his office. To quote Heflin, "I turned quite a bit of stuff over to... Mr. Masters."

Scheele continued with yet more irrelevant questions about Starkweather:

"Do you recall one of the items that you gave Mr. Masters being a letter or a note of some kind in an envelope?" Scheele is clearly referring to Starkweather's Version 1 account of his murder spree, his "For the law only" note inside an envelope taken from Starkweather's pocket, purporting to be written by both Starkweather and Caril at the Wards' house.

"Yes, sir," Sheriff Heflin replied.

"And where was that obtained from?"

"From the coat that Caril Fugate had."

This is not likely what Scheele expected to hear! Sheriff Heflin had just revealed that Caril had a note in her coat. There is now testimony before the jury about two notes given to Eugene Masters—one note from Starkweather's pocket and a second note from Mrs. Ward's suede jacket which Starkweather made Caril put on before they left the Wards' house.

It would appear that the prosecution's plan had not included having the jury hear about another note found in the coat Caril was wearing. This is the note that said, "Help. Police. Don't ignore." Having this note before the jury might help to prove Caril's assertion that she was a hostage. Unfortunately, Caril forgot she had transferred the note from her blue coat into Mrs. Ward's jacket before leaving the Wards' house. She had mistakenly told authorities that she left this note in her blue coat, and, while on the witness stand, she would also testify that she left this note inside her blue coat pocket. Apparently, Caril never made the connection when Sheriff Heflin testified about finding a note in the suede jacket she was wearing after escaping from Starkweather.

The prosecution must have been fairly certain that they could keep the existence of Caril's note away from the jury. Scheele defused Heflin's bombshell about there being a second note by implying with his next question that Heflin is referring to Starkweather's note (Version 1 of his many accounts of his murder rampage). Starkweather's note was found inside an envelope addressed to "For the law only." Caril's note was not inside an envelope addressed to anyone; it merely said, "Help. Police. Don't ignore."

"For whom was it addressed, do you recall?" Scheele asked Heflin.

"No, I don't recall."

"Do you recall whether it was addressed 'To the law only,' or something to that effect?"

"Well, it was addressed to some law."

Scheele was attempting to confuse Heflin and the jury into thinking that Caril's "Help. Police. Don't ignore" note that Heflin was referring to was actually Starkweather's "For the law only" note.

Scheele next handed Sheriff Heflin an envelope marked as "Exhibit 29" and requested that Heflin remove the contents. Heflin identified the contents as the "clippings found in the jacket pocket that Caril Fugate was wearing at the time."

Scheele next asked Sheriff Heflin what he did with the clippings, to which Heflin responded, "I'm sure I mailed these from Douglas [Wyoming] to the Sheriff here," he said referring to Sheriff Karnopp, who was sitting in the courtroom.

Now Sheriff Heflin revealed that the clippings he found from the coat Caril was wearing were mailed to Sheriff Karnopp. It may be that Sheriff Heflin also mailed Caril's note along with the clippings to Sheriff Karnopp. The note and the clippings were both found in Caril's coat pocket. Earlier, when Sheriff Heflin testified that he gave Caril's note to assistant police chief Eugene Masters, he may have been confused. Starkweather's note, Version 1, was given to Masters in Sheriff Heflin's office. The contents of Caril's jacket were mailed to Sheriff Karnopp. It is likely that Caril's note was mailed along with the newspaper clippings because they both came out of the same coat.

On cross-examination Caril's attorney, John McArthur, asked Heflin whether Starkweather said anything about Caril upon his capture. Heflin replied, "He said that Caril didn't have anything to do with it....I guess I asked him about these killings....He said that she had nothing to do with it."

McArthur also pinned down Sheriff Heflin as to whether he provided either one or two notes to the Lincoln authorities by asking, "There was one, if I understand you accurately, you found one in Caril's pocket and you got one from Starkweather?"

Heflin replied, "Yes, sir."

McArthur asked, "And did you turn them both over to the officers?"

Heflin responded, "Yes, sir."

McArthur asked, "You don't have either of them now?"

Heflin responded, "No."

The important thing to remember is that Sheriff Heflin did testify that, among other things, he turned a note taken from Starkweather and a note taken from the coat Caril was wearing—two separate notes—over to the authorities from Nebraska. Whether he turned Caril's note over to Masters in person, or whether he mailed her note to Karnopp along with the clippings contained in Exhibit 29, is irrelevant. The fact that the existence of Caril's note was never turned over to the defense team smacks of deliberate deceit.

Next to testify for the prosecution was Eugene Masters, the assistant chief of police of the Lincoln police department, who, among other reasons, was called to testify about the evidence that was handed over to him by Sheriff Heflin in Wyoming.

"Now prior to your departing Douglas, Wyoming, were any items turned over to you by Sheriff Heflin?" Scheele asked.

"Yes, sir."

"Will you tell us what those were?"

"Sheriff Heflin turned over to me a number of .22 caliber shells, some .410 shells, a hunting knife, and a note which had been taken from the person of...."

But before he was able to finish telling the jury that the note came from Starkweather, defense attorney John McArthur objected, saying, "Let's not go into where you got these, just what he turned over to you."

"A note was turned over to me," Masters answered.

Masters was not asked about where the shotgun shells and the hunting knife were taken from. He was just asked about the note.

"And can you identify that note in some way, that is, the envelope it was in?" Scheele asked.

"Yes, sir."

"To whom was it addressed?"

"I believe it said, 'For the law only.' "

Scheele was quick to make sure that he asked Masters to identify the envelope the letter was in, even though Masters hadn't said it was inside an envelope. Caril's note was not placed inside an envelope, and Scheele would have known this. By asking Masters to identify the envelope the note was in, Scheele was asking Masters to mislead the jury in thinking that only one note existed—Starkweather's Version 1 note which was in an envelope. If Caril's note were put before the jury it would have helped to show the jury that she was not a willing accomplice.

When the defense attorney, John McArthur, cross-examined Masters, he asked, "Mr. Masters, do I understand you received only one note from Sheriff Heflin?"

Masters answered, "From Sheriff Heflin, yes." This answer contradicted Masters's testimony at Starkweather's trial where he testified that he received a total of three notes from Sheriff Heflin.

Note: Was Masters so intent on denying that he received the note Caril wrote that he forgot that he earlier stated at Starkweather's trial that he received three notes from the Wyoming authorities: Version 1 from Starkweather, marked "For the law only"; Version 3, which was Starkweather's handwritten confession written in his jail cell; and Version 4, Starkweather's letter written to his parents in his jail cell?

Next, Vance Rogers, a doctor of divinitY and the president of Nebraska Wesleyan University, was called to testify for the prosecution. He relayed that on Saturday, February 1, 1958, deputy county attorney Dale Fahrnbruch called him in the morning asking him to attend a meeting taking place with Caril Fugate at the state hospital. Rogers stated that he viewed his role as having a humanitarian interest by observing the way Caril was being treated.

Note: Why would Fahrnbruch take the time and effort to get the university professor to attend this meeting as a "humanitarian," but not a defense counsel who would have temporarily represented Caril on a *pro bono* (free) basis?

Others present at the meeting included Fahrnbruch; Dr. Coats; Eugene Masters, the assistant chief of police; and Gertrude Karnopp, the sheriff's wife.

Rogers was asked what Caril had stated regarding the teenager Robert Jensen. Rogers recalled a question being asked about a gun in the car being held on Caril's lap. He did not recall what else was said about the gun or whether it was loaded. He remarked how Caril was allowed breaks to go to the bathroom and get a sweater because she was cold. When Scheele asked him about Caril's demeanor, he said she appeared "terribly frightened."

Rogers also stated Caril answered questions in a "direct manner," and was told by deputy country attorney Fahrnbruch that all he wanted was the truth and the reason why she was there was to find out from her what had truly happened during her time with Starkweather. Rogers said Fahrnbruch's attitude toward Caril could be compared to a father questioning a daughter rather carefully.

On cross-examination by defense attorney McArthur, Rogers admitted that, in his presence, Fahrnbruch did not say anything to Caril about filing a first degree murder charge against her. Neither did Fahrnbruch tell her that he intended to seek the electric chair for her. Nor did he tell her that anything she said could be used before a court and jury as evidence against her.

The sheriff's wife, Gertrude Karnopp, was called next to testify for the prosecution. She was to attest to Caril's willingness to provide a statement, transcribed by a court reporter. Mrs. Karnopp stated that on the drive back to Lincoln she sat in the backseat with Caril and that the two men in front couldn't hear what they were saying.

Mrs. Karnopp testified that at some point during the drive to Lincoln, Caril asked her if her folks were dead. Mrs. Karnopp didn't respond. Then Caril asked her who killed them.

Mrs. Karnopp asked, "Don't you know, Caril?"

Caril then told her that the first she heard about her family was in the Gering jail.

Mrs. Karnopp stated that Caril began talking about the "series of events" and began with August Meyer's murder and the teenagers.

Mrs. Karnopp testified that Caril told her about getting stuck at August Meyer's and how the teenagers came along and offered them a ride to a telephone. Robert Jensen started driving, and Starkweather directed him to drive to the cellar. According to Karnopp's account, Caril said the King girl thanked them "for being nice to them," and then, as they walked down to the cellar, Starkweather shot them.

Mrs. Karnopp testified that Caril said Jensen acted very nice while they were driving along, even slowing down at corners, "as if nothing was wrong."

However, it was Elmer Scheele's job to convict Caril Fugate as an accessory to the robbery and murder of Jensen, and he followed up with a leading question, "Was anything said in reference to any money in connection with Robert Jensen?"

"Yes," Mrs. Karnopp replied. "She said they did take some money from him."

Scheele then asked Karnopp whether Caril said anything about the Ward house.

Mrs. Karnopp said, "Caril said Starkweather went in first and then motioned for her to come inside. He told the women, Clara Ward and her maid, Lilyan Fencl, they weren't going to hurt them, and Mrs. Ward said she liked helping people in trouble." Karnopp said Caril told her about Starkweather telling Caril he went upstairs and came down to tell her Mrs. Ward went for a gun, and he threw a knife at her.

Mrs. Karnopp stated that Caril said the maid was nervous and still alive when Mr. Ward came home. She also said that they (Starkweather and Caril) took the maid upstairs and put her on the bed, and she (Caril) said that she thought the maid would never die. Then Caril told about getting clothing and answering the phone and saying how Mrs. Ward's clothes wouldn't fit her (Caril).

Scheele next asked Mrs. Karnopp, "Was anything said with reference to any writing Caril may have made?"

Mrs. Karnopp answered, "She told about writing a letter or note of some kind and said it should be in her blue jacket."

Note: This statement about Caril's note is critical. Caril thought her note was still in her blue coat. However, the prosecution knew the note was actually inside of Mrs. Ward's jacket that Caril was wearing, but they made sure this note never got before the jury because it would help to prove Caril was Starkweather's hostage. As noted earlier, Caril initially had the note inside her blue coat pocket, but when she and Starkweather were leaving the Wards' house, Starkweather made her put on Mrs. Ward's suede jacket. Caril grabbed the note in her right hand and, while she put on Mrs. Ward's jacket, she transferred the note into Mrs. Ward's jacket pocket. Unfortunately, Caril didn't remember she transferred the note until years later.

Caril's forgetfulness turned out to be a lucky opportunity for the prosecution. Scheele had been shocked earlier when Sheriff Heflin testified he found a note in Mrs. Ward's jacket. Scheele deflected this bombshell by confusing Heflin with the "For the law only" note taken off Starkweather. At Starkweather's trial, Heflin testified that he never read Starkweather's "For the law only" note. Heflin's undersheriff was the person who removed the note from Starkweather's person and handed the note to Heflin, who in turn gave it to Eugene Masters.

Note: The whereabouts of Caril's note to the police has never been determined.

Mrs. Karnopp was being used by Scheele to further quash any suspicions that might have been raised by Sheriff Heflin when he said he took a note out of the jacket of Mrs. Ward's that Caril was wearing. A juror might think, what note is he talking about? By stating that Caril told her the note asking for help should be in her blue coat, Mrs. Karnopp dispelled any notions that somehow the note found by Sheriff Heflin was Caril's cry for help.

Mrs. Karnopp's testimony continued. She said that Caril answered deputy county attorney Dale Fahrnbruch's questions during several interrogations at the mental hospital. She also asserted that Caril was well aware that charges of first degree murder had been filed against her and that the penalty was either life in prison or the electric chair. Mrs. Karnopp took pains to mention how considerately Caril was treated by stating that the questioning was stopped whenever Caril needed a break to get a drink of water or to put on a sweater. Mrs. Karnopp mentioned that only one of Caril's statements was recorded. But Karnopp made sure to say that in an unrecorded discussion, Caril admitted that she handed Starkweather a gun from the Packard to the Buick out in Wyoming on January 29, 1958.

Under questioning by prosecuting attorney Scheele, Karnopp brought up Caril's remark about not liking her stepfather. Karnopp also stated that Caril admitted she held a gun on Jensen and that money was taken from him by Starkweather and Caril before he was shot. Karnopp also testified that Caril said she thought the maid at the Ward house would never die.

Note: This statement by Mrs. Karnopp about the maid made Caril sound callous. However, it was Starkweather who told Caril after he bludgeoned the Ward maid to death that he thought she would never die. Karnopp further stated that Caril told her that Carol King thanked them for not being mean. But Caril said Carol King never said this. Caril Fugate remembered Carol King being paralyzed with fright and not being able to say anything.

Continuing with her testimony, Mrs. Karnopp stated that upon arriving in Lincoln they stopped at the penitentiary to drop Starkweather off, then continued to the county jail and the state hospital to drop off Caril.

Mrs. Karnopp saw Caril the following day, on February 1, 1958, a Saturday, at the hospital. Present were deputy county attorney Dale Fahrnbruch; Lincoln assistant chief of police, Eugene Masters; Dr. Vance Rogers from Wesleyan University; Dr. Coats, a psychiatrist from the hospital; Caril; and Gertrude Karnopp.

Karnopp said Fahrnbruch asked Caril questions during this meeting, and Mrs. Karnopp assured Scheele that no one there made any threats, promises, or inducements in order to get Caril to talk and that she answered questions "very willingly." This meeting lasted about one hour.

Mrs. Karnopp testified that she next saw Caril on Sunday, February 2, 1958, in the late morning. She and the sheriff first picked up Caril's father, Bill Fugate, and his wife, Dot. Their meeting with Caril lasted fifteen minutes. They left for lunch and returned at 2:00.

Mrs. Karnopp testified that at that time, Barb, Caril's sister, was also present. Karnopp testified that Lancaster County's deputy attorney Dale Fahrnbruch once again made no threats, promises, or inducements to get Caril to talk. He asked her to tell her side of the story and to tell the truth. He also informed her that there could be charges filed against her on this. Her family told her to tell the truth. Fahrnbruch told Caril he would be back that night to take a statement from her.

That evening, February 2, between 8:00 P.M. until 10:50 P.M., in the presence of Gertrude Karnopp, Audrey Wheeler— the court reporter, and Dr. Coats, Fahrnbruch took Caril's statement. Mrs. Karnopp, when prodded by Scheele, assured the jury that Caril was allowed several breaks to get a drink or a sweater or make a trip to the ladies' room. When Caril said she was tired, they quit for the night.

Karnopp said that the next day, Monday, February 3, 1958, she joined her husband, the sheriff, in picking up Caril and driving her to county attorney Scheele's office. Present were Mr. and Mrs. Bill Fugate, Caril's sister Barb, Sheriff Karnopp, and Mrs. Karnopp. Scheele read the charges filed against Caril from a book and said something about aiding and abetting. He asked her if she had an attorney, and her dad said they couldn't afford one. Scheele then said something about Legal Aid and that the county could appoint her one. Caril was then returned to the state hospital where her second of two statements was taken from 12 P.M. to 1:30 P.M. by Fahrnbruch, with Mrs. Karnopp, Dr. Coats, and the court reporter present. Caril was then taken to the courthouse and arraigned before Judge Ronin.

Mrs. Karnopp testified that the next time she saw Caril was on Wednesday, February 5, 1958, at the hospital at 9:00 A.M. Present were Fahrnbruch, Eugene Masters, Dean Edmund Belsheim of the Nebraska Law School, and an attorney, Mr. William Blue from the local Legal Aid office. Dean Belsheim and Mr. Blue had volunteered to serve as Caril's *pro bono* lawyers on a temporary basis.

As her testimony continued, Mrs. Karnopp reported that Caril's transcribed statement was read to Caril. Dean Edmund Belsheim and Legal Aid's William Blue informed everyone that they told Caril to make oral corrections but not to sign it. Once again, Karnopp said, no threats, promises, or inducements were made. Caril made oral corrections to the statement, and Eugene Masters took notes. Fahrnbruch asked Caril if the statement was true and voluntary, and Caril said "Yes."

The next time Karnopp saw Caril was on Friday, February 7, 1958, at the state hospital around 12:30 P.M. Present were Dale Fahrnbruch, Dr. Coats, and Gertrude Karnopp. Karnopp testified that Caril said that when they were in Wyoming, she took Starkweather a gun from Ward's car and gave it to him.

Karnopp also remembers vividly that Caril said she packed a suitcase before she left her Belmont Street house with Starkweather. She said that Caril explained that she first packed a blue suitcase but thought it was too big, so she used a small red gym bag. Caril also stated that she practiced throwing a knife with Starkweather in the kitchen by the washing machine; she also looked for keys in her mom's purse that was on the piano.

Mrs. Karnopp next saw Caril on Tuesday, February 11, 1958, at the hospital with Dale Fahrnbruch and Dr. Coats. She stated no threats, promises, or inducements were made this time either. This time Caril told Fahrnbruch she didn't like him and that she wouldn't talk to him anymore.

Mrs. Karnopp forgot to tell Scheele that on Sunday morning, February 2, the sheriff asked Caril if she wanted to see Charlie because he had asked about her, but she said she didn't want to see him. She had even written a note telling him so.

Caril's lawyer, John McArthur, was a seasoned attorney, and he must have sensed Mrs. Karnopps's vulnerability. He began his cross-examination.

Prior to being cross-examined, Karnopp did admit that she had never before been asked to be present when formal statements were taken from a prisoner under accusation. She also admitted that Caril's temporary *pro bono* attorneys, William Blue of Legal Aid and Dean Belsheim of the law school were not present on February 7, 1958, when Caril talked about throwing knives and a blue suitcase. Karnopp said her memory was failing her when it came to the issue of whether these gentlemen were notified of the meeting.

McArthur asked, "When there's a serious lawsuit pending and you want to talk to the persons in trouble, isn't it customary to kind of let their attorneys in on it and let them be there too?"

"Well," she said to the attorney, "I don't know about the legal things."

"You don't know that a prosecutor that's trying to electrocute a fourteen-year-old should let her attorney know about it or not then?"

"I don't know about such things."

McArthur reminded her that she was there trying to help convict a teenaged girl.

Karnopp was silent.

"Was there anything about the routine in the steps of the taking of this statement that impressed you particularly, Mrs. Karnopp?"

"The routine of it?"

"Yes."

"Well, of course, not having had the experience before I probably wouldn't notice it, I don't know of anything."

McArthur continued, "Well, let's take it step by step now. When was the first time that you can recall, and think of this carefully, that Caril Ann was actually told that a formal charge of first degree murder had been filed in court against her?"

"Well, I don't remember when they said that it had been, but I can remember that it was explained that this was a very serious matter."

"When, when was that?"

"Well, I would say that from the very beginning and all the way through."

"What I'm trying to find out if you'll just try your best to remember, the very first time that you can definitely say that Caril Ann was told that a first degree murder charge was filed against her, had been filed against her?"

"Well, I...I remember when her...when her father and stepmother were there, them talking about it, and I don't know whether they said it had or could be, I can't remember for sure." Mrs. Karnopp looked uncomfortable. "Well, I know definitely in Mr. Scheele's office," Karnopp stated.

McArthur's questioning continued. "All right, in Mr. Scheele's office, and that was on the day that she was arraigned, was it?" (February 3, 1958)

"That's right."

"All right, and at that time her statement had already been taken, had it?"

"Yes, sir."

"Now, do you know, Mrs. Karnopp, that as early as the 29th day of January a formal charge of first degree murder had been filed in court against Caril Ann Fugate?"

"I remember that there were charges filed against..."

"You knew that?"

"From reading it in the paper, yes, sir."

"Do you recall the date of this arraignment in county court?"

"I believe it would be the third of the month."

"That would be Monday. You are unable to say positively that Caril Ann was ever advised that a charge of first degree murder had been filed against her prior to February 3, would that be an accurate statement?"

"At each occasion that Mr. Fahrnbruch talked with her, that was the very first thing that was said practically."

"All right. Now are you going to say that Mr. Fahrnbruch did tell her that a formal charge of first degree murder had been filed?"

"On the Sunday when her parents were there." (February 2).

"Mrs. Karnopp, I want to know if you heard Mr. Fahrnbruch tell her that she had been charged with any crime in any court."

"Yes, sir."

"Now you tell us what he said."

"Well, I can't say it in the legal terms, Mr. McArthur."

"I appreciate you can't, but..."

"That he told her that she had been charged with murder and that murder was a serious thing."

"Now you are willing to say that he absolutely did that, is that true, you heard that?"

"Why, I'm sure he did."

"All right. And in the presence of who?"

"Her family."

"And that was on the second day of February, 1958?"

"Well, he may, he may have mentioned it before, I don't remember it specifically, there's been so many times, and I can't say positively."

"I'm trying to find out, Mrs. Karnopp, if the state took this girl's statement and got her to waive her rights out in Wyoming, did all these things without her knowing that she had been previously charged with murder."

"But I don't know that."

"When was the first time that you can recall that Caril Ann was told in your presence that she could have a lawyer of her own?"

"The very first time that, that Mr. Fahrnbruch...that would be on the first morning that we went out to the state hospital, when Dr. Rogers and Dr. Coats and them were there." (February 1, 1958)

"But now you heard Mr. Fahrnbruch tell this little girl on the first of February that she could have an attorney, is that true?"

"That she had a right to have an attorney."

"She was told that, that she could have a right to an attorney?"

"Yes."

"And you don't know what she said, she didn't say yes or no or anything?"

"Well, I don't remember specifically what she might have said."

"You do remember that Mr. Fahrnbruch told her on the 1st that she could have a lawyer on the 1st, but you don't remember what she said about it?"

"I believe that she said she did not have any."

"That she did not have any?"

"That's right."

"What else did she say about it?"

"Well, I don't remember."

"Well you knew she was fourteen years old?"

"Yes, sir."

"And what was done about getting her an attorney that you know of?"

"Well, I don't know anything about it except when, at the time that the law school dean, Belsheim, came in."

"Well, Caril Ann was in custody every minute, wasn't she?"

"Well, I would say she was, yes."

"She was told she could have an attorney, but she had no attorney until after the statement was all taken, isn't that what really happened?"

"Well, I have nothing to do with that, I don't know anything about that."

"All right, the fact that a fourteen-year-old child is charged with a crime that carries a death penalty is a little unusual, isn't it?"

"Yes, sir."

"And if they, if they're told they can have an attorney but nothing is done about it, do you think it's all right to go ahead?"

"Well, that was my understanding that Dean Belsheim (from the Nebraska Law School) was doing; it was his interest in it."

"Isn't it true that he was allowed in there after the questions had been asked and the answers given?"

"Oh, after the statement had been taken, yes, that's right."

"She was told she could have an attorney before the statement was taken, but she got one after it was taken?"

"She was told and her family was told, yes, sir."

"But after she did have an attorney, she was contacted and questioned in the absence of an attorney, was she not, on two occasions?"

"There was not an attorney present on the 7th and on the 11th."

"Now, Mrs. Karnopp, do you know the purpose of having several sessions of questioning of Caril Ann before a written record was made of it?"

"No, I do not."

"You were present when this 'thing,' was read to her, weren't you?" By "thing," McArthur was referring to the recorded statement Caril had given on February 3rd.

"Yes."

He continued questioning Karnopp, referring to the statement transcript. "I'll ask you whether these questions were asked and these answers given."

He first asked, "Question: 'Now, after you got out to the farm, what happened out there, Caril?' "

"Answer: 'Do you want me to tell the story?' "

"Question: 'Yes.' "

"Answer: 'I am all mixed up. I don't know whether I can tell it straight or not now.' "

"Do you remember that?" McArthur asked Mrs. Karnopp.

"I can remember occasionally that she said that, yes... I remember times when she would stop; she'd say she was mixed up. I can't remember specifically each question and answer, but I do remember that that happened."

"I just would like to have you acknowledge, if you will, that when you talk about this girl talking so freely and willingly and so unhesitatingly, that she was at the same time all mixed up?"

McArthur continued, "And did you do some of the questioning yourself?"

"No, sir."

"You did none of the questioning?"

"Not during the taking of the statement, I may have."

"You mean by that, that your question should have been left out?"

McArthur then showed Mrs. Karnopp the page in the statement indicating where she had conversed with Caril.

"Oh, this was during the break, as I remember it, and Mr. Fahrnbruch and Dr. Coats were out of the room," said Mrs. Karnopp.

Even though they were taking a short recess during the interrogation and Fahrnbruch and Dr. Coats were out of the room, the court reporter continued taking notes on what was being said between Caril and Mrs. Karnopp.

McArthur asked Mrs. Karnopp to read from the transcript.

"I don't remember what went on in the Bartlett house," Caril said.

"What went on in the house?"

"No."

"What do you mean, Caril?" Karnopp asked.

184

"I don't remember it all."

"You don't remember it all?" Karnopp asked again.

"I don't remember it all," Caril said.

"What do you mean, you don't remember it all?"

"I don't remember what went on."

"Can you remember what you told me when you talked to me?"

"I don't remember."

At this point, the recess ended and Fahrnbruch and Dr. Coats returned to the room.

Although Mrs. Karnopp would refresh her memory by reading this dialog, her conversation with Caril would not be read at that time to the jury.

"When there's no perfect record made of questioning and answering, it's very easy to be in error, is it not?"

McArthur played on the fact that Caril was confused, just as Gertrude Karnopp was now confused. Mrs. Karnopp denied having asked Caril any questions, but then McArthur showed her the page in the statement where she had talked to Caril.

McArthur moved on to discuss the death penalty. He wanted to question whether the young, frightened defendant had been made aware that she was facing the electric chair.

"Do you remember what Caril was told, what you heard?" McArthur asked, referring to the penalty for first degree murder.

"Well, I can't remember exactly, Mr. McArthur. I have it in my own mind, and I don't know specifically if that's what was said."

"Well, you're trying to be fair; you see, it's so easy to say that she was told what the penalty was, but if you don't know what was told, you have no memory."

"Well, I'm just sure it was gone through completely."

"Yes, I know, but what can you remember Mr. Scheele telling her the penalty was?"

"Well, the penalty for first degree murder was life imprisonment or death in the electric chair, I think."

"Did you hear Mr. Scheele tell her that?"

"Yes. I said he followed through the entire procedure."

"What did he say to her about the penalty?"

"Well, I don't remember specifically."

"Can you remember him saying anything about life imprisonment?"

"I wouldn't say absolutely I can remember that."

"Can you remember hearing him say anything about the death penalty?"

"The same applies to that. I wouldn't say absolutely that I could remember both, I remember him reading to her out of a book."

"I'm still not absolutely sure whether you have said that Mr. Scheele told her that she could get either death or life imprisonment or not?"

"What I said is that I did not remember and could not say positively."

"And when you say that Caril Ann was answering freely and voluntarily, your testimony has to be in the same shape, doesn't it?"

"What do you mean?"

"Well, is there any way you can say whether it was free on her part or not?"

"Well...it...then it would...I would say that it appeared to be that she answered them willingly and with no hesitation when she did answer them."

"It's just a kind of an opinion you have, isn't it?"

"That's what it would be. Yes, that's what it would be."

"And two people can see the same thing and get just opposite opinions on that, can't they?"

"That's possible, sure."

"You wouldn't question Dr. Rogers's integrity when he said she appeared terribly frightened, of course?"

"Why, of course, I wouldn't."

"And yet you can see the same child at the same time and form the opinion that she didn't appear terribly frightened?"

"I had seen her previous to that."

"But you could see her when Dr. Rogers did and observed no evidence of fear, did you not?"

"I didn't think of it as fear."

"Would you be willing to say this, Mrs. Karnopp, that in stating your recollections of what Caril said to you there's as much room for error or doubt as when you try to remember what Mr. Scheele said about the death penalty?"

"I think that was rather, well, impressed upon my mind somehow."

In effect, McArthur was saying that it appeared that Mrs. Karnopp could remember everything Caril told her in the backseat of the car, but that she couldn't remember what Caril said during a proceeding in the county attorney's office later on.

Chapter 14

The prosecution planned to introduce the transcribed "formal statement" taken from Caril on February 2, 1958, using her own words to convict her. This statement was marked as "Exhibit 40" and was read almost in its entirety to the jury. Portions of the statement describing the agonizing death of Lilyan Fencl and Starkweather's attempted rape of Caril would be excluded as being too prejudicial and inflammatory.

In order to use Caril's statement, the prosecution had to show that Caril had answered questions freely and voluntarily, without hesitation, and that no threats, promises, or inducements had been given to her in order to get her to talk. Gertrude Karnopp previously testified that Caril answered freely and voluntarily but she had crumbled when pressed about this issue by Caril's attorney, John McArthur. Now the prosecutors needed to present other witnesses to show how nicely everything was done in the questioning of Caril.

William P. Dixon, who at the time of Starkweather's capture, was County Attorney of Converse County, Wyoming, was called to the stand. He was questioned by county attorney Elmer Scheele. Dixon described a conversation with Caril on January 30, 1958, in the jail, a meeting at which Deputy William Romer was also present.

Dixon stated that upon meeting Caril, he handed her a telegram from her sister, Barbara, which said "We love you and we're going to stand behind you. Cooperate with these people and tell them anything they want to know, and do everything you can to help them."

Caril then asked Deputy Romer what he thought she should do, and he responded that the advice in the telegram was good advice and that she should fully cooperate with all the authorities involved.

Dixon said, "We then explained to Caril Fugate that since she was in custody in Converse County, Wyoming, that in order to take her back to Lincoln, Nebraska, it would be necessary to extradite her, and I explained in quite some detail the extradition process. We asked her if she were willing to go back to Lincoln, Nebraska, at that time and was willing to do so of her own free will, and if she would sign a waiver of extradition. I personally explained this as carefully as I could to her, having in mind her youth and her age and what I thought she could understand, and I explained it to her as well as I thought I could, in terms of what I thought a fourteen- or fifteen-year-old girl would understand."

Dixon continued, "Her reply to that was what did she think that, or, what did we think she should do. I told her at that time that I could not advise her because I was county attorney, that if she needed legal advice, she was entitled to an attorney at this time....I believe at that time she indicated willingness to come directly to Lincoln. She asked that if she did sign this waiver of extradition, how long would it be before she could get back to Lincoln and see her relatives; and I said, 'If you sign it you can leave immediately.' As a matter of fact, that was the plan for you," he said referring to Scheele, "to take them that afternoon."

Dixon next described a second meeting with Caril later that afternoon when Scheele, Deputy Romer, and Harry L. Wise, the justice of the peace, were also present.

Scheele asked Dixon, "Specifically, do you recall whether or not she was told at that time whether any charges were filed against her in Nebraska?

"It wasn't told in quite those words," Dixon responded.

"Can you relate it as best you can?" Scheele asked.

"Yes, I believe I can. I believe you," again referring to Scheele, "told Caril Ann Fugate after first the two of us, you and I, explained separately the extradition process. We explained her rights to her, and I might say that we doubled up on each other, I would explain it first from the Wyoming standpoint, and you would explain the Nebraska standpoint. At that time you told her words to the effect that she was in deep trouble, that this was a terrible mess, and that when she got back to Nebraska you were pretty sure that charges would be filed against her; and that is to the best of my recollection, Mr. Scheele."

Dixon finished answering the questions from Scheele by stating that Caril willingly signed the extradition papers and that no threats or promises or inducements were used to get her to sign the waiver.

Next, it was Caril's attorney John McArthur's turn to question Dixon.

McArthur asked, "She did waive every right that she had under the law of Wyoming, sir, did she not?"

"Well, no, sir. I'm not sure I understand that question," Dixon replied.

"Well, of course, my question now is what he," referring to Scheele, "told her about any charges that had already been filed in any court; what did you hear him say about that?"

"I don't recall hearing him saying anything about that."

"If I were to tell you that on the 29th of January a first degree murder charge had been filed against this girl in this county, would you say that Caril Ann then was fully apprised of what she was heading into?"

"Yes, sir, I think she was."

"You don't think that a fourteen-year-old child that isn't told specifically that there has been a first degree murder charge filed has been misled by not being told that?"

"She was not misled, sir, at any point in that procedure."

"How did she find out that there had been a first degree murder charge filed against her, Mr. Dixon?"

"Well, I don't recall whether it was ever placed in exactly that language to her."

"In any language?"

"Yes, sir, in any language."

"You tell us what the language was and who said it."

"Mr. Elmer Scheele said to Caril Ann Fugate in the kitchen of the sheriff's house that she was in serious trouble, that this was a terrible mess, that when she got back to Lincoln the proper steps would be taken to handle it."

"What did he say about steps that had been taken against her in Lincoln?"

"To the best of my recollection, I don't know that he said anything."

"Is it possible even to extradite a person if there isn't a criminal charge filed in the state that's asking for them?"

"Well, not to my knowledge."

"Yes, as a lawyer you know it couldn't be."

"That's right."

"Did anybody tell Caril Ann that?"

"Tell her that there could not be extradition if there were no charges filed?"

"That there had to be a criminal charge filed or that they couldn't extradite her, did anybody mention that to her?"

"I didn't...." Dixon paused.

"You didn't hear it?"

"I didn't hear it."

Next, Scheele wanted to establish that Caril's written statement was given voluntarily.

Dr. Edwin Coats, psychiatrist and acting assistant superintendent of the Nebraska state mental hospital, was called to the stand. Could he repair the damage Dr. Rogers had created for the prosecution earlier in the trial by testifying that Caril was not informed that a murder charge had been filed against her in his presence, nor was she told that any statement she made could be used as evidence against her?

According to Dr. Coats, on February 1, Caril seemed rather friendly, knew what she was saying, and did not appear extremely frightened. She answered Fahrnbruch's questions without hesitation, freely and voluntarily. No threats, promises, or inducements were made in order to get her to speak. The interrogation began at 9:45 A.M. and ended at 2:00 P.M.

Dr. Coats said he next saw Caril the following day, Sunday, February 2, 1958, at 9:45 A.M. in the Admission Building with Sheriff Karnopp and Mrs. Karnopp. The session lasted about twenty to twenty-five minutes. He explained that he next saw her at 10:45 A.M. with Mrs. Karnopp and Fahrnbruch. Sheriff Karnopp had left to give Starkweather the note Caril wrote, telling Starkweather she did not want to see him because she would be afraid of what she might do to him. Dr. Coats also testified that Caril's sister, father, and stepmother visited with her for a few hours.

Coats continued that later on at 8:00 P.M. he saw Caril again. This time, those present were Fahrnbruch, Mrs. Karnopp, and Audrey Wheeler, the court reporter. Coats said, once again, no threats or promises were made to Caril to get her to talk, and Caril answered questions "very freely." She was quiet and cooperative and rather friendly. She did not have any tendency to "embellish or go into any great description about details of what happened; she knew what she was saying and was completely in contact with reality," Dr. Coats said.

According to Dr. Coats, he next saw Caril on Monday, February 3, 1958, from 12:30 P.M. to 1:30 P.M. Present were Fahrnbruch, Mrs. Karnopp, and Audrey Wheeler. At this meeting, Caril completed her statement. He said, once again, no promises or inducements were made and Caril answered questions freely and voluntarily. She was in contact with reality and did not appear to be frightened.

On February 5, Dr. Coats reported that he attended another meeting with Fahrnbruch, Caril, Mrs. Karnopp, and Eugene Masters of the Lincoln police department. Also present were William Blue from Legal Aid and Edmund Belsheim, the dean of the Nebraska Law School in Lincoln. These men had spoken with Caril earlier that day. During this meeting they read Caril's statement as transcribed by Audrey Wheeler. Fahrnbruch read all 166 pages of the statement, and Caril made oral corrections as he read.

Coats said Lincoln deputy police chief Eugene Masters took notes every time Caril made an oral correction. At the end of each page, Fahrnbruch would ask Caril whether the transcribed statement was true and correct. If she made any oral corrections, she confirmed that their corrections were accurate. No inducements, threats, or promises were made. She answered freely and voluntarily.

In response to Scheele's question about whether Caril was advised about any charges filed against her, Coats answered that she was advised on Saturday, February 1, that Fahrnbruch said to her she would be charged with first degree murder and murder in the perpetration of a robbery in connection with Robert Jensen. Coats said she was also advised that she was entitled to have an attorney when she appeared in county court.

Dr. Coats was then cross-examined by Caril's attorney, John McArthur.

Dr. Coats was asked to quote what Fahrnbruch had actually said in connection with the charges against Caril.

Coats responded, "The essence was that this was a serious situation, that I believe at that time the statement was that charges had been filed, and she asked if there would be a trial. And it was then that the matter of first degree murder, and, again, I don't know too much about the legal aspects of these things, and, second, was the perpetration or murder in the perpetration of robbery, and, if, I believe that she, something was said on that occasion about it being Robert Jensen that Mr. Scheele had...."

Before Dr. Coats could finish his sentence, McArthur interrupted him and asked whether it was his recollection and testimony that Fahrnbruch told Caril that there were charges already filed against her. Coats responded that the attorney's statement was correct.

Coats continued on about Caril also being told she was entitled to counsel, and "something about the county court and the appointment of an attorney at that time."

McArthur asked, "In the county court?"

Coats stammered, "No, I don't believe it was the...that an attorney....I'm not familiar enough with it, but it seems to me that when she was to go to county court it would be decided then about the appointment of an attorney."

When McArthur asked Dr. Coats whether Caril was told she could have an attorney of her own present at the taking of her statement, Dr. Coats was evasive.

"I don't remember as to that. I, I don't know whether... here again it's a matter of what she assumed, I assume from what was said that if she's asked for a lawyer at that time that one could not have been appointed because of the fact that she had not yet been arraigned."

Continuing, Dr. Coats stumbled a little, "She wasn't offered one, no, because I don't think she requested one." He continued, "I felt that there would be somebody available if the family would get busy and try to go through channels to get one. I don't know the mechanisms provided by law or by any Legal Aid bureau. But I felt that that was what could be done or would be done."

McArthur cut to the chase and asked if anyone offered to wait and hold off on taking the "formal" statement until Caril did get a lawyer.

"That question wasn't even brought up," Coats responded.

Audrey Wheeler, the court reporter who transcribed Caril's statement in shorthand, was called next to testify about the 166-page formal statement. She had taken shorthand notes on, February 2nd and 3rd of the interrogations.

Audrey Wheeler basically testified that Caril answered questions freely and voluntarily and was made no promises or threats. Wheeler testified that after taking the shorthand notes, she typed the statement and gave it to either Fahrnbruch or Scheele.

Handing her a document that was marked "Exhibit 40," Wheeler identified the document as the transcription of the statement taken from Caril.

Next, Prosecutor Scheele asked the court reporter whether there was any further conversation after the "formal" statement ended.

"Yes," she replied, explaining that she was still taking shorthand notes when the statement ended but the conversation continued on February 3rd. Wheeler stated that the conversation lasted no more than twenty minutes and ended at 1:45 P.M.

Scheele asked her if she still had the original shorthand notes in her possession and whether she could produce them. Then he rephrased the question, asking Wheeler whether she was able to recall word for word everything that was said during the conversation.

Wheeler responded, "I'm afraid not."

Scheele asked her to read from her shorthand notes the conversation that took place.

McArthur objected, in part, because these notes had not been furnished to the defense previously in compliance with the court's order requiring all written statements to be supplied to the defense prior to the start of the trial.

After a sidebar conference, the judge asked Audrey Wheeler to type up her notes so that the court could "inspect it before we get into it."

Prosecutor Scheele was likely hoping to do with this conversation what he did with the rest of the non-transcribed interrogations—have his witnesses recall how fairly Caril had been treated. He never intended for McArthur to read this conversation in its entirety. Therefore, he now tried to get the court reporter to say all the right things about the prosecution and their dealings with Caril.

Audrey Wheeler was called back to the stand by the prosecution after her notes were typed and provided to Caril's attorney John McArthur.

Scheele asked Wheeler whether Fahrnbruch made any explanations to Caril and to tell what they referred to.

Wheeler responded, "Well, he first explained to her that she would be taken to the county attorney's office that afternoon, at which time her father and her sister would be present, and she would be given an opportunity to visit with them before she was taken over to county court for arraignment. He told her that this was a very serious charge; she said that she understood that. He told her that she would be taken to county court and arraigned; he explained the charges that would be filed against her, which would be first degree murder and murder committed in the perpetration of a crime."

"He asked her if she understood that, and she said she did. He then told her, asked her, if she knew that at the time these things were going on they were wrong. She said she did."

"He then told, explained, the arraignment to her, what she would be charged with, and let's see, oh, at that...he explained to her that, that she would be arraigned on these charges even though she had not actually participated in the actual killing, that she would be arraigned as an accessory. And he told her that she could have an attorney if she wanted one, that at the preliminary hearing it would be up to her folks or friends to provide such an attorney. If she were bound over from county court to district court for trial, that then the state could provide her with an attorney."

In response to Scheele's question asking whether Fahrnbruch said anything to her with reference to any possible plea she might enter, and over McArthur's objection, Audrey stated that Fahrnbruch "told her that in the county court she would be asked whether or not she was guilty or not guilty. She remarked that she would plead...."

Scheele interrupted her to confine her testimony to only what Fahrnbruch told Caril.

Wheeler continued, "He told her that if she felt that she was not guilty that she should say so, that she had a choice of pleas; that if she did plead not guilty that she would be bound over to the district court for trial to a jury."

When Scheele asked Wheeler whether anything was said with reference to a plea of not guilty, Audrey responded, "Yes. He told her that a plea of not guilty could not be held against her in court if she decided to plead not guilty."

Scheele next asked Wheeler whether anything was mentioned about a conversation he (Scheele) had with Caril in Wyoming, and Wheeler responded, "Mr. Fahrnbruch asked her if she had been told by you in Wyoming that she could have any attorney."

"What did she say?" Scheele asked.

"She said 'Yes,' " Wheeler responded.

Asked whether Caril had asked Scheele or anyone else to provide her with an attorney, Audrey answered, "No, she had not." According to Wheeler, in this conversation that Fahrnbruch didn't know was being take down in shorthand, Caril had been provided with every courtesy under the sun. Even as early as out in Wyoming Scheele had informed Caril that she could have an attorney, and she said "No."

The jury was left with the impression that Caril, with full knowledge that a first degree murder charge was being filed against her, did not want an attorney of her own to represent her during interrogations when her answers could lead her straight to the electric chair.

Wheeler, like all the witnesses for the prosecution, had assured the jury that, as with the previous unrecorded interrogations, Caril answered freely and voluntarily.

Note: No one pointed out that Caril's interrogations began shortly after having witnessed a patient across the hall being given shock treatments, and that she not only wondered why she was in a mental hospital, but feared if she did not cooperate fully, she, too, would be subjected to shock treatments. No one pointed out that Caril also wondered why she appeared to be in trouble despite having told the authorities the truth about Starkweather.

That truth included the fact that, obeying Starkweather's orders, she had taken money out of young Jensen's billfold and given the money to Starkweather, and she held the gun on Carol King. Caril also told them that she had asked Carol King to get out of the car in obedience to a maniac she had just seen shoot a farmer in the back for no reason. Nor did any of the witnesses report that Caril told them that Starkweather had said he would kill her and kill her family if she didn't obey him. Instead, all the prosecution's witnesses had reported that Caril was "friendly" and "cooperative," that she answered questions freely and voluntarily, and that she was in complete touch with reality.

It should be noted that it was only several hours prior to her statement being transcribed that Caril learned with certainty from her sister that her family had, indeed, been murdered by Starkweather. The news prompted her to remark that she wished he had killed her, too, so she could be with her mother.

It was now Caril's attorney's turn to question the court reporter, Audrey Wheeler.

"Miss Wheeler, wouldn't you say that the way you have related this conversation is quite misleading?"

Wheeler answered that she didn't understand what he meant by "misleading."

McArthur asked her to refer to her notes. "Will you refer to those, please. I'll ask you whether this question was asked by Mr. Fahrnbruch and this answer given at the time and place you have testified about. 'And did Mr. Scheele explain to you, and he did explain to you in Wyoming, did he not, that you could have a lawyer if you wanted one?' And the answer 'Yes.' Is that true?"

"Yes, sir," Wheeler responded.

McArthur quoted further from the transcribed notes, " 'And you told him at that time that you did not want a lawyer?' " he said, referring to Caril's interrogation. "And the answer, 'No, I never. I didn't know what he meant at the time by that. I thought he meant by the district attorney.' "

"That's correct," Wheeler said.

McArthur said, "And the next question and answer: 'And were you aware at all times, Caril, that you could have a lawyer if you wanted one?' And her answer, 'No, I wasn't.' "

"Yes, sir." Wheeler answered.

"And the next question and answer: 'Did your father tell you that yesterday?' Answer: 'No, I don't think he did.' "

"Yes, sir," Wheeler nodded.

"And the next question and answer? 'And you want a lawyer now, is that right?' And the answer, 'Yes, but who would take it?' "

"Yes, sir."

On redirect examination, Scheele asked Wheeler, "And the next question and answer: 'Caril, in the county court it is up to the person being charged or it is up to her friends to get her a lawyer...after the preliminary hearing, and if you are bound over to the district court then you are entitled to have a lawyer appointed by the court. Do you understand that?' Answer: 'Yes.' "

"Yes," Wheeler said.

Scheele continued. "The next question, 'You have not made any requests for a lawyer, have you, Caril?' Answer: 'No.' "

"Yes, sir."

"The next question: 'You haven't asked me for a lawyer?'
Answer: 'No.' "

"Yes, sir."

On recross-examination McArthur asked, "Then what really happened, Miss Wheeler, is that she first said she did want a lawyer, and they kept questioning her about it and she said she didn't, isn't that about the way it worked?...And they wouldn't leave that alone, well, they kept on until she said no, that she'd never asked anybody for one....That's what your notes show, isn't that right?"

Note: McArthur had essentially exposed what he considered the bullying of the teenager Caril Fugate. Wheeler had been placed in the position of being honest and truthful—that, essentially, Caril been talked into proceeding with the interrogation without an attorney present.

Over John McArthur's objections, both Exhibits 40 and 41, transcripts of Caril's statement, were admitted into evidence.

CHAPTER 15

The prosecution's main witness against Caril was none other than Charles Starkweather, the man who was a known liar and a convicted murderer, who had already been sentenced to die in Nebraska's electric chair. However, before examining Starkweather's testimony, it's important to review the statements given by another inmate, Otto Glaser. Starkweather's jail room was approximately three feet from the door of Glaser's room, so Glaser could clearly hear what was being said in Starkweather's cell.

Guards warned Glaser many times to stay away from his door and to stay toward the back of his room, but during the conversations that took place with Starkweather all parties would be talking in a loud voice that Glaser could hear from any portion of his room without intentionally attempting to do so.

After he was released from prison, Glaser contacted Caril's attorney, John McArthur, and provided an affidavit about things he overhead coming from Starkweather's cell prior to Caril's trial. Yes, Glaser was a convicted felon, but still, it is indeed telling to compare Glaser's description of how Starkweather was coached on what to say at Caril's trial with what Starkweather actually said. The two stories match.

Otto Glaser, being first duly sworn and under oath, stated that he was discharged from the state penitentiary of the State of Nebraska on March 14, 1959, and that he immediately contacted the attorneys for Caril Fugate because he had personal knowledge of the actions of the State of Nebraska in influencing Charles Starkweather to testify falsely as a witness against Caril. Glaser was shocked and disturbed at the things that he heard Starkweather say immediately prior to and during the trial of Caril Fugate.

Glaser stated that he was removed to the hospital ward in the state penitentiary on approximately the 14th day of October, 1958, and occupied room 4 therein continuously thereafter to and including the 12th day of December, 1958. During all this time, Charles Starkweather occupied room 5 of the hospital ward which adjoined room 4 on the north. On many occasions Glaser saw and talked with Starkweather, and on many occasions Glaser could observe and hear what other persons said to Charles Starkweather and what he said to them.

Glaser stated that during the early days of his confinement in the said hospital ward following approximately October 14, 1958, Charles Starkweather appeared to be treated exactly as other prisoners on the ward. He was not allowed access to newspapers, nor was he permitted radio earphones or magazines, and the television was so located that he could not see it through his door. Starkweather was allowed to receive books from the prison library. During the early days of his imprisonment, Starkweather was given cigarettes, one at a time, to a total of about seven or eight cigarettes per day. Glaser was in a position to see and hear and did see and hear every visit made by anyone to Starkweather, and each person going to or from Starkweather's room went past Glaser's room to get there.

Glaser stated that at about the time that Caril Fugate went to trial in the District Court of Lancaster County, Nebraska, the treatment of Starkweather changed abruptly and from that time forward he was granted numerous and continuing favors. Starkweather was given the *Lincoln Star* newspaper each day and the *Omaha World-Herald* each day; he was given a carton of cigarettes and a bag of candy to take into his room at noon on the day he testified; in the evenings, he was given another carton of cigarettes to take into his room.

On the second day that Starkweather testified against Caril Fugate, he took more candy of different kinds and cigarettes into his room: he had Camel, Chesterfield, L&M, and Lucky

Strike cigarettes and at least one other brand. Glaser further stated that Starkweather was given earphones and was permitted to listen to the radio whenever he wished, both day and night. Also, he could order coffee at various times of the day and night and it would be brought to him by an attendant.

Prior to this time, the television set was located at the north end of the ward and near the west wall, where Starkweather could not see it; nor could Glaser see the television. But immediately after Starkweather completed his testimony against Caril Fugate, the television was removed to the east end of the ward and set in the corner facing Starkweather's room. From that time forward, Starkweather watched television any time he pleased, and Glaser's room, which adjoined that of Starkweather's on the south, was so located that Glaser could also see the television through his door.

Glaser stated that from the time Starkweather testified up to and including the 12th day of December, 1958, when Glaser was removed from the hospital ward, Starkweather continued to receive the newspapers, the use of the radio earphones, cigarettes in abundance, and the privilege of watching television at any time. Prior to his testimony, Starkweather was only allowed to go to the bathroom to take a bath occasionally in the daytime. Later on, he was permitted to go to the bathroom to take a bath whenever he so requested, either day or night. Glaser said Starkweather stated to the guards that Elmer Scheele had promised him that he could take a bath at any time he saw fit, and it appeared to Glaser that he did so.

Glaser stated that approximately one week before the case of *State of Nebraska vs. Caril Ann Fugate,* three persons whose names Glaser did not know but whom he could readily identify on sight, spent practically all of each day including the meal periods there at the door of Starkweather's room, and the three persons would take turns talking to Starkweather about Caril Fugate and her case. These three persons were not all present all of the time every day, but at least one of them was present all of the time and sometimes two at a time, and occasionally all three would be present.

Glaser heard these men tell Starkweather repeatedly and on different occasions on practically every visit that a great deal depended upon him, that there were certain things he must not say and that it was just as important to omit the things he was told not to say, and to testify to the things he was supposed to say.

Glaser particularly recalled one of the men telling Starkweather repeatedly that he would not get the electric chair if he said exactly what he was told to say in the Caril Fugate case. This man said that Elmer Scheele was a man of his word and would see to it that Starkweather did not get the chair.

Glaser stated that Starkweather was told on many occasions by the three persons that there were certain things he definitely must not say on the witness stand. When they discussed these matters the voices usually got louder, and Glaser could more readily hear what Starkweather was told not to say than what he was told to say.

Glaser recalled specifically that Starkweather told the men about using violence on Caril Fugate in the Meyer home and that Starkweather said he almost shot Caril at the Meyer home because she tried to escape and because she would not do what she was told there. Starkweather said he used considerable force on her at the Meyer home, and Glaser said Starkweather was warned repeatedly and emphatically by the three men that he must not say any of those things on the witness stand.

Glaser further specifically recalled that Starkweather told the visiting men that he almost killed Caril in the Ward home, too, that he felt he had to. He treated her violently in the home because she attempted to escape and because she would not obey him, but he was prevented from killing Caril by some circumstance that Starkweather did not make clear. Glaser said the three men who visited Starkweather warned him that he must never make any such statements on the witness stand.

Glaser also reported that he heard Starkweather tell the three men that he had to threaten Caril with death at the time of the Collison (the traveling salesman) killing in Wyoming and that he intended to kill her there, and would have done so, had he not been interrupted and captured. Again, the three visitors warned Starkweather repeatedly that he must not repeat these facts nor admit them under any circumstances.

Glaser stated that Starkweather told the three visitors that he should have killed Caril in the Bartlett home and had contemplated doing so. He believed he could have made his escape more easily if he had done so. Again, the men repeatedly warned Starkweather not to make any such statements on the witness stand.

Glaser further recalled that the three attendants told Starkweather repeatedly and emphatically almost every day that he must never admit on the witness stand his reason for killing Mr. Bartlett, the stepfather of Caril, but that he must claim and testify that he killed Bartlett in a sudden fight and that the killing was the first of his crimes.

Glaser particularly remembered that the three men had a spirited quarrel with Starkweather about what he should say and what he should not say about the killing of Robert Jensen. During this discussion, Starkweather became excited and talked in a loud voice with considerable profanity. Glaser said the men continued to talk to Starkweather each day about the Jensen killing and told Starkweather repeatedly that everything depended upon him and that he must testify as he was told, and that if he would "play ball," Elmer Scheele would keep his word and Starkweather would be saved from execution.

Glaser stated that Starkweather would on many occasions become excited and obscene and would insist that he wanted to tell the story his own way. The men would continue to talk to him and repeat that his welfare depended on testifying the way he was told and omitting the things he was told to omit.

Glaser also said that on the first day Starkweather testified in the Caril Fugate case, that evening, the three men told Starkweather that on the following day he would be questioned by Caril Ann Fugate's attorney and that he must be extremely careful and that he must not answer any question that he had previously been told not to answer and that he must be particularly careful to say only the things he had been told to say. The men told him that after each question by Caril's attorney, he should attempt to decide before answering whether he could say the things he had been told to say and, if not, he should refuse to answer the question.

Glaser stated that from the time Caril Fugate went on trial on October 27, 1958, until her trial was over, Starkweather would be taken from his room at approximately 9:00 A.M. and be away from the ward until noon. Then, he would be returned to the ward during the noon hour and would be removed from the ward again at approximately 2:00 P.M. and returned to the ward at approximately 4:30 P.M. During the time Starkweather was in the ward, he was constantly being talked to by the three men about the Caril Fugate case. They would talk to him about what Starkweather might be expected to say.

When the Fugate case was submitted to the jury, Starkweather was no longer removed from the hospital ward. Glaser said he asked Starkweather where he was taken when he left the ward each day of the Caril Fugate trial, and Starkweather told him that he was taken to a consultation room to be in constant contact with the prosecution.

Glaser stated that although it is impossible for him to know personally, it was generally believed and discussed on the hospital ward by both prisoners and personnel that all during the Caril Fugate trial a phone line was constantly kept open between the county attorney's office and the penitentiary to keep in constant contact with Starkweather.

Glaser reported that before and after Caril's trial and all during the time Glaser was in the hospital ward, the invariable practice was for the guards and other attendants, including the three persons who constantly interviewed Starkweather, to stay outside Starkweather's room in the hall and talk to Starkweather through the door which had bars and a screen on it.

According to Glaser, the three men at times taunted Starkweather. Glaser said that on many occasions and practically every day the three men talked to Starkweather, they would mention to him that Caril Fugate had stated that Starkweather was bowlegged and that he liked to play cops and robbers and liked to play cowboys; they also told him that she said that he could not dance because of his crooked legs and that she thought he was insane. Starkweather would become extremely angry and frenzied and would curse and repeat over and over again that he should have killed Caril Fugate on the different occasions that he could have done so.

Glaser stated that he talked to Starkweather on several occasions while in their cells. Glaser said Starkweather told him that he realized he should have killed Caril Fugate in the Bartlett home along with the rest of her family or at the Meyer farm or at the Ward home. Starkweather said he also nearly killed her in Wyoming and that he intended to let her know that during her trial. Starkweather told Glaser repeatedly that he had realized at the Meyer home and was fully convinced by the time they got to the Ward home that Caril would escape or would tip off the police or would in some manner get him captured. His big mistake was in not killing her when he had the chance.

Glaser further stated that when Starkweather was returned to his cell after testifying at Caril's trial, escorted by three guards, he would have candy in hand and appeared to be in an extremely happy mood. He made the remark that he had everybody eating out of his hand.

Starkweather told Glaser that he had been promised leniency for testifying as instructed against Caril Fugate and for withholding certain facts in his testimony; he had been assured that he would get a hearing before the parole board and he would not be executed. Starkweather said he had been assured repeatedly that the county attorney was a man of his word and was able to fulfill these promises. Starkweather said he would never be executed because he had done as he was told.

Glaser said that he had heard Starkweather say on several occasions that he would be happy to have Caril Fugate sitting in his lap if he was electrocuted and that his one last wish was that she be electrocuted. Glaser also said that when it was announced that a verdict had been reached in the Fugate case, Starkweather put on his radio earphones and for a period of one half hour Starkweather was talking about how anxious he was that it be a guilty verdict condemning her to death. When Caril's verdict was announced on the radio, Starkweather shouted and laughed, saying his only disappointment was that Caril did not get the chair. But still, he had gotten his way in the case.

Otto Glaser's signed affidavit was notarized on March 14, 1959.

Note: Starkweather kept telling the men he wanted to tell the story "his way." It was inherently wrong for the prosecution to pick and choose which of his versions of the events they wanted Starkweather to testify about on the stand. They warned Starkweather not to say that he almost killed Caril several times, and he was not to mention he used violence on her at the Wards' house. Their behavior descends to the level of fabrication of testimony.

These men also employed the possible commutation of his death sentence as an incentive for him to go along with their "coaching." They gave him false hope. Starkweather knew his appeal was being heard on the day after McArthur cross-examined him. He likely thought the court could and would commute his sentence to life.

However, on the eve of Caril's trial, Starkweather completely refuted the notion that Caril was a willing accomplice. The prosecutors finally heard from Starkweather's own mouth that Caril was acting under duress and threats—something she had been telling them all along. Now they knew it, but instead of bringing the truth to the attention of Caril's lawyers, which they were obliged to do, they encouraged him to lie on the stand to get her convicted. A prosecutor's goal is not to get a defendant convicted on a false charge!

Many years later, on January 16, 1992, Paul Douglas, then Lancaster deputy county attorney, working with Elmer Scheele, was interviewed for the television series, *Murder in the Heartland*. In this interview, Douglas corroborated Otto Glaser's affidavit. Douglas said, "Early on we sensed the hostility between Charlie and Caril, and…well…we brought things to Charlie's attention, such as things Caril was saying about him (to get him) to testify against her. And we could do that, he was our witness."

If a witness is told to say something that is *not* true, the crime being committed is suborning perjury. If a witness is encouraged to *not* tell something that *is* true, there may also be criminal activity, whether obstructing justice or witness tampering.

There is an appropriate, legal way to coach a witness. When an attorney coaches a witness, he or she does not strive to change the witness's testimony. The lawyer only provides the witness with basic suggestions such as try to relax, listen very carefully, volunteer nothing, answer only the question asked, and don't be afraid to disagree with leading questions. Attorneys often assist witnesses in the strong points of their testimony, but that is very different from encouraging them to lie. Coaching should never give a witness the substance of what to say. That is the line between witness coaching and subornation of perjury or fabricated testimony.

Glaser's affidavit was later used by Caril's attorneys, John McArthur and Merril Reller, to seek a new trial; however, their efforts would be unsuccessful.

CHAPTER 16

It is shocking that the key witness at Caril Fugate's trial was Charles Starkweather, a serial murderer and a known liar who had already been convicted and sentenced to die in the electric chair. Moreover, he had already given numerous, conflicting versions of what had happened.

In the months preceding Caril's trial, Starkweather had turned against her. Now he was being called to the witness stand at her trial. However, just as he had already changed his story numerous times as to how the murders occurred, he was now on the brink of giving yet another version when he took the witness stand at Caril's trial. This latest version would sink any hope of exonerating Caril.

As Starkweather entered the courtroom in handcuffs and leg irons, the jurors and spectators watched him in stunned silence, as if a movie star had entered the courtroom. Caril wanted to scream in fear and disbelief, and she held onto her attorney Merril Reller's arm, tightly twisting the sleeve of his suit to control herself.

Caril held her head down and thought, I failed, I failed, I failed. Stupid. I was so stupid. So stupid. How could I have been so stupid to believe him? How? How could he do this? What made him do this? Liar. Liar. Liar.

Starkweather took the witness stand for the prosecution. Asked what happened at the Bartlett home, Starkweather said he arrived at the Bartletts at 1:30 P.M. All three of them—Caril's parents and baby sister—were at home. He said he stayed a half hour and then left to drive around the block. He drove back to the Bartletts and got into an argument with Mr. Bartlett who kicked him in the rear end out the door. He then went to Hutson's, a nearby small grocery store, and made a phone call to Mr. Bartlett's work to tell them Bartlett was sick. He returned to the Bartletts and remained there until 3:00 or 3:30, when he left to pick up Caril after school.

Something was wrong with his car so he left it at the Griggs' house, a few blocks away. He walked back to the Bartletts' house and knocked, but no one came to the door. So he sat on the back porch playing with their dogs. According to Starkweather, Caril arrived home at 4:00. He heard Caril and her mother yelling so he went inside the house. Mrs. Bartlett slapped him, and Starkweather hit her back. Mrs. Bartlett screamed, and Mr. Bartlett came in. Starkweather said he shot Mr. Bartlett with his brother Rodney's .22 rifle.

Scheele asked, "And did you do anything to Mrs. Bartlett?"

"Well, I shot her, too."

"With the same gun?"

"Yes, but I didn't kill her," Starkweather said.

"And did you do anything to Betty Jean?"

"Yes. I threw a knife at her."

"And was Caril in the same room when you shot Mrs. Bartlett?" Scheele asked.

"Yes," Starkweather replied.

"Was Caril in the same room when you threw a knife at Betty Jean?"

"Yes."

"Did you throw a knife at Betty Jean more than one time?"

"No."

Note: Betty Jean's autopsy report indicates there were two puncture wounds to her neck and multiple skull fractures of her head, information known to the attorneys. Allowing Starkweather to lie about throwing his knife at Betty Jean only one time would give the jury the impression that the second knife wound and skull fractures were done by Caril.

Starkweather next testified about the two teenagers, Robert Jensen and Carol King, who stopped to help them on the country road. Starkweather said Carol King thanked them for being nice; he also said that Carol King's statement made Caril Fugate mad and she told King to turn around and shut up. Starkweather's lie about King saying this could contribute to the jury's thinking that perhaps Caril had a motive to kill Carol King because she was jealous.

When prompted by Scheele about a billfold, Starkweather stated, "Caril asked if I already asked Jensen for his money, and I said 'No.' " Starkweather continued with his new story by stating that Caril held a loaded .410 shotgun on the King girl.

Starkweather next described how he killed Robert Jensen. He said Jensen came running up the cellar stairs and so he shot him. That would mean Jensen would be shot from the front. However, Dr. Zeman, the pathologist, had previously testified that the bullet wounds entered from the back of Jensen's ear, therefore proving that Starkweather shot him from behind.

Starkweather described Caril as a willing accomplice in the robbery of Jensen and King.

"What did Caril say?" Scheele asked.

"She said, 'You do as we tell you or you'll find out, and I'll shoot the girl to show you that we will.' Them ain't the exact words, something like that," Starkweather said.

"Now that was Caril Fugate that said that?"

"Yes."

Starkweather frequently went into detail about how Caril was an active participant rather than a passive hostage.

Scheele continued, "Now what did Caril Fugate do with Robert Jensen's billfold?"

"She just took the money out and handed it back to him; Carol King took the billfold."

"Caril took the money from it and handed the billfold back to whom?" Scheele asked.

"She held it up between Carol King and Robert Jensen, and Carol King took it."

"Now, what did Caril Fugate do with the money that she took from Robert Jensen's billfold?"

"Well, she asked me for my billfold, and I gave it to her, and she took the money and put it in mine and gave it back to me."

Starkweather continued by testifying that after Jensen was shot, Carol King was standing outside the cellar's entrance and

Starkweather told her to go down into the cellar. He walked over to the car and got it stuck in the ditch. Starkweather and Caril walked back to the cellar and told Carol King to come out. Starkweather left Caril holding the .22 and telling her to watch King. He went back to the car and got it out of the ditch.

Note: Nothing more was asked about Carol King, leaving the jury with the impression that Caril not only killed her, but stuck a knife up Carol's vagina with such ferocity that it punctured her rectum. The jury had already been shown the photograph of the young woman with her breasts exposed and her pants pulled down with blood running down her legs from the knife wounds. Jurors were left to ponder whether Caril Fugate performed this heinous act because she was jealous of Carol King.

The defense attorney, John McArthur, immediately began cross-examination of Starkweather with the following question, "Charles, is your own case now pending in the State Supreme Court?"

"As far as I know."

"And does that come up for hearing in the Supreme Court of Nebraska tomorrow?"

"As far as I know."

This question was crucial. McArthur was preparing to show Starkweather's bias against Caril and his intent to ingratiate himself with the prosecutors in the hope that they would help get his sentence commuted.

McArthur then concentrated on the numerous contradictory statements Starkweather provided to the prosecution and read quotes from his prior statements, including this one from Starkweather's Version 4 account.

"I wrapped them up and put them in the little house out behind the house. Caril came home about four o'clock that afternoon. I told her a line that they were somewhere. I was going to tell her about what happened, but I let it go by, and before I said anything the days went by so fast I never did say anything to Caril."

"Do you recall writing something like that?" John McArthur, asked Starkweather.

"Yes," Starkweather said.
"You did?"
"Yes."

McArthur also read one of Starkweather's statements (Version 6), in which he said Caril did not get home from school until sometime after three o'clock:
"Did you make any phone calls from any place that afternoon?"
"Yes, right after I killed them, about 2 o'clock, I think it was, I went back up to the Hutson's Store and I told them that Mr. Bartlett wouldn't be to work for a couple of days, he was sick."
"Who did you tell that to?"
"Some lady on the phone down at Watson Brothers."
But Starkweather had testified that he had killed Mr. Bartlett in front of Caril, after he called Mr. Bartlett's work. There were dozens of such contradictions in Starkweather's testimony.

McArthur began another rounD of questioning. He pressed the fact that Starkweather had given numerous inconsistent statements, asking if there was any testimony Starkweather had given that was not embellished or incorrect.
"Well, things that I said that Caril didn't do this and didn't do that, well, when she did do it, is that the 'false' that you are talking about?"
McArthur said, "Perhaps that's a little confusing. What I'm trying to find out is this: Were every one of your statements false in some respects?"
"A lot of hogwash in some respects."
McArthur pointed out that Starkweather acknowledged that every time he gave a version of his confession, he stated it was true at the time. Given that fact, it was extraordinary Starkweather had any credibility whatsoever.
"All right. Every time you have made a statement or made a confession or signed something in the past have you told the people that you gave it to that it was all the truth?"

"A few of them," Starkweather stated.

"I beg your pardon?" McArthur asked.

"A few of them."

"Well, did you ever deliver one and tell them it wasn't the truth?"

"No."

"You have always said it was the truth at the time, haven't you?"

"Yes."

Note: Let's step back a moment and remember the statements made by prison inmate Otto Glaser who claimed that he overheard the three men who visited Starkweather prior to Caril's trial tell him to be extremely careful and not to answer any questions he was told not to answer and to say only the things he had been told to say. Starkweather was told by them that after each question he should attempt to decide before answering whether he could say things he had been told to say; if not, he should refuse to answer at all. The segments of questions that follow are from both the prosecution and defense attorneys.

The following is from cross-examination by defense attorney John McArthur:

"And, Charles, why did you kill Mrs. Bartlett?" McArthur asked.

"I shot Mrs. Bartlett, but I didn't finish killing her."

"Well, why did you shoot her?"

"Mr. McArthur, in these murders, I wish not to talk about them."

"I beg your pardon?"

"These murders, I wish not to talk about them."

Regarding the murder of Robert Colvert, McArthur asked, "Would you just tell us briefly the circumstances, how you happened to be there?"

"No," Starkweather answered.

"You don't want to do that?"

"No."

With regard to the murder of August Meyer, McArthur asked, "I just want to know what you can tell us about his taking a shot at you, Charles."

"Well, I didn't want to talk about these crimes."

"With respect to the murder of C. Lauer Ward, Charles, would you say that C. Lauer Ward made some attack on you before you shot him?"

"Yes."

"Would you tell just briefly what he did?"

Starkweather did not reply.

"I beg your pardon?"

"No."

"You mean you can't recall?"

"I told you this morning I wasn't going to talk about it."

"Would you tell us what C. Lauer Ward did that you felt you had to shoot him?"

Starkweather did not reply.

"You will not do that?"

"No."

"With respect to Merle Collison making a threatening movement towards you, what was the nature of that movement?"

"Well, I'm not going to talk about that either."

"With regard to what you would have done to Caril had she tried to escape or tip anybody off, you testified yesterday, Charles, about the farmer that pulled your car out of the mud out at Bennet?"

"Yes."

"And at that time I believe you had a knife?"

"Yes."

"Did you have in mind what you would do if Caril told Mr. Genuchi some of the things you had done?"

"You mean some of the things we both did? Maybe she should have."

"I beg your pardon?"

"If she did, maybe Bob Jensen and Carol King wouldn't have got killed."

"What I'm asking you is this, did you have in mind what you would do if she should suddenly speak up?"

"She could talk anytime she wanted to."

215

"Yes, she could talk, but what I'm asking you, do you know what you would have done if she had?"

"I don't care what she did, she wasn't going to talk."

"Do you know..."

"She was worried about not getting to the cops, she wasn't going to."

"You're not answering me. What would you have done if she had?"

"She wasn't going to do it."

"Well, of course, you realize that she wasn't going to talk, and everybody knows she didn't talk, but what I'm asking about what would you have done if she had?"

"I wasn't worried about her talking. I wasn't worrying about what she did; she wasn't going to talk."

"Well, you're kind of dodging me a little bit."

"No, I ain't."

"Do you know what you would have done if she had?"

"Well, I wasn't worrying about her doing it, so I didn't think about it."

Upon further questioning from prosecuting attorney Elmer Scheele:

"Now, Charles, has anyone told you or tried to tell you what to say here in this courtroom?"

"No."

"And what did I tell you to do before you came down here to testify?"

"Just to tell the truth."

"And have you told the truth?"

"Yes."

In his recross-examination, defense attorney John McArthur asked, "Charles, why is it that when I ask you about these specific killings you refuse to answer, and when Mr. Scheele asks you, you are willing to answer? Did Mr. Scheele, the prosecuting attorney, ask you which version you were going to testify to on any of these different transactions?"

"No."

"Then, as far as you know, Mr. Scheele had no idea of what you were going to tell him the facts were?"

"Well, maybe Mr. Scheele knew what he was going to say, but I didn't know what he was going to ask me."

"Well, what I'm getting at is this: Mr. Scheele didn't ask you which of the several statements of fact you were going to claim as the truth when you went into court, did he?"

Note: As pointed out earlier, Charles Starkweather had given multiple stories of how the murders had occurred. As he gave each version, he claimed it was true.

CHAPTER 17

The defense called Caril Fugate to the witness stand.

Many commentators have written that Caril was not the model witness. Perhaps the jury and onlookers expected to see her appearing childlike, terrified, vulnerable. In those days people did not understand much about adolescent psychological development; people had never heard of post-traumatic stress disorder. Nobody on the jury or among the reporters covering the case knew what it had taken for Caril to hold together the vestiges of sanity and personal dignity during Starkweather's rampage. Consequently, as a matter of self-preservation, neither her face nor her voice showed much emotion. In short, she looked the way many soldiers look when they return from a combat patrol, and this is most likely not what the jury expected to see in an innocent girl. So she came across as hard, defiant, tough.

Caril's attorney John McArthur had her explain to the jury that as an eighth grader, she had decided that she wanted to be a nurse when she grew up. She was above average in intelligence. She had been well behaved and compliant during the time she was being held at the state hospital. He also explained that even though Charles Starkweather was behind bars, she was still "scared to death" of him. To humanize Caril further, McArthur had her identify a number of her family photographs which he passed around the jury.

Caril testified that she had broken up with Starkweather and that she had become afraid of him. She testified that she had told Starkweather to leave and not come back when she had broken off the relationship; that had been on January 19, the Sunday before the murder of her family. She testified about her fear and exhaustion, her fright.

McArthur had to deal with the fact that Caril did in fact hold a .410 shotgun as she was walking down the road with Starkweather after Meyer was killed. But Starkweather was holding Caril by her left arm as he carried two rifles, a pistol, and a knife. McArthur was proving that the fact that she had possession of a weapon did not necessarily mean she was in command of it.

In 1958 and to this day, there are plenty of people in Nebraska who imagined themselves and imagine still how brave and daring they would have been if they were in Caril's situation and had the gun—how they would've leapt forth, killed Starkweather, and driven for help.

But, in reality, most people do not react in a heroic manner. Most people—including many well-trained soldiers on the battlefield—find themselves to be in a state of paralysis the first time they are faced with any gunplay.

Caril testified how the teenager Robert Jensen stopped the car, how they got into the car. She also spoke of her fears that Starkweather was going to kill her because he already had killed Mr. Meyer. She also feared that he would have her family killed.

Caril described how Jensen handed over his billfold. Starkweather ordered her to take it, so Caril took it. She testified that at first she wouldn't take it but that Jensen had said, "Do what he says so no one will get hurt," and she took it after Starkweather had screamed at her again. When Starkweather told the couple to get out of the car and Carol King did not move, Caril whispered to her that she better get out, that she (Caril) was afraid he was going to kill them all. She further testified that Starkweather had ordered Jensen to go down into the storm cellar. Caril testified that she was shaking when she heard the shots, that she didn't run away, that "I couldn't move, after I heard the shots, I couldn't move."

Caril testified that on the drive back to Lincoln she noticed some schoolbooks in the backseat, and she threw them out because she knew somebody would find them and start looking for the two students. She was trying to leave a trail.

She had written a note in the filling station, "Help. Police. Don't ignore." She stated that she never had the chance to slip the note to anyone. She testified that Starkweather took Jensen's car into Lincoln and to the Bartletts' neighborhood and would not let her out of it.

McArthur asked the question that the jurors and the general public wanted to know: Why did she not jump out and run? But the fact was Starkweather was armed, and she was very young and very terrified. McArthur asked her if there was any time at all that she was with Charles that she did not want to get away, and she answered no. She stated that she always wanted to get free, but he had told her if she ever got loose her family would be killed and it would be her fault.

Caril's fatigue began to show, and McArthur requested the court's permission to excuse her and recall her later.

It is not unusual to excuse witnesses with the intent they will be called back later, and it is also not unusual for witnesses to be called out of turn. McArthur called pathologist Dr. Edwin Zeman. It was Zeman who testified that Carol King had been stabbed several times in the vagina, stabbed so deeply that a wound had gone through the internal walls into the rectum, where the blade had been twisted.

McArthur then offered into evidence the testimony of Dr. John O'Hearne, who had testified for the defense at the Starkweather trial. McArthur wanted the jurors to better understand the situation Caril was in as Starkweather's hostage.

O'Hearne was a psychiatrist from Kansas City who had given Starkweather a physical and neurological examination, and, as a psychiatrist, developed certain opinions. One of his comments about Starkweather was, "If things would come at him one at a time, slowly, as in a routine job, he would be able to handle these things, but if things began to flood in on him, such as work not going right, the sprinkler on the ceiling coming on, or somebody yelling and whistle going on all at once, I don't think he could function."

O'Hearne went on to comment that Charlie would behave like a frightened animal, that, although he "walks around in the body of a human being," he could not think or function as a human being, that he had never quite "learned to be a person." O'Hearne described Charlie quite clearly as a kind of subhuman creature. McArthur, of course, was reminding the jury that Caril was the hostage of a monster with whom none of the adults on the jury could have coped.

Although McArthur was ostensibly putting this evidence forth for the purpose of impeaching the credibility of Starkweather's testimony on the grounds he was insane, as with any good trial lawyer he had a double motive: it was his desire to make certain the jury was fully aware that Caril was at all times dealing with a real maniac. McArthur called Alice Lauer, a relative of the Wards, who testified that Mr. and Mrs. Ward had been healthy, intelligent people. The next two witnesses testified that Robert Colvert was smart, strong, and able-bodied.

McArthur called witnesses who testified that Caril Fugate was a nice, friendly young girl, her family was affectionate, she loved her baby sister, she was a generally nice person—and now she was a ward at the state hospital.

McArthur pointed out that strong, sophisticated, intelligent people had not been able to deal with Starkweather and had not survived him. It would be unreasonable to expect that a gentle, sweet, young girl such as Caril could be able to handle him. This was McArthur's theme throughout the trial: Nobody had been able to handle Starkweather. How could the jury demand it from this young girl?

Caril's grandmother, Pansy Street, testified that on Monday morning, January 27, she took a taxi to 924 Belmont, Caril's house. She saw Caril there, who looked very white and frightened. Caril told Pansy to go away, "Oh Granny, go away...." The grandmother remembered that Caril put her hand up over her mouth, stepped back toward the gas heater, and moved her fingers as if she were pointing in the corner. Pansy was screaming for her daughter Velda to come to the door, or at least for her to come to where Pansy could see her. But Velda did not come, so Pansy said she would go and get a search warrant. Pansy went to the police station and asked them if she could get somebody to go out to the Bartlett house, and the police finally assigned two men to go out to the house with her. The officers took her back to the Bartlett house, climbed inside through a window, and opened the door to let her in. The house was deserted and clean.

Pansy Street continued to worry, but the police officers told her she shouldn't stick her nose in the affairs of her married children. After Pansy Street was excused, McArthur continued to call witnesses to show that the Bartletts were a decent, typical family.

On Friday morning, McArthur called to the stand Hazel Heflin, the wife of the Douglas, Wyoming, sheriff. Hazel described Caril as being in a state of shock and explained that she had asked that Caril be sedated. "She cried and screamed for her mother and little half-sister and wondered why they wouldn't call."

Barbara Von Busch, Caril's sister, and Barbara's husband, Bob, testified next. They reiterated McArthur's image of the Bartlett family as harmonious and getting along. Their testimony was about their visit to the house on Saturday, January 25. Barbara said Caril had come to the door and shouted to her to go away, saying, "Go away if you know what is good for you, or mother will get hurt." Barbara remembered Caril as looking very pale, and Caril ran to them and said she was sorry she was cranky, but they had to leave.

Then, the next-door neighbor testified that on the Tuesday the Bartletts had been killed, she had left work at 4:00 and stayed at home for the rest of the afternoon and had heard nothing unusual.

Caril was then recalled to the witness stand. Once again McArthur did everything he could to soften her image, to humanize her, but Caril was clearly compensating as best she could as she had to relive her nightmare from the witness stand. She simply could not come across with a soft, sweet voice—the way she might have talked before she had been subjected to the ordeal that Starkweather put her through. She had faced further despair when the state locked her in solitary confinement in a mental institution where she was subjected to brutal interrogation by the prosecutorial team and saw people undergo shock treatment. There was simply not enough strength left in Caril to present herself as the victim she really was. She was coping, just barely, as best she could

Defense attorney McArthur cannot be criticized for not being able to undo the public image Caril presented because of the astonishing psychological damage that had been done to her. McArthur did as good a job as possible back in the days before psychiatric and psychological witnesses were available who could have explained that Caril was testifying behind the protective mask of shock; perhaps they could have explained her demeanor in a way that showed she was simply trying to survive emotionally.

Later, under questioning by McArthur, Caril testified how she and Starkweather had driven from Lincoln to the lane by Meyer's farm, where the car got stuck. They went to Meyer's to borrow his horses to pull the car out. Meyer came out to meet them, agreed to lend the horses, and Starkweather shot Meyer. She was terrified of Starkweather. When McArthur asked Caril how she felt when Meyer was shot, she simply said, "I couldn't move." She then stated she had never seen anybody shot or killed before. Of course, this was a bone of contention in court because the prosecution depended entirely on the notion that she had already seen her family killed and had participated in it.

Caril testified that she had a kind of paralysis, an inability to move, as Starkweather ordered her around. She related how Starkweather ransacked Meyer's house, eating, changing socks, taking money. She testified that a neighboring farmer offered to help while they were trying to get their car unstuck, and how she feared saying anything to him.

When the court resumed on Monday morning, Caril continued her narration, and with McArthur's encouragement continued to explain that she had acted constantly through fear, not only for her life but for the lives of her family and everyone with whom they came into contact.

She spoke of her fear of fleeing, explaining that she felt forced and coerced into holding the gun on the housekeeper at the Wards' house. She felt forced to alert Starkweather when Mr. Ward's car came into the driveway, buy hamburgers, and bring Starkweather the gun when he shot Merle Collison in Wyoming. She had the same motive in each instance—she had to act as a kind of obedient zombie under his control or he would make a phone call, and her parents and little sister would be killed.

McArthur expounded on the fact that Caril was already terrorized when the police came while she was in the Bartlett house. She said and did what she thought she needed to do to keep herself and her parents alive. Caril explained that she wrote a note about the family having the flu and put it on the door. She had signed it "Miss Bartlett," which was the name of her baby sister, who of course could not read or write; it was meant as a hint or a clue or a warning that something was wrong in the house.

John McArthur completed his direct examination of Caril by the noon hour.

When Caril returned to the stand, prosecuting attorney Elmer Scheele cross-examined her. Upon seeing Scheele approach the witness stand, Caril flinched. That filthy man! I hate him, she thought to herself. He said I had "it" (Starkweather's penis) in my mouth, my mouth. He makes me want to vomit.

Scheele tried to take her back to conversations they had had in Wyoming. Scheele's initial intent was to make it clear that her extradition was voluntary. Scheele asked Caril if she had in fact returned to Nebraska willingly, and she agreed that she had. Of course, she did not have an attorney at the time, and nobody had told her that she could fight extradition. Nor had anyone told her that Wyoming did not have a death penalty, in the event she were tried in connection with the shooting in Wyoming.

Scheele was single-mindedly advancing the prosecution's theory of the case: Caril could simply have escaped. His total lack of empathy for an adolescent girl in horrifying circumstances would not be possible in a courtroom today. Even most laypeople know something of the Stockholm Syndrome, the notion that even mature, tough, combat-hardened prisoners of war—who have been trained to withstand all conceivable pressures—may become compliant to their captors.

Scheele hammered away. He noted that Caril had been alone in the car at the service station when the car was being greased. He asked where Bartlett's gun was when they were at the filling station. He asked why she didn't run when she went to get hamburgers. He questioned her about returning to Bennet, and the second time the car got stuck, and how they asked Robert Jensen for a lift. He confirmed that Caril did in fact take money from Jensen's billfold and put it into Starkweather's.

Caril was a young girl who, fearing for her life and that of her family's, had done as she was ordered. But Scheele knew that his jury had been subjected to enough pretrial publicity that they all assumed that under similar dire circumstances they would have behaved more wisely and heroically. And so it went. Caril confirmed that at Starkweather's instructions, she had pointed the gun at Carol King and had ordered King out of the car. Then Scheele talked about when Starkweather, King, and Jensen were in the storm cellar.

The next morning when the court reconvened, Scheele began needling Caril about the gang that Starkweather claimed to be a member of, which he said would harm her family with a simple phone call from him. Scheele tried to get her to say that she had never heard of such a gang until she came home from school January 21 and Starkweather was waiting in her house and threatened her. When she said she had heard about the gang before, Scheele asked her why she continued to go out with Starkweather.

Caril was not sophisticated and did not know that the jury would see her as being evasive, when in reality she was simply trying to respond truthfully to a trained and merciless prosecutor.

Scheele continued, "Even after you left the Wards' home while you were on the way to Wyoming, did you tell Charlie Starkweather you loved him?" Caril replied, "Yes, I did; I was afraid he was going to kill me." Scheele established that Starkweather had kissed Caril after that, but she denied kissing him back.

After McArthur rested his case, Scheele called rebuttal witnesses. Dr. Edwin Coats from the state hospital stated that Starkweather, though disturbed, was not legally insane. William Dixon, the county attorney in Wyoming, again assured the court and the jury that Caril was told, while still in Wyoming, that she was entitled to an attorney.

The next day, attorneys delivered their closing arguments. In his closing remarks, defense attorney John McArthur was preaching the obvious to the unwilling. It would not have been possible to have picked a jury in Lincoln, Nebraska that had not already been sold on the notion that Caril could have quite calmly and easily escaped any time she wanted. After all, it happened in movies all the time.

They had seen enough movies to know that Errol Flynn or Randolph Scott could have escaped—when left alone briefly in a gas station, when getting hamburgers, when people came to the house and Starkweather was holding a loaded weapon, at the Meyer's farm, or at the storm cellar. She could have escaped out in the country during a Nebraska winter, or at the Wards' residence near the Lincoln Country Club. In movies, people even leap from moving cars. The fact that Caril was fourteen, and not a very mature fourteen, at the time she was subjected to Starkweather's violence was not going to faze the Lincoln, Nebraska, jury. Twelve citizens, good and true.

Scheele asked Caril why she didn't attempt to escape when policemen came to her house. Never mind that Starkweather was present and armed. Scheele wanted to know why she didn't escape when Starkweather was asleep.

Scheele ignored the possibility that this child was living in shock and fear. He shrugged off the rare circumstances of having a child on trial for murder. "Even fourteen-year-old girls must realize they cannot go on eight-day murder sprees." He let the jury know that this would be a good lesson for other teenagers—that they would be held responsible for their crimes.

McArthur rose in what he must have known was an exercise in futility, but he gave it all he had, and he did a good job in a hopeless situation. He said that Caril was being blamed for the acts of a madman. He pointed out that the public disgust at the manner in which law enforcement had failed in its duties was visited upon Caril, that she was the recipient of the kind of anger that would be directed to any scapegoat. Although nobody would listen, McArthur reminded them that Caril had been persuaded to sign away her legal rights in Wyoming. She had, in her youth and inexperience, given statements without benefit of counsel. It was McArthur's hope that the jury could imagine themselves being in a situation like the one Caril had found herself in—believing her family to be in danger and having been subjected to the brutal treatment of a madman. McArthur went on to say that when Caril saw August Meyer killed she became "a piece of putty" in Starkweather's hands. And by the time she arrived at the Wards' house, all of her reservoirs of independent action had been completely depleted.

By now, however, nothing could have stopped Caril's conviction. Judge Spencer did his job, charging the jury with his instructions. Caril was being tried on two charges: first degree murder (in the murder of Robert Jensen) and murder in the perpetration of a robbery. For this, there must have been some intent on her part to be an accomplice. This gave the jury two different ways of giving her a life sentence. The jury could find her guilty of second degree murder if they found there was no premeditation.

Judge Spencer was a careful-enough judge to give the jury the required instruction that if it found that Caril had accompanied Starkweather under duress, she must be found not guilty.

The jury went out at 10:01 A.M. on November 21, 1958. Caril was taken to the state hospital, where she had remained in solitary confinement, to await the jury verdict.

Although this was a very tense time for the defense, the prosecution knew if Caril were acquitted they could simply file additional murder charges against her for the other victims, and there was no doubt that would happen.

When the jury filed back into the courtroom later on that day, the jury made its announcement. Caril was found guilty of Count 2, first degree murder in the perpetration of a robbery in the death of teenager Robert Jensen. The conviction meant life in prison for Caril. The jury made no finding as to Count 1, for the premeditated murder of young Jensen. Judge Spencer made no inquiry as to the jury's failure to do so, nor did he seek the reactions of the prosecuting attorney or the defense attorney.

Caril sobbed on Attorney Merril Reller's shoulder. Looking at the jury she cried out, "If you really thought I was guilty, why didn't you give me the chair. Someday they're going to find out they made a mistake!"

A reporter at KMTV television news, Ninette Beaver, of Omaha, Nebraska, spoke with several of the jurors after they found Caril guilty. In her book, *Caril,* released in 1974, Beaver reports: "The deliberations had been difficult, reporters learned from a few jurors who were willing to talk. After the jurors had listened to Judge Spencer's lengthy instructions, they retired to the jury room, where the foreman tried to get a discussion started. But nobody seemed willing to speak first.

"Finally somebody voiced what was bothering everyone in the room. It was not the verdict; it was the sentence—life in prison or death—which the jury, under Nebraska law, would be required to determine. After all, the girl was only fifteen years old. Only after the jurors reached agreement that the sentence would be life in prison and not death in the electric chair, were they able to talk about the girl's guilt or innocence."

When Caril was tried in 1958, Nebraska law stated that anyone convicted of first degree murder shall suffer death or shall be imprisoned in the penitentiary for life. The decision was left to the jury.

Judge Spencer instructed Caril's jury that her presence alone with Starkweather during his murder spree in and of itself was not sufficient to find her guilty; they must also determine whether Caril remained with him under duress, in other words, whether she was under the unlawful restraint, intimidation, or compulsion of Starkweather to such a degree that would induce her to do or perform an act contrary to her will.

Judge Spencer further instructed Caril's jury that she was not on trial for failing to run away from Starkweather, for failing to report his crimes, or for failing to prevent his crimes.

It appears that the jury made two serious errors. First, the jury disregarded Nebraska law by deciding on the penalty *before* they deliberated on her guilt or innocence. And secondly, the jury disregarded Judge Spencer's instructions, as well.

Beaver quotes a conversation she held with a former juror while she was researching her book, *Caril*. She asked the juror how Caril appeared to him when he first saw her.

"Well, I think *that* was one of the things that contributed to us being a little more lenient, she being that age. It's understandable how they can be frightened and really not know what's actually going on. I felt there was a possibility that she was being led more than doing it on her own volition."

Beaver than asked, "But you still had to bring in a conviction?"

"Well, that's true. That's right. She was guilty. They didn't ask us why. It was whether she was guilty or not. I mean, circumstances wasn't supposed to enter into it."

"In Nebraska," said Beaver, "the jury sets the penalty in a first degree murder case, so you had two options: life or death. Did you or any other members of the jury stop to consider the implications of a life sentence?"

"To a certain respect, yes," answered the juror. "We knew that a life sentence never had meant a life sentence in Nebraska or anywhere else, as far as that's concerned. But we didn't think that she deserved the death penalty, even if she had been guilty. I guess her age had a lot to do with influencing us. I know it did with me."

Beaver then asked, "Some people look at a life sentence and say it was the mind of the jury or the judge that they (the convicted person) stay in prison until they draw their last breath. That wasn't the feeling of your jury?"

"I don't think so," replied the juror. "No, I really don't think so."

It wasn't until 1974, when the book *Caril* was released, that anyone learned the reasoning behind the jury's conviction of Caril. According to the jurors interviewed by Beaver, they decided that Caril should be given life in prison before they deliberated on her guilt or innocence. They also knew that a life sentence would never really mean being imprisoned for life. In addition, they neglected to consider the issue of whether Caril was Starkweather's hostage, as directed to by Judge Spencer.

Perhaps knowing that one day Caril would be released from prison somehow relieved the jury's conscience in not only failing to obey the law, but also failing to uphold their duty as citizens selected to perform such a sobering and momentous act as serving on a jury.

CHAPTER 18

June 25, 1959

Today was the last day of Charles Starkweather's life. His execution was scheduled for midnight. As custom dictated, the prison would allow him to order a last meal. He was offered a steak dinner, perhaps intended as an act of kindness, even generosity. But kindness and generosity had no place in Starkweather's bleak world. He refused the steak dinner, and instead he chose cold cuts. "I choose two slices of sausage and salami and a slice of roast beef and turkey."

Prison employee Dewey Thompson took Starkweather his last meal. Thompson had heard from another inmate on death row that nearly every man in the Adjustment Center, where death row inmates resided, had begged Starkweather to tell the truth about Caril's innocence and to "Cut that girl loose!" Starkweather's response had been, "Hell, no! If I am going to ride the lightning bolt, she's gonna ride it with me."

As the clock neared midnight, final preparations were made for Starkweather's execution. One of the people who would witness the execution was Lincoln police lieutenant Robert Sawdon, a friend of the deputy warden, who had asked him to attend the execution. Sawdon was there that night as an unofficial witness to the execution.

It was a clear, starry night when Sawdon got behind the wheel of his car and headed to the penitentiary. He still couldn't shake the irony of what was happening—he had known Charlie

Starkweather when Charlie was a kid of eight or nine. Now, the little scrapper he'd often talked to on the streets of Lincoln was about to be put to death for the most unthinkable crimes. As he pulled into the prison parking lot, Sawdon had a hard time finding a parking spot; there were already dozens of cars parked alongside the highway in front of the prison. A few cars had loud music blaring but, for the most part, the crowd was quiet. Groups of people in twos and threes strolled past the prison's front gate but weren't allowed to linger.

"Let him through. This is a friend of mine, Lieutenant Bob Sawdon," Deputy Warden John Greenholtz said. Known to his friends as "Big John," Greenholtz had been waiting for Sawdon's arrival at the front gate.

Out of habit, Sawdon flashed his police badge for the guards to see as he drove past the front gate. Sawdon parked the car and met up with Big John at the main entrance to the prison. Greenholtz threw a half-smoked Lucky Strike onto the sidewalk and ground it out with his heel. Together they went inside.

It was quiet in the prison corridor. Security regulations called for all inmates to be in lockdown tonight. The only people on the floor would be prison personnel and about forty other people—mostly press—whose names were randomly selected from a lottery of hundreds of applicants from all over the country.

Greenholtz ushered Sawdon into his office and poured him a cup of coffee, which Sawdon was unable to drink—his stomach was too queasy. Both men made small talk about their kids and summer vacation plans, until an older man, Beverly A. Finkle, M.D., the seventy-five-year-old prison physician, knocked and walked into the room. Dr. Finkle was a prominent, well-liked doctor in Lincoln who was also a close friend of Big John's. Dr. Finkle was on hand to declare the prisoner dead after the execution.

Sawdon hadn't seen Finkle in a while. The elderly doctor wasn't looking very well, he thought. He wondered how a man Finkle's age had the stomach for this sort of thing anymore. Greenholz called for a security guard to escort Sawdon down to the basement. With neither man speaking, the guard directed Sawdon into a drab, gray-walled room where about six rows of folding chairs had been temporarily set up. Because the seats were already taken, Sawdon stood in the back of the room. To his immediate right was an open door leading into a room that housed a control panel. Sawdon heard someone in there clearing his throat.

Nobody in the audience was speaking. Everyone's eyes were unavoidably drawn to a single four-legged chair constructed of massive oak timbers that was anchored to the concrete floor by four heavy bolts. The chair stood eight feet in front of the first row of folding chairs. Two conduit wires connected to the chair ran along the floor, leading into the room with the control panel. An iron neck rest and ankle rest were attached to the chair.

Sawdon checked his watch. It said 11:51 P.M. What on earth was he supposed to do while waiting for something like this? Strike up a conversation? Most of these people in this room were strangers to one another. They didn't know one another's names or where they lived. They most likely would never see one another again and probably had nothing in common. Yet, at that moment, they all shared something—the seemingly never-ending awkwardness of just waiting.

Sawdon found himself again thinking of the Charlie Starkweather he once knew as a kid on the streets of Lincoln. A little red-headed guy with a speech impediment and bowlegs. After Sawdon got promoted to lieutenant, he no longer patrolled the neighborhoods, but he would still see Charlie, as a teenager, now and then. By then, Sawdon wore street clothes and drove his own red Plymouth convertible, a car Charlie came to recognize. When Sawdon would see Charlie walking out of a bar late at night, he'd toot the horn and offer him a ride. Charlie would look around to make sure nobody saw him and jump in. Charlie became a snitch of sorts and would divulge information like, "So and so broke into this place and stole some copper wire," or "So and so stole a radio out of a car." And Sawdon would act pleased and say something like, "Well, thanks, for the tip, Charlie. We've been wondering about that down at headquarters for a while, now." Then he'd slip Charlie a few bucks.

Sawdon always tried to build Charlie up. He always made a point to ask Charlie about something mechanical because he knew Charlie was very good with cars. The last he had heard about Charlie before the murders was that he was hauling trash for a living and not too happy about it. But Sawdon could never have dreamed that it would come to this—watching the young man he once knew as little Charlie being executed for mass murder.

Just then, Sawdon noticed a short man walking quietly next to the wall, carrying a screwdriver in his right hand. Sawdon realized this man was the executioner. He shuddered at the thought of having the man's job, but the executioner was just doing his job. He was tightening a few screws on the electric chair.

The door on the left opened and Deputy Warden Greenholtz entered. Sawdon was surprised to see tears in the deputy warden's eyes.

Greenholtz held the door open and six other men walked in. One was a minister. Four were prison security guards. The sixth man was Charles Starkweather. He wore a blue shirt, blue jeans, and a pair of loafers without any socks. His shirtsleeves were rolled up, and one pant leg was slit up the side. He was flanked by guards and was shackled with handcuffs chained to a steel belt clamped around his waist. The leg irons forced him to move awkwardly. The crown of his skull had been shaved. He was young, just twenty years old.

Greenholtz asked Starkweather whether he had any last words. The condemned man slowly shook his head no. The guards ushered him to the chair.

Starkweather sat down in the electric chair just as casually as though he was visiting a barbershop. He seemed unfazed as he smirked at his audience while the prison guards unlocked the leg irons and removed the handcuffs. Looking as if the routine had been rehearsed, the guards fastened leather straps around Starkweather's chest, lap, wrists, biceps, and ankles, anchoring him to the chair.

One guard removed two sponges from a bucket; the sponges had been soaking in a salt solution so strong that not all of the salt had dissolved. The sponges were soaked in brine to aid in the conduction of electricity, to provide good contact support, and to prevent the sponge from catching on fire.

One sponge was placed on Starkweather's right calf. The other sponge was placed on the shaven spot of his skull. "This strap's a little loose," Starkweather said, wiggling his left hand. "Tighten it up," he ordered. The guards placed a copper electrode over each sponge and then wrapped a leather strap around the electrode and sponge to keep them attached to his body. The strap that was placed around his head and chin now hid most of his face.

A curtain was draped over the upper part of the prisoner, leaving his hands and legs showing. The four guards, having finished their tasks, lined up against the wall on the right side of the room. The minister approached the chair and whispered something into the ear of Starkweather, whose fists were clenched. Then both Deputy Warden Greenholtz and the minister walked away and stood next to the security guards. The executioner had disappeared. All Sawdon could hear was the sound of his own breathing. It was now 12:01 A.M.

Even after seventy years of having used the electric chair to deliver the death penalty, state officials still kept their fingers crossed that just the right amount of electrical current would be administered to kill a condemned man quickly and cleanly.

The first jolt of electricity was supposed to be strong enough to render the subject brain dead, but not so strong as to light him on fire. The next jolt, delivered at a weaker dosage but at a much longer cycle, was supposed to cause the body organs to swell by a rapid rise in temperature so that actual death would be due to asphyxia when the enlarged organs crushed the larynx and lungs. To be on the safe side, the cycle was then repeated because experience had taught that each individual has his own unique physiological resistance to electric current and may cling to life even after the first jolt is administered.

The executioner pulled the switch. He administered 2,000 volts for ten seconds. The next 480 volts surged for twenty-two seconds. The executioner repeated the procedure and turned off the current.

The left side door opened and a doctor approached Starkweather, now slumped over in the chair. The doctor placed a stethoscope to his chest, checking for a heartbeat. "This man has expired," he announced. It was 12:04 A.M.

235

While he had waited for his date with the executioner, Charles Raymond Starkweather had smirked that it was "a good thing that they can't send me to the chair for all my murders. If I'd killed twenty, the state could kill me only once." For Starkweather, that was a good thing. But plenty of Nebraskans would have favored a longer, more torturous death for him. He had left a path of death and destruction the likes of which the country had never seen. Having murdered eleven people in cold blood, he had gained the reputation as one of the nation's first spree killers.

After Starkweather was pronounced dead, and the witnesses filed quietly out of the room, Sawdon hurried back to his car. Once behind the wheel, he took several deep breaths and tried to quell the nausea he felt. He thought about what he had seen tonight and wondered how he would ever be able to reconcile the Starkweather he had just witnessed slapping violently against the chair with each electric jolt with the red-headed little scrapper Sawdon watched grow up on the streets of Lincoln, Nebraska.

Sawdon regretted not being able to visit with Charlie while he was on death row, but regulations just did not allow it. He wondered what he would have said to Charlie. He wondered if Charlie noticed him standing in the back tonight, and if so, what he could have been thinking.

About fifty miles west of the Lincoln penitentiary, fifteen-year-old Caril Fugate had just heard that the execution of Charles Starkweather had actually occurred. Feeling totally dejected, she sat in her narrow prison room, starring out a steel-mesh-covered window at the Nebraska Correctional Center for Women, in York, Nebraska.

With Starkweather dead, she had now lost all hope of the truth ever being told. He was the only other person in the world who knew the truth—that she was not involved in any of the eleven killings. And now, he was dead. He died without even attempting to clear her name. She wondered if the truth would ever be told.

Her days in confinement were monotonous and lonely. According to Nebraska law, she had to remain in isolation until she turned sixteen. She had only a little more than one month to wait, but, at that moment, it seemed like a million years away.

Throughout the day, she spoke to no one but the warden and a school teacher who was assisting her with an eighth-grade correspondence course. She awoke at 6:30 a.m., made her bed, and straightened her cell room. Breakfast was always taken to her because she was not allowed to eat with the other inmates. She was then escorted to the shower, and one day out of the week, she was given shampoo. On Mondays, Wednesdays, and Fridays, at 8:30 A.M., she was escorted to another building on the premises to study with her teacher for forty-five minutes. The rest of the day she was isolated in her cell.

As she looked out her window, she would watch the cars drive along the road that lead into town and would imagine that she was in one of those cars driving away from the prison.

A criminal trial is not a game in which the State's function is to outwit and entrap its quarry. The State's pursuit is justice, not a victim...

–Giles et al v. *State of Maryland*
United States Supreme Court, 1967

SUMMARY

by
John Stevens Berry

When I ponder the story of Caril Fugate and think about the decades' worth of comments I have heard about "what she *should* have done," it brings to mind an incident I learned of in Vietnam. At the time, a young but experienced infantry lieutenant was in a combat crawl, cradling his weapon, intent on his mission. Suddenly one of Vietnam's many venomous snakes appeared next to him, ready to strike. Instinctively, the lieutenant reared up and was immediately sawed in half by the enemy's automatic rifle fire.

Armchair combatants, people who have never faced the real pressure of combat or other extreme danger, might well ask, "Why didn't he just...?" Some people who have never been in real danger or under extreme pressure ask the same question about Caril Fugate, "Why didn't she just...?"

We all have fears: fear of hurricanes, snakes, heights, confinement. Fear is a thing we live with in varying degrees and do not always conquer.

However, most fears pale compared to the actual terror felt by the people in Lincoln, Nebraska, and surrounding communities in 1958, when Charles Starkweather went on his eleven-person murder spree. The Nebraska National Guard was called out. Parents hustled their children into their homes. Men with shotguns voluntarily patrolled the streets. Farmers sat on their front porches with their hunting rifles at the ready.

The fear felt in the Lincoln area at the time affected any juror or panel of jurors who would have judged Charles Starkweather and Caril Fugate. But there was another kind of fear felt that year in Lincoln—the fear fourteen-year-old Caril Fugate experienced when Charles Starkweather took her captive and told her that her parents and baby sister were being held by his gang and would be killed if she didn't go with him and do exactly as she was told. All he had to do, he told her, was to make one phone call to his gang and the "job" would be done. Caril managed to survive that fear, though she was in a state of absolute panic and nervous collapse by the time she escaped Starkweather and ran toward a law enforcement officer, begging for help.

There have been many disturbing issues raised over the years about the ruthless and improper handling of Caril Fugate's arrest and trial. Below, we briefly summarize the most egregious of these conditions and the seemingly illicit steps that were taken in the prosecution's determined effort to secure Caril's wrongful conviction.

Caril's Mental State

Caril Fugate was only fourteen years old, in eighth grade, when she was taken captive by Starkweather. She was emotionally and psychologically immature. She had no prior arrests. And at Starkweather's hands she witnessed a series of hideous murders that, naturally, traumatized her.

In the years since Caril's trial, great progress has been made in understanding psychology in general and adolescent psychology in particular. It is now recognized that every human being has a breaking point. This holds true even among the best-trained soldiers when they are captured. In current thinking, the fact that Caril Fugate, just a child, survived her ordeal with Charles Starkweather would no longer be held against her, as it was in 1958, but would be seen as kind of a personal heroism, even though she was unable to escape or overcome Starkweather.

In 1958, Caril Fugate was the youngest person ever to be put on trial in the United States for first degree murder. But in that era our nation did not understand the mindset of this child, who had been witness to a murder spree. Nor did anyone know of the phenomenon that has come to be known as "post-traumatic stress disorder."

Neither did the public acknowledge at that time the fear that a courtroom can cause in some people. The great trial lawyer Gerry Spence has stated that the atmosphere of fear in the courtroom is so great that no plant can live in a courtroom. It was in such a frightening atmosphere that Caril had to face Charles Starkweather while she was on trial for murder. We can now understand that from the moment Caril came home from school to discover a weapon pointed in her face, she was in a state of shock and subsequently suffered from *post-traumatic stress disorder (PTSD)* , for which she was later diagnosed.

A reference book known as the *Diagnostic and Statistical Manual of Mental Disorders* defines and discusses various psychological disorders. To quote briefly from section 309.81 "Post-Traumatic Stress Disorder":

> [An] Essential feature of post-traumatic stress disorder is the development of characteristic symptoms following the exposure to an extreme traumatic stressor involving direct personal experience of an event that involves actual or threatened death or serious injury, or other threat to one's physical integrity; or witnessing an event that involves death, injury, or a threat to the physical integrity to another person; or learning about unexpected or violent death, serious harm, or threat of death or injury experienced by a family member or other close associates.

Caril Fugate was a textbook case, a poster child, for post-traumatic stress disorder. Since the war in Vietnam, we have recognized that even mature, well-trained, battle-hardened men and women can suffer from PTSD. The diagnostic text states that "traumatic events that are experienced directly include such events as military combat, violent personal assault such as sexual assault, physical attack, robbery, mugging, being kidnapped, being taken hostage...." PTSD often leads to what used to be called a "personality disintegration."

Caril's personality disintegration may have caused her negative image in the media.

Many observers of Caril Fugate's testimony on the witness stand said that her personality did not come across well to the jury during the trial, that her comments to the media came across as cold and impersonal. In hindsight, we realize that few, if any, fifteen-year-old girls would have the skill to communicate with the media in a smooth, articulate manner and in the appropriate tone of regret. A clinical psychologist and practitioner of the Erickson method of hypnosis examined Caril in 1990 and concluded his report by saying:

"I saw film clips of Caril Fugate during the trial when she was fifteen. In my clinical opinion Caril Fugate had and still does have a problem of connecting her thinking to her feelings. She was experienced as hard, calloused and cold in those 1959 film clips. When hypnosis helped her with an affect bridge, that is when her feelings and thoughts connected, people thought she was innocent. I have reason to believe if proper psychiatric help were available in 1959 that had done the same connecting of affect she would have been found not guilty."

Caril Fugate Was a Hostage, Not a Participant

Many have argued over the years that Caril had plenty of opportunities to escape from Starkweather. However, even if she had chances to escape, she feared that if she did Starkweather would have her parents and baby sister killed. He had made this very threat to her when she first arrived home from school to find him holding a gun in her face. Then, having seen him murder people in cold blood, she had no reason whatsoever to doubt his threat. And Starkweather would not even allow Caril to urinate without him watching her. She was a child who went along on a "ride from hell" with Charles Starkweather so that her family would not be killed.

Many newspaper readers at the time believed that Caril could have somehow subdued or escaped Starkweather, defied him, or evaded him during his murderous rage.

A similar question could be asked about Mrs. Ward and her maid, Lilyan Fencl. Why didn't they try to escape? Could they not have run out the back door instead of fixing breakfast for Starkweather? Mrs. Ward and Ms. Fencl knew who Starkweather was—they had seen the headlines about the killings and the search that was underway for him. Yet Mrs.

Ward was so frightened that she did not even try to reach out for help when she went upstairs alone to change her clothes. Why didn't she try to make a phone call or lock herself in a bedroom or the bathroom, or open a window and scream for help? Perhaps she, like Caril, believed that if she did as she was told, she would not be harmed. If this was her thinking, she was also probably unaware that the "bad guys" do not play by the "good guys'" rules.

Still, many people who have never been in a situation in which their life or the lives of people close to them were threatened are certain that *they* would have escaped.

The Disappearance of Caril's Note to Police Asking for Help and Her Letter to Her Mother—Tampering with Evidence?

A key piece of evidence—one that could have helped prove Caril Fugate innocent, disappeared. When Starkweather first left the Bartlett house, taking Caril with him, she wrote a note that said, "Help. Police. Don't ignore." She kept it in her jacket pocket, hoping for an opportunity to give it to someone along the way. But she never had what she considered a safe opportunity to give the note to anyone without putting her family at risk.

A Wyoming law enforcement official testified under oath at Caril's trial that he saw that note and that it was made available to the Nebraska authorities. The prosecutors never acknowledged receiving that note. Nor was it shared with the defense attorneys. In fact, to this day, no one knows what happened to that crucial note.

Another piece of potential evidence that demonstrated that Caril only obeyed Starkweather in order to save her family was a letter she had begun writing to her mother after her arrest. Because there was no appropriate jail in Nebraska in which to lock up a fourteen-year-old girl, Caril was held in a mental hospital. While being held there she wrote a letter to her mother asking her to come and visit her in the hospital.

Mother,
Please come and sea me. I am very lonely hear.
Barbara, Bob has been out to sea me so has dad. I mean Bill and dot. Please come out and bring Betty

243

Jean. I want to sea her. Winnlin has been out to. But I want to see you please come out. I am fine but I want to come home. Please come and get me. I am afrade to be alone. Tell daddy I said that will you come out and take me home. I don't really like it hear. Every body is good to me. But ther is no body my age hear just old people. I wish Billy was hear. Mother please come out and get me. Or I will come to you or you will come and take me a way from hear and take me home with you. You know how I feal so I am asking you to come please. All thes people are so strange. I don't think they like me a all. So please come as soon as you can.

Love Your Dother
Caril Fugate
Lincoln State Hospital

The letter indicates Caril's confused and emotional state. This letter, which was found in the bed stand next to the cot in the hospital where Caril slept, was never turned over to the defense, who could have used it to show Caril thought her mother was still alive.

More than half a century after Caril's conviction, the co-authors of this book were only able to obtain this letter from the Lancaster County attorney's office by writing several letters invoking the *Freedom of Information Act.*

Caril Ran to Police in Wyoming, Not Away from Them

When Starkweather finally encountered the police in Wyoming, he fled, but Caril Fugate ran to the police, begging for help in preventing Starkweather from having her family killed. She ran toward Deputy Romer in a zig-zag fashion, hoping she would become a harder target for Starkweather—because she fully expected him to shoot her in the back. Even if he did shoot her, she had decided it would be a better fate than remaining his hostage.

Linda Battisti & John Stevens Berry

Sheriff's Wife: "I Don't Think She Knows Her Family Is Dead"

After Caril's escape from Starkweather, Sheriff Heflin's wife, Hazel, who first cared for Caril immediately after her arrest, was quoted as saying, "I don't think she knows her family is dead." When various officials mentioned to Caril that her family had been murdered, she refused to believe it. She had been given sedatives, and through the fog of the medication, she refused to believe her family could be dead. After all, she had done everything Starkweather ordered her to do. She believed the horrible truth only when she was told by her sister Barbara that her parents and baby sister were dead.

Legal Mistreatment of Caril Fugate:
Interrogation without Legal Counsel

What we now know as *"Miranda* rights," which are read to people when they're arrested, were not yet in effect in 1958. Essentially, *Miranda* states that "You have the right to remain silent. Anything you say can and will be used against you in a court of law. You have a right to an attorney. If you cannot afford an attorney, one will be appointed for you." But because the *Miranda* case did not occur until 1966, Caril's rights were not explained to her. However, the Fifth Amendment has been around since 1791 when it was ratified in the Bill of Rights, and it contains this phrase: "No person...shall be compelled in any criminal case to be a witness against himself." The point is, that there should be due process, or what is commonly thought of as "fair play." Originally, it was generally considered that the Bill of Rights only applied to the federal court system and not to the state court system. But in the 19th century, after the U.S. Civil War, the Fourteenth Amendment was passed, and it stated, among other things, that no state may "deprive any person of life, liberty, or property, without due process of law; nor deny to any person within its jurisdiction the equal protection of the laws."

On the face of it, it would seem that with the passage of the Fourteenth Amendment in the 19th century, the Bill of Rights now applied to people in all states. But that was only in theory.

In the 1950s, after President Eisenhower appointed former Governor Earl Warren as chief justice, the "Warren Revolution" began—it profoundly expanded constitutional rights into state courts. But it did not extend into criminal law until the 1960s, too late for Caril.

At the time that Caril was first incarcerated and had not yet appeared in county court, there was no system in place for paying attorneys to represent those who could not afford an attorney. Yet, it was not uncommon for lawyers to represent indigent defendants, especially minors, without compensation. A lawyer could have been found for Caril.

However, prior to hours of interrogation, Caril was not made aware that she was being charged with first degree murder and that she faced a possible death penalty. In fact, she was astonished to learn this. Caril was completely unaware of the availability of *pro bono* lawyers to assist her during the period between her arrest (after fleeing Starkweather and running to the authorities) and her district court arraignment. Caril also had the misfortune of trusting her very unsophisticated sister, Barbara, who thought that law enforcement would act honorably and told Caril to cooperate and tell the investigators everything.

One can argue that the county attorney's office was legally accurate in advising Caril that funds would not be provided for a counsel for her until after she was bound over to district court, but they did not tell her that there were attorneys who were willing to work without compensation. The tradition of representing indigent defendants runs very deep into the Anglo-American tradition. In old England, barristers (trial lawyers) were not paid, but rather wore a cloak with a hood, and grateful clients would occasionally place a coin in the back of the hood.

Caril was not represented by counsel from the time of her arrest until after her statement had been taken, a period of six days. She requested counsel as early as January 29, 1958, when she waived extradition in Wyoming, and renewed the request for counsel on at least two subsequent occasions. Furthermore, it appears she was misled into believing that she could have counsel only if she or her parents could retain counsel. The record is not entirely clear as to whether Caril was properly notified that she could refuse to answer questions, and that anything she said could be used against her at trial.

This warning does not appear until page 126 of the 165 pages of the recorded interrogation. Toward the end of her long interrogation, Caril did ask for an attorney. This initial request was recorded in shorthand by the court reporter, Audrey Wheeler. This request did not appear in the official transcribed copy of the statement; however, the truth did come to light when Wheeler was on the witness stand, as explained in an earlier chapter.

Vicious, Unethical Interrogation?

Although it is quite possible that the investigators and prosecutors all believed that they were "doing the right thing," the atmosphere regarding this case may have led them astray from their normal course of conduct. There is no doubt that Caril was subjected to a brutal interrogation at a time when she should have been tended to medically. In today's more enlightened atmosphere, victim-witnesses are often given mental status evaluations and thorough physical examinations. They are not incarcerated in a mental hospital, as Caril was, and where, just before she was interrogated, she saw a woman given shock treatments. By the time interrogators finished their brutal grilling of the fourteen-year-old-girl she was willing to say whatever they wanted to hear.

The record of the Fugate case is replete with illustrations of the prosecution's apparent disregard for the rules of law, ethics, and common decency.

Any American should be astonished at the brutality and sheer viciousness to which the prosecutorial system subjected Caril, who, at fifteen, was the youngest American ever to be tried for first degree murder in the United States. Prosecutor Dale Fahrnbruch grilled her for many hours without counsel in a mental hospital, where she was being held.

In his interrogation, Fahrnbruch obsessed over sexual details. Yet he did not recommend that this child undergo a medical examination. She was called a "tramp and a whore" by the public and was portrayed as Starkweather's mistress. Yet no physical examination was performed on her. It was only after Caril's parole in 1976, after eighteen years in prison, that she underwent a physical examination, which showed that her hymen was intact—she was still a virgin. She had never had sexual intercourse with Charles Starkweather.

From the numerous brutal hours interrogating Caril, the prosecutors cobbled together a statement that still did not amount to a confession.

Unrelated Evidence Permitted at Caril's Trial

Caril was charged with being an accessory in the murder of the teenager Robert Jensen. She was never charged with any crime related to Carol King's murder, yet the jury was deliberately told about Carol King's brutalization and the stab wound that went through her vagina and into her rectum. They were even shown the photograph. Starkweather's other murders should never have been brought to the jury's attention.

For unknown reasons, the unfairly prejudicial "uncharged misconduct"—evidence unrelated to the crime for which the defendant was charged—was never directly attacked on appeal.

A Convicted Murderer as Chief Witness at Caril's Trial

One wonders how Charles Starkweather could have ever been called as a credible witness at Caril's trial. He had been convicted of murder, sentenced to death, and had given nine different versions of how the murders occurred. Yet he was called as "chief witness" in Caril's trial and testified that Caril had participated in some of the murders.

Did Witness Bribing and Tampering Occur?

Since Charles Starkweather had been sentenced to the penitentiary and had been ordered to be kept there until the date of his execution, it seems strange that he would be going back and forth between the penitentiary and the county/city building. A. James McArthur, as a young man, had watched his father defend Caril Fugate. One evening, as A. James was driving south on 9th Street in Lincoln, he passed Deputy Les Hansen's car and saw Starkweather in the backseat. Hansen made evasive driving maneuvers to get away from the young McArthur, who went home and told his father what he had seen. At first, the elder McArthur did not believe that Starkweather was being transported back and forth between the penitentiary and the county/city building, which would be in violation of the sentence of the court. But months later, a former guard at the penitentiary contacted Caril's attorney John McArthur and co-attorney Merril Reller and informed them of the visits Starkweather had made to the county courthouse for meetings with prosecutor Elmer Scheele.

The guard's statement gives further credence to the statement of Otto Glaser, an inmate who had been held in a cell near Starkweather's. After Glaser was released from prison, he gave a sworn statement to Caril's attorney about how Starkweather had been coached on how to testify at Caril's trial.

Given the fact that Charles Starkweather had been determined to be weak-minded and have no moral capacity, it is easy to see how the prosecution could have shaped his testimony against Caril. The reader who does not think that was possible may be interested in a sworn affidavit given by Otto Glaser about what he overhead during his confinement in a cell near Charles Starkweather from October 14, 1958, until December 12, 1958.

Glaser talked with and saw Charles Starkweather on many occasions, and he could observe and hear conversations between Charles Starkweather and visitors to his cell. It was during this time that Glaser observed three men routinely visiting Starkweather and continuously coaching him on what to say— and what not to say—on the witness stand during Caril's trial. For example, Starkweather was told to never mention the fact that he considered killing Caril on three separate occasions, including once in the Ward house in Lincoln.

The three men who coached Starkweather to testify against Caril at her trial had no justification for doing so in that manner. What they did at the very least approached witness tampering. As prosecutors, they represented *only* the people of the State of Nebraska. The behavior of the prosecution and its agents during the course of preparation for Caril's trial may have crossed the line from witness coaching to subornation of perjury (encouraging a witness to fabricate testimony under oath).

It is one thing to coach a witness. It is another thing entirely to take a person of such low intelligence and no moral structure—Starkweather—and mold his testimony into a fiction that would convict a young girl and result in her receiving a life sentence. How easy it must have been to turn Starkweather from a defender of Caril Fugate, in his original statements and letter to his parents, into the witness who convicted her.

As mentioned earlier in this book, it would seem easy to dismiss Glaser's story—he was, after all, a jailhouse snitch. However, Glaser was not reporting what he had overhead in order to cut a deal for himself. He had already been released from prison when he contacted Caril's attorney to report how Starkweather had been coached. Furthermore, what Glaser reported as being said during the coaching sessions with Starkweather actually occurred on the witness stand when Starkweather testified. It's difficult not to believe Glaser.

The sworn affidavit of Otto Glaser showed that Stark-weather's testimony was fabricated to fit the prosecution's story line. For his cooperation, Starkweather received special gifts—such as candy, cigarettes, and a clear view of a prison television set. Starkweather also was led to believe that his cooperation would help him avoid the electric chair.

Even if we disregard the sworn testimony of Otto Glaser, we cannot ignore (as the prosecution did) the difference between Starkweather's statement on February 1, in which he admits that Caril was not home when he killed her family, and that she was unaware that he had killed her family, and his statement of February 27 (his seventh version). In this version, he said Caril was involved in the killing of her family, and he stated that she was aware that her family was dead at all times.

There will be those who will be reluctant to believe that the prosecution would, through its attorneys and investigators, totally remake Charles Starkweather's testimony. However, this pattern of behavior has more than a hint of suborning perjury, which would be a felony. Through the prosecution's coaching, Starkweather repeatedly changed his story of what happened. He testified against Caril and secured her conviction.

Similarly, there will be those who will be reluctant to believe that the prosecution would cobble together something that looked like an admission from Caril as she was in a state of shock throughout the vicious, constant grilling by Fahrnbruch and others under terrifying circumstances. But this is what happened.

Linda Battisti & John Stevens Berry

Manipulating Caril and Defying Rules

Almost immediately after Charles Starkweather was captured, he told Sheriff Earl Heflin that Caril had nothing to do with the killings. He also wrote a letter to his parents in which he commented about Caril, saying, "don't hate her...she had not a thing to do with the killing." That was the position he took, though his statements changed from time to time until the prosecutors and investigators worked on him and coaxed him into testifying against Caril.

Starkweather's sixth statement, which completely exonerated Caril in the murders of her family, was made shortly before her arraignment. In that era, once a person was arraigned in district court, they were then entitled to receive appointed counsel. Because Starkweather had made a statement exonerating Caril immediately before her arraignment, and with the prosecutors expecting that Caril would soon get counsel to represent her, the prosecution team must have become alarmed. Once she had a lawyer, the prosecutors would not be able to manipulate her further. Before Caril had a counsel appointed, they needed to manipulate her into doing something that would cause Starkweather to change his statement and testify against her.

So, with the blessings of prosecutor Elmer Scheele, Sheriff Merle Karnopp called on Caril, whom he knew to be terrified of Starkweather, and asked her if she would like to see him. Caril told Karnopp that she never wanted to see Starkweather again, so Karnopp encouraged her to write a letter to Starkweather telling him how she felt about him. The ruse worked. Caril wrote the letter, and Karnopp immediately delivered that letter to Starkweather, who, from that point on, incriminated Caril in all of his subsequent statements and testimony.

It should also be pointed out that Starkweather himself would soon be represented by counsel T. Clement Gaughan and an assistant. The office of the county attorney had been eager to manipulate Starkweather before he had his own lawyer.

This manipulation of Caril by the prosecutors was an act of bullying that violates all concepts of justice and due process as laid out in the Fifth Amendment to the United States Constitution, a concept that has been around since the Magna Carta of 1215.

251

The prosecutors knew that once Caril was appointed an attorney, there would be no way her lawyer would have allowed her to send a letter to Starkweather. Additionally, the absurdity of Caril even being allowed to send a letter to Starkweather in that manner puzzles people who are aware of the strict regulations regarding incarcerated people receiving and sending correspondence. A letter hand-delivered from Caril to Starkweather simply would not have been allowed.

Lack of Evidence

If Caril had, as Starkweather previously stated, participated in the killing of her parents (for which she was not charged) in the manner in which he described, certainly there would have been blood spatter evidence somewhere in the Bartlett house. There is no mention in the record of any such evidence.

Should the Same Judge Have Heard Both Cases?

Presiding Judge Harry Spencer was the judge on the bench during the Starkweather trial. He was also the judge overseeing Caril Fugate's trial. One wonders why Judge Spencer did not recuse himself and step down as a judge in Caril Fugate's case, because he had heard such vicious stories about Caril by the man whom he had seen sentenced to death.

Years later, it also came to light that Judge Spencer had actually coached prosecutor Scheele and Fahrnbruch during the course of the trial. Jeff McArthur, grandson of Caril's attorney John McArthur, and author of the book, *Pro Bono—The 18 Year Defense of Caril Fugate,* learned about the coaching from Lincoln attorney Paul Douglas shortly before Douglas' death in 2012. Douglas, a young attorney at the time of the trial, was a member of the prosecution team, and later became the attorney general for the state of Nebraska.

Could Caril Fugate Ever Have Received a Fair Trial in Lincoln?

With the character assassination Caril Fugate received in the press, along with Starkweather's accusations against her, is there any way Caril could have received a fair trial in Lancaster County...or *any* county in Nebraska? Should the trial have been moved to a different city? One wonders if there were a venue anywhere in Nebraska where Caril could have received a presumption of innocence, which is the basis for a fair trial anywhere in America.

At the time of Caril's trial, under the Nebraska statute, her trial could only have been transferred to an adjacent county. That clearly would have made no difference, as Harry Spencer would have been the judge in any event. It is interesting to note that although two attorneys were appointed for the murder case of Charles Starkweather (in murder cases it has always been customary that there be at least two counsel for the defendant), Caril was afforded only one. She had requested that Merril Reller be appointed to assist John McArthur. McArthur had also made that request, and Reller was ready and eager to participate. But Judge Spencer ruled that Reller could not be appointed co-counsel. Reller would be allowed to sit at the table with McArthur during the trial, and perhaps be allowed to whisper to McArthur, but Reller could not actively participate in the trial. There was no way that Judge Harry Spencer was going to allow the possibility of an acquittal in this case.

Inadmissible Evidence Introduced

It is worth noting that one prosecutor at Caril's trial asked Starkweather, while he was on the witness stand, whether he had taken a polygraph test. Starkweather answered that he had taken the polygraph test, and one may assume that the jury would have thought he had passed the polygraph, because the prosecutor brought it up. (The results of that lie detector test were never made public.)

However, polygraph evidence is not admissible in Nebraska, so this question was obviously posed simply to further confuse the jury and to further trample on whatever presumption of Caril's innocence may have existed in the courtroom.

Juror Took Bets on Verdict

After the trial had concluded, it was learned that a week before Caril's trial started, one man, who became a juror, made a bet that Caril would get the death penalty. Apparently the juror was less than honest about having no opinion on the case when he was being questioned as a potential juror. This impropriety did not bother Judge Harry Spencer; nor, as it happens, did it bother the Nebraska Supreme Court. Today, such betting would result in an immediate mistrial or other judicial action.

Did the Jury Follow All Instructions?

A close examination of instructions to the jury suggests that the jury disregarded some of the judge's instructions. Instruction 12 read: "You are instructed that one who is merely present at the time a crime is committed, and who does not unlawfully aid, assist or abet its commission, cannot be held guilty of such crime. In this case the defendant says in substance that at all times material herein she was acting under duress of the compulsion of Charles Starkweather.

"Duress may be defined as an unlawful restraint, intimidation or compulsion of another to such extent and degree as to induce such other person to do or perform some act contrary to his will or inclination.

"You are instructed that if the evidence shows the defendant did the things with which she is charged under duress or the compulsion of Charles Starkweather, you could not find she voluntarily aided and abetted in the commission of any crime and it is then your duty to find the defendant not guilty of any degree of homicide under both the first and second counts."

Further, Instruction 13 to the jury read, "The defendant in this case is not on trial for failure to run away from Starkweather, for failing to report such crimes as he may have committed, or for failing to prevent such crimes. If you find from the evidence that she failed to do one or more of these things, such circumstances are relevant only for the purpose of determining the state of her mind at the time Starkweather killed Jensen."

After the verdict came back finding Caril guilty, one of the jurors explained that Caril was present during the crimes, and "circumstances were not supposed to enter into it."

"Circumstances were not supposed to enter into it"? The court clearly gave the jury instructions to decide whether Caril was a hostage. The jury clearly disregarded this instruction if they believed that her actions alone proved Caril aided and abetted Starkweather. The hostage issue was crucial to their

determination of guilt. The jury avoided giving Caril the death penalty and let her live, but delivered the guilty verdict the public was expecting.

Caril's Appeal

Are there any circumstances under which Caril Fugate could have received a fair trial in 1958? It's hard to know the answer. It was more than fifty years ago. It was a different time, perhaps a simpler time. People were different. Starkweather was one of the nation's first spree killers. No one in Nebraska had seen the likes of such a crime.

Still, the fact remains, the child Starkweather took along with him on his rampage was herself a victim—a victim who would be convicted by public opinion and who would spend many years of her life in prison.

Caril's attorney, John McArthur, worked hard and diligently on her behalf. He appealed to the Nebraska Supreme Court. When that did not succeed, he and Caril made the decision to move laterally into the federal system by filing a Petition for Writ of Habeas Corpus in the federal district court for the District of Nebraska. When that did not succeed, they appealed to the United States Court of Appeals for the Eighth Circuit, which includes the State of Nebraska. In 1971, this court denied the appeal. However, one of the judges of the appeals court, Judge Gerald Heaney, wrote the only dissenting opinion. He agreed that Caril Fugate deserved to have her conviction reversed. In looking at the case as a whole, he believed Caril's statements were not given voluntarily.

Judge Heaney wrote in his opinion, "The county attorney's office may have been legally accurate in advising Caril that appointed counsel could not be provided to her until after she was bound over to District Court; but I have too much respect for the Nebraska Bar not to feel confident that a simple request to that bar from the county attorney's office to provide free counsel for Caril until she was bound over to the District Court would have met with immediate acceptance."

Judge Heaney continued, "The presence of two prominent lawyers, Dean Belsheim and William Blue, at the signing ceremony, when the confession had already been given, is clear evidence of the willingness of the bar to assume its responsibility if asked. Furthermore, the county attorney's office, by delaying the arraignment for eight days, provided its own excuse for not furnishing counsel."

"I am totally unimpressed with the facade of fairness that the county attorney erected to shield the interrogation process. The fact that Dr. Vance Rogers, an educator, was present as an observer at the first interrogation, and that Mr. Blue and Dean Belsheim [from legal aid] were present to advise Caril as to whether she should sign the transcribed question-and-answer statement of February 2 and 3 only serve to strengthen my conviction that counsel could have been obtained for Caril if that had been the objective."

Among the other points Judge Heaney made in his opinion:

- Caril was only fourteen at the time, and had just witnessed or been party to ten murders, which had to have traumatized her.

- She asked for counsel early on, but did not have a lawyer until six days after her arrest.

- She was misled into believing that she could have an attorney only if her family could retain one.

- She was held in a state mental institution during the interrogation proceedings and witnessed shock treatments to patients.

- The record is not clear that she was properly warned that she did not have to answer questions.

Finally, the dissenting opinion of Judge Gerald Heaney argued that the state took advantage of a fourteen-year-old girl, put her in uncomfortable settings, and misled her until she made the statement which was used against her.

Letters of Support Withheld from Caril

Many letters of support and Bibles were sent to Caril during the time of her trial, but were never given to her. They eventually ended up in the possession of Gertrude Karnopp, wife of the Lancaster County sheriff. Years later, these letters were purchased at a garage sale. It took the authors of this book a few years to get copies of them. We don't know what happened to the Bibles.

Of course, these letters had no evidentiary value, and their historical importance is small. But one cannot help but wonder if a terrified young girl may have gotten some consolation in reading these letters of support from complete strangers. Here are quotes from a few of the letters that Caril did not see until decades later. One letter to Caril started, "Dear Caril... You don't know me, nor I you, but you have been in my thoughts a bit the last few days. I want you to know we have been praying for your safety and for strength and comfort to come through your experience without it ruining your young life. If you were a girl that has gone to Sunday School and church, you know you can tell all your heartaches and griefs to our dear Lord Jesus and he will give you peace." (Wyoming)

Some letters were five or six pages long, handwritten. One very lengthy letter simply concluded: "God Bless you, Caril. I pray that things work out well for you." Another letter said: "Mother across the miles cares about your soul and is praying for you when I read all the terrible crimes that had happened to you." Another says: "You are only fourteen...if I could help you in any way, I would. I know how one can be drawn into sin when young—too young to have what it takes to pull away from the wrong and turn to the right....I wish you were in my house. I believe I could bring you up right. We would go to Sunday School, and church together...Romans 13:10: Love fulfills the whole law. So practice loving everybody....Each day you will be a better Christian...God is love." (Ohio)

A letter from Kansas City said: "I am a mother and I have heard the very sad story....God will forgive you, provided you ask him and tell him your mistakes. God has Apostles here on Earth. A Catholic priest can tell you all about it." Someone visiting Lincoln and staying in the Cornhusker Hotel wrote Caril a letter on hotel stationery: "We think of you often, and pray for you more....We do know God understands. Pray to Him! Caril for the strength you will need and for the weeks ahead. Trust in Him and He will comfort and keep you. Yours in Prayers."

A gentleman from Fremont, Nebraska sent a five-page, handwritten letter stating he was about to turn eighty-two years old, had been a Christian for about sixty-five years, and told a little bit about his family and his love of the human race: "Be a good girl, Caril, have faith in God. Try to obey Christ's teachings....God bless you." By way of postscript he said: "I am not a minister, just an old deacon."

A letter addressed to Mrs. Karnopp was written by a lady who told Mrs. Karnopp: "I wrote Caril a little note. I would be so glad for suggestions of some little things I could do to help. I told her I would pray for her and I hope her mother and granny have taught her to pray. May the Lord bless you for your kindness to her." It concludes with a postscript that she was sending a Bible and some magazines to Caril.

A lady from Seward, Nebraska also wrote to Mrs. Karnopp: "I see your picture with Caril Fugate, and you look like a kind person. That poor child needs love and affection and kindness if ever anyone did. I feel sorry for her, because I believe she was a victim of those terrible things that happened. I would like to give her a little Bible with my love."

There were numerous letters, some from boys wanting to be her pen pal. Some letters were laden with hatred, but many were loving and supportive and declared their sympathy for Caril. They expressed their belief in her and said they were praying for her. Caril received none of these letters, Bibles, or other items that were sent to her. Many years later, the authors of this book made copies of all the letters available to Caril. We hope they were, finally, of some comfort to her.

Support from Those Who Knew Caril

A number of years ago, I had a daily radio program, *The John Stevens Berry Show,* on KLIN radio, in Lincoln, Nebraska. One day my guest was A. James McArthur, the son of Caril's attorney. The son had unsuccessfully tried to get a full pardon for Caril Fugate. As McArthur was talking about Caril's case, we were surprised when Caril herself called into the show from her home in Michigan. No one involved in my radio talk show knew she would be calling in.

Caril pointed out some further discrepancies that had occurred during her trial. She said, "Mr. Detective Sawdon, who went on television, and I saw it, and he said to the Nebraska people, 'Well, she must have known her family was dead, the house looked like a slaughterhouse.' But, in fact, there was no evidence in the house to indicate foul play. There was no blood. There were no bullet holes."

What happened following Caril's two call-ins on two consecutive days to the radio program was astonishing. So many supportive calls came in for Caril, it was stunning! The sympathy for Caril, and the belief in her innocence, were spontaneous. There were impassioned calls from listeners giving their various reasons for believing Caril to be innocent.

Classmates of Caril at school had known she had broken up with Starkweather and that she was afraid of him. One student called into the show and spoke about Caril trying to hide from Starkweather, who was looking for her. However, this fact never came to light during the investigation and trial. The student's parents didn't want her to get involved.

One caller, Marian, said about Caril, "I remember her very well, and I want to tell her that I can attest to the fact I've seen Caril hide in the bathroom as she'd try to get away from Charlie; I've seen her dragged off the bus by him. I've seen her personally abused, and I believed her forever."

One woman caller stated that she knew Caril was trying to hide from Starkweather whenever she got out of school, and she wanted to testify to that, but her mother would not allow her to involve their family in the case. Another caller said "There were a lot of us—it's just that the news media didn't choose to select any of us, and we've been standing up for you, and I'll continue."

Another caller who identified herself as Louise said to Caril, "I remember you so well. Well, Caril, what I have to say is that our family has talked time and time again about how you were railroaded. It was just terrible. Your grandmother came to see my dad before they found your parents, and she thought something was wrong there." The caller went on to say, "My dad was there. He said there was no evidence of anything happening in the house, it was out back, and he was wanting to tell the police and talk to them, you know, tell them what he saw. They would not allow it. They would not listen to him one bit. They just didn't want evidence. They didn't want the truth."

My coauthor, Linda Battisti, an attorney, befriended Caril and visited with her occasionally over a period of perhaps ten years. Linda was convinced that Caril had been wrongfully convicted, and when Linda was a guest on my radio show, she invited me to join her in writing this book expressing her belief that Caril was innocent.

Caril Passed Multiple Polygraph Tests

Polygraph test results are not allowable as evidence in a court of law in Nebraska. However, since her release from prison, Caril Fugate has always been willing to take lie detector tests. She has taken at least seven polygraph tests over the years. Her story has never changed, and she has passed every lie detector test she has taken, including the ones she took on national television in 1983 with famous defense attorney F. Lee Bailey, who had a television series at the time called *Lie Detector.*

Bailey questioned Caril whether or not she had been under duress while she was with Starkweather, whether she believed that her parents were being held and would be murdered if she did not do everything he said, and whether she was unaware that they had been murdered when Starkweather took her with him on the murder spree. She answered yes to the questions. The polygraph showed that she answered all of the questions truthfully. So she was tested again. And once again the polygraph showed that she had answered the questions truthfully.

Changes in Law Since 1958

Most Nebraskans would probably agree that Charles Starkweather deserved the death penalty. However, it is noteworthy that the statute under which Charles Starkweather was executed, and Caril Fugate was sentenced to life imprisonment, has since been found to be unconstitutional. The Nebraska statute in effect at the time left the question of the death penalty or life imprisonment up to the discretion of the jury. Nationwide, objective standards for the determination of the death penalty have been established and the death penalty may no longer be discretionary either by a judge or a jury.

In 2005, in the legal case *Roper v. Simmons,* Supreme Court Justice Anthony Kennedy noted that "a lack of maturity and an underdeveloped sense of responsibility are found in youth more often than in adults, and are more understandable among the young. These qualities often result in impetuous and ill-considered actions and decisions." Kennedy quoted from a study from *The American Psychologist,* "As legal minors, juveniles lack the freedom to extricate themselves from a criminogenic setting." In another legal case, *Graham v. Florida,* the comment was made, "Developments in psychology and brain science show fundamental differences between juvenile and adult minds. For example, parts of the brain involved in behavior continue to mature into late adolescence."

In 2012, in *Miller v. Alabama,* the United States Supreme Court held that mandatory life without parole for persons who were juveniles when their crime was committed was unconstitutional. In 2014, the Nebraska Supreme Court vacated the life sentences previously given to several men for crimes they committed as juveniles. So, fortunately, the law, psychology, and sociology have evolved considerably since Caril's trial in 1958.

The Attorneys and the Judge: After Caril's Trial

Based on their "behind-the-scenes" behavior, it would seem as though prosecutors and some law enforcement officials lost their moral and ethical compasses in Starkweather's wake. What became of the men who made up the legal teams in the trials of Charles Starkweather and Caril Fugate? Judge Harry Spencer and deputy county attorney Dale Farnbruch were both elevated to the Nebraska Supreme Court, though at different times. As they sat at the bench, their backs were to the native walnut wall, whereon it is carved, "Eyes and ears are poor witnesses when the soul is barbarous."

Lancaster County Attorney Elmer Scheele became a district court judge; even after a diagnosis of cancer he continued serving on the bench during a period of time when he was severely disabled and in great pain. Paul Douglas, the third member of the prosecution team, became Lancaster County attorney, then Nebraska state attorney general and was in the private practice of law at the time of his death.

John McArthur, defense counsel for Caril Fugate, lived out his life as a successful lawyer; his practice was eventually taken over by his son A. James McArthur, a successful attorney, who followed in his father's tradition of advocating for Caril. Merril Reller, whom Judge Harry Spencer specifically had forbidden from speaking aloud in his role as second chair of Caril's defense, died on an African hunting safari at age sixty-five.

The Twelfth Victim

Starkweather killed, corrupted, or destroyed anything decent in his path. He carried with him a virtual aura of pure evil. He killed eleven innocent people during his rampage. So many victims. Caril Fugate was Starkweather's twelfth victim.

In the end, the Nebraska legal system survived the Caril Fugate trial. But, perhaps more importantly, Caril survived—not only her ordeal under the control of a spree killer, but she also survived her victimization at the hands of a flawed and ruthless justice system.

Caril prevailed and has continued to live out her life with dignity.

Epilogue

Caril Fugate was thirty-two years old when she walked out of prison. After serving eighteen years of her life sentence, she was granted parole and left the Nebraska Correctional Center for Women, in York, Nebraska, on June 8, 1976. Having been a model prisoner, she told the parole board, "I just want to settle down, get married, have a couple of kids, dust the house, and clean toilets. I just want to be an ordinary little dumpy housewife. I'll wash the socks and burn the toast."

At that time, the superintendent of York women's Reformatory, Jacqueline Crawford, told the board "She has earned her parole...society has gotten its pound of flesh.'"

While in prison, Caril worked in a Nazarene Church nursery, taught Bible classes on Sunday, and delivered sermons. Caril also trained as a geriatric aide in a work-release program.

Upon her release from prison, one of the first things Caril did, along with her sister Barb, was visit the graves of her parents and baby sister, Betty Jean. The Wyuka Cemetery, in central Lincoln, is more than 100 years old. The cemetary is made up of 140 acres of rolling hills with trees, shrubs, and flower gardens. Caril's family, the Bartletts, had a single headstone, with the names of Caril's stepfather, her mother, and baby sister, Betty Jean.

Caril and Barb held each other and wept at the grave site. Barb told Caril that Betty Jean had been buried in her mother's arms. Barb cried, saying that she felt guilty for what had happened to Caril. Barb had dated Charles Starkweather, but had developed a crush on another boy. To make breaking up with Charlie easier, Barb set up a date between Caril and Starkweather. Barb believed that if Caril had never met Starkweather, Caril would never have suffered the horrific experience with Charlie. Shortly thereafter, Caril moved to Michigan, where she worked as a surgical orderly in a hospital. She also became a nanny to two little girls. She would leave the hospital after an eight-hour day and work as a nanny in the evenings. Despite working a sixteen-hour day, Caril claimed that those days were the happiest in her life.

Caril maintained a very private life and guarded her privacy zealously. However, in 1993 she made a rare public appearance to discuss the release of the TV series *Murder in the Heartland,* a fictionalized account of the Starkweather murder rampage. Caril told the *Lincoln Journal Star* newspaper that watching the program "made the fear real again." Even more difficult than watching it, she said, was being forced to relive her tragedy when she had to explain her involvement with Starkweather to her nieces and nephews.

When Caril told them her story, she gave each niece and nephew a Lincoln-head penny with a heart engraved on it because, she said, Lincoln told the truth and because she loved them. She also told reporters, "I would be happy if people would say maybe, just maybe, they were too quick to judge me." For a number of years, Caril lived with her parakeet, "Moses," a pet that gave her much joy. She and Moses would often play hide-and-seek; Moses would walk around the doorway to the kitchen, peek at Caril, and hide by the wall where she couldn't see him. When Caril would peek around the doorway, Moses would squawk.

In addition to the two little girls she cared for as a nanny, Caril's passions in life were her family, garage sales, and casual casino trips. In fact, it was at a casino where she met her husband, Fred Clair, whom she married in 2007. The newly married couple settled down to life in a small town in northwest Ohio. They spent their married years traveling across the country and going to casinos. Speaking of their lives together, Caril said, "All we do is laugh."

Tragedy struck Caril and Fred on August 6, 2013. While driving to Michigan, their car went off the road, killing Fred and critically injuring Caril. She spent months recovering.

Linda Batissti

> *We live in the given. Consequence,*
> *and lack of consequence, both fail us.*
> *Good is what we can do with evil.*
>
> —J.V. Cunningham
> American Poet

Caril, along with her attorney James McArthur, had always believed she deserved a pardon from the state of Nebraska—not only because she was innocent, but also because of the way she was legally mistreated after her arrest. In 1996, McArthur filed an application for a pardon for Caril, however, she was denied a pardon.

Over the years, my wife and I became friends with Caril. She and her husband visited our home often. It was later that I became Caril's legal counsel. We never gave up on getting her a pardon. On August 23, 2017, we filed another application for Caril to receive a full pardon by the state of Nebraska. My team and I spent months preparing the application. The process was rigorous. We completed the pardon application, giving detailed information about Caril's life since her release. We submitted related court documents, including Caril's sentencing order, probation order, release from probation order, and five letters, verifying the applicant's good character. It was required that some of these letters come from citizens of the community where Caril had resided.

One letter that was submitted was from a woman for whom Caril had served as a nanny for several years. She had nothing but positive things to say about Caril, to whom she entrusted the care of her children.

Perhaps one of the most notable letters of reference was from Jackie Crawford, who had been the director of the Nebraska Correctional Center for Women, where Caril was held during her seventeen-year incarceration. Crawford said, "Caril was a model citizen at the correctional center, and in all the years I knew, she never moved toward conflict. She always moved away from it."

Another key person who submitted a letter was Liza Ward, whose grandparents, the Wards of Lincoln, and their maid were murdered by Starkweather. My wife, Margaret, and I met Liza in 2017. We were impressed by her personal quest to learn more about her grandparents. She was also seeking more information about Caril Fugate. She realized how much misinformation about Caril had been propagated in court and in media. She has always been committed to setting the record straight. Liza believed that Caril had been unjustly convicted. Liza sent a letter to the Board of Pardons, which, one suspects, the Board never bothered to read.

Liza's letter was especially powerful, considering her grandparents were victims of Starkweather. Her father, an only child and teenager at the time, was away at boarding school when his parents were murdered. Liza's letter read in part:

> I see this opportunity to pardon Caril Fugate Clair as a chance to right the wrong long-held presumption of guilt concerning a young girl, orphaned herself and under the control of psychopath wielding three rifles and a knife. This was a boy she had known, dated at the vulnerable age of thirteen, and broken up with. A boy to whom, when she said no, turned on a dime, and blew away her family while she was at school. He claimed her family was still alive somewhere; that their safety depended on her obedience. What choice was left to her other than to believe him?
>
> To answer the question as to why a pardon matter after all this time, I feel it is a matter of human decency and integrity. It matters to the family members who remain behind. It matters to Caril Fugate Clair that her name be cleared of this heinous crime. To give a very old woman the peace she so rightly deserves has become for me, a moral obligation. I fell that it is my duty to speak up for what I have found to be true. The truth is owed as much to the memory

of grandparents who were people of deep faith and grace, as it is owed to Caril herself.

I've spent my life uncovering the facts. I have read every document available to the public. Every line in the thousand pages of her trial transcript. I have visited every crime scene. I have listened to countless stories, and I find myself as yet to uncover a single shred of evidence that suggests beyond reasonable doubt that Caril Ann was guilty. What I have found instead is that she should never have been charged with a crime—tried as an adult at fourteen with the death penalty on the table. Caril Fugate was not an accomplice in the Starkweather homicides. No the mastermind. And never a willing participant in any of these murders.

That Starkweather himself, a psychopath responsible for eleven deaths, who changed his story at least four times before his conviction—was presented as lead witness for the prosecution is inconceivable. Why was Starkweather given a voice while Fugate's version of the story was disbelieved? I find this not only unjust but unfair to Caril Fugate, but disrespectful to the victims who were murdered by Starkweather.

Why should a mass murderer's version of events prevail in our consciousness? Why are we predisposed to hate her? To judge her by the fact that she didn't cry at the trial? Or by her tough expression in a photograph? She should've been sitting on his knee when he got the chair. She was the mastermind. She had his baby in prison...Guilty as sin. These are all things that have been said to me. I don't believe the people who said these things are bad or cruel, only misinformed, which in 1958, it was almost impossible to be.

Liza Ward, Granddaughter
C. Lauer and Clara Ward

The pardon application concluded with Caril's statement. "The idea that posterity has been made to believe that I knew about and/or witnessed the death of my beloved family and left with Starkweather willingly on a murder spree is too much for me to bear anymore." One would like to believe that perhaps one member of the Board of Pardons glanced at this. She concluded, "Receiving a pardon may somehow alleviate this terrible burden."

As my legal team wrapped up details for Caril's pardon application, I believed that if I were to lay out the facts, during the hearing, there was a considerable likelihood that Caril could receive a full pardon. Still, I was concerned about the recent performance of the Nebraska Board of Pardons. It had held only thirteen hearings over the past three fiscal years. In contrast, there had been 345 hearings during the three years prior, during a previous administration. The Board, which used to meet six to eight times a year for numerous hearings, met only twice during 2019.

As the date and time of the hearing approached, I was recovering from a spinal fusion surgery. I had service-connected disability from my days in Vietnam. I had written to the Board, explaining that it would be difficult and painful for me to come to the hearing, and the pain medication I was taking dulled my thought processes.

Similarly, I wrote to the Board to explain that that Liza Ward, the granddaughter of the Wards, who were murdered, wanted to attend the Pardon Board hearing. She was flying into Nebraska from her home in Massachusetts. She had a husband and two small children, and concomitant obligations. The trip would be a personal, emotional, and financial hardship for her.

I asked the Board to please let me know if our case would not be heard. If the Board had no intention of hearing our case, neither I nor Liza Ward would attend. We heard nothing. So, we both attended. Liza flew out at her own expense, and I, without pain medication, and with the assistance of a walker, made it to the hearing room.

Liza and my wife, Margaret, had arrived early and were sitting in the front row. Because it had been so long since there had been a hearing by this board, the room was crowded beyond capacity. People stood in hallways or adjoining rooms. Margaret and Liza had arrived early enough to sit in the front row.

One of Caril's stepsons had volunteered to bring her to the Pardon's Board hearing, but I had told him that it would most likely simply lead to further heartbreak for Caril and would be more fuel for the people who had exploited her life in so many ways.

February 18, 2020

When it came time for Caril to be heard at the hearing, I was prepared to speak. However, the Pardon's Board refused to hear me. They even refused to hear from the descendants of Starkweather's victims. No one was allowed to testify. The pardon application for Caril was denied.

The attorney general inaccurately stated that Caril's request was beyond the scope of the Nebraska Board of Pardons. This was a misstatement of the law. Not only was the statement contrary to the Nebraska Supreme Court's ruling on the matter, but it was contrary to my experience in fifty-seven years as a member of the Nebraska Bar. I had appeared in more pardon hearings than this Pardons Board combined, and I had never seen the board of pardons take such a cavalier attitude in rejecting hearings. The afternoon produced the rejection of pardons that would have been granted by any other pardons board I had ever appeared before.

Further, the Pardon's Board had made a mistake in listing the crime for which Caril was seeking a pardon. Caril had been convicted of felony murder; at Starkweather's order, she had counted the money in the wallet of one of his victims. She was never convicted on count 1, first degree premeditated murder. Yet, the Pardon's Board stated that she was requesting pardons on two counts. This was clearly inaccurate. So, I asked if I might be permitted to correct the record.

A one-word answer came from Pardon's Board member, Nebraska Governor Pete Ricketts, "No!" I later heard that as he was shouting "No," from the dais, he was shaking his ballpoint pen at me!

The governor had spent perhaps a third of a million dollars of his own money to get the death penalty reinstated in Nebraska, after the legislature had eliminated it.

As time has passed, many attitudes about the guilt of Caril have changed. More Nebraskans seem more open to the realization that Caril was railroaded. To be clear, I have never held Caril out as a paragon. I suspect that to do so would cause her embarrassment. That has never been the issue or the intent of this book. We have described a very real person, held hostage first by Starkweather, then by the Nebraska legal and political system.

John Stevens Berry

Appendix

In Memoriam

To the memory of the victims of Charles Starkweather:

Robert Colvert, 21, service station attendant, Lincoln Nebraska

Marion Bartlett, 57, Caril Fugate's stepfather, Lincoln Nebraska

Velda Bartlett, 36, Caril Fugate's mother, Lincoln, Nebraska

Betty Jean Bartlett, 3, Velda and Marion Bartlett's daughter, Lincoln, Nebraska

August Meyer, 70, Starkweather's family friend, rural Lincoln

Robert Jensen, 17, Carol King's boyfriend, Bennet, Nebraska

Carol King, 16, Robert Jensen's girlfriend, Bennet, Nebraska

C. Lauer Ward, 47, wealthy industrialist, Lincoln, Nebraska

Clara Ward, 46, C. Lauer Ward's wife, Lincoln, Nebraska

Lilyan Fencl, 51, Clara Ward's maid, Lincoln, Nebraska

Merle Collison, 37, traveling salesman in Wyoming

Timeline of Events
Charles Starkweather's Murder Rampage

July 30, 1943: Birth date of Caril Fugate, born in Lincoln, Nebraska.

1956: Caril was thirteen when she was introduced to Charlie Starkweather; he began visiting her every day after school, Whittier Junior High School in Lincoln.

Dec. 1, 1957: Starkweather commits his first murder. He kills Lincoln gas station attendant Robert Colvert. He told Caril that he had only robbed the man.

Jan. 21, 1958: While Caril is at school, Starkweather murders Caril's mother and step-father, Velda and Marion Bartlett, and their three-year-old daughter, Betty Jean. Starkweather hid the bodies in an outhouse and chicken shed behind the house.

Jan. 27, 1958: Before police could arrive at the Fugate home to investigate, Starkweather and Caril, his hostage, flee to Bennet, Nebraska, a small town in southeast Nebraska. They stop to visit a Starkweather family friend, August Meyer, 70. Starkweather shoots and kills the farmer as he was walking toward his house; he also shoots and kills the farmer's dog.

Starkweather and Fugate, while on the run, get their car stuck on a muddy country road. Two area teens, Robert Jensen and Carol King, stop to offer help. Starkweather forces them at gunpoint into an abandoned storm cellar. There, he shoots and kills seventeen-year-old Jensen. He also shoots and brutally stabs sixteen-year-old King. Starkweather would later say that Fugate shot the girl.

Jan. 28, 1958: The two enter the home of Lincoln businessman C. Lauer Ward and his wife, Clara. Believing the Wards to be wealthy, Starkweather hopes to steal money so they could flee Lincoln. Starkweather stabs Mrs. Ward and her maid, Lilyan Fencl, to death. Later, when Mr. Ward arrives home, Starkweather shoots and kills him.

Jan. 29, 1958: Starkweather and Fugate flee to Wyoming. As news of the murder spree spreads, residents of Nebraska fear for their safety. On a highway outside Douglas, Wyoming, the pair find traveling salesman, Merle Collison, who was sleeping in his parked car. Starkweather shoots and kills him.

Starkweather was at the wheel of the Ward's car, but the brake was stuck. A passing motorist, area resident Joe Sprinkle, stops to help. When Starkweather aims his rifle at Sprinkle, the two struggle and Sprinkle manages to get the gun away from Starkweather. A deputy sheriff comes upon the scene, and Fugate runs to the deputy. Starkweather flees in a high-speed chase that exceeds 100 mph. Only after sheriffs shoot at Starkweather, shattering the windshield and cutting his face, does Starkweather stop the car and surrender.

May 23, 1958: Starkweather is found guilty and sentenced to death.

Nov. 21, 1958: Fugate, the youngest female to be tried for first degree murder in the United States. She was sentenced to life in prison for first degree murder in the perpetration of a robbery. Starkweather, who originally claimed that Fugate had no involvement in the murders, had later testified that she was a willing participant in several of the murders.

June 25, 1959: Starkweather is executed in Nebraska's electric chair.

Oct. 31, 1973: State Pardons Board commutes Fugate's sentence to thirty to fifty years in prison. She became eligible for parole in 1976.

June 1976: State Board of Parole votes to parole Fugate. She moves to Michigan, where she works as a hospital orderly and as a nanny for two children.

1981: Fugate is discharged from parole, making her free of the prison system.

1993: Fugate visits a school classroom, telling students to avoid dumb choices. Hers was believing Starkweather as a thirteen-year-old. "I thought I was really hot stuff," she says. "It was the biggest mistake I made in my life." Fugate says she unsuccessfully tried to kill herself by ingesting pills.

1996: Fugate calls into a Lincoln radio talk show. Host John Stevens Berry, a local attorney, is surprised by the number of listeners who believe her story of innocence.

2007: Fugate gets married to Fred Clair of Michigan.

2012: An Internet news site, citing an unnamed stepson, says Fugate suffered a series of strokes and is partially paralyzed. A friend says she's okay and not in a wheelchair or hospital.

August 6, 2013: Caril and her husband Fred, who was at the wheel, were in a one-vehicle, rollover accident. Fred was killed immediately. Caril was critically injured and spent months recovering.

ABOUT THE AUTHORS

Linda M. Battisti is a trial attorney with the United States Department of Justice; she prosecutes bankruptcy fraud cases in the Northern District of Ohio. She attended Rollins College in Winter Park, Florida, where she earned a bachelor of arts degree in Spanish and French with a minor in philosophy. Battisti studied abroad for one year at the Universidad de Madrid in Madrid, Spain. She received her Juris Doctorate degree from Cleveland-Marshall College of Law, Cleveland, Ohio.

Her personal interests include her Catholic faith, family, friends, and her English bulldog, Chrissie. She works out with "Physique 57," and is a great fan of Alfred Hitchcock and Steven Tyler. Battisti enjoys travel to Paris and would like to live there.

 **John Stevens Berry Sr.** is an attorney and the founder of the Berry Law Firm in Lincoln, Nebraska. A native of Onawa, Iowa, Berry graduated from Stanford University, Stanford, California, with a bachelor of arts degree in English with minors in philosophy and religion. He earned his Juris Doctor degree from Northwestern University in Chicago, Illinois. He is a graduate of the Infantry Officer School at Fort Benning, Georgia, and the Judge Advocate General (JAG) School in Charlottesville, Virginia.

In 1968 and 1969, Mr. Berry was the chief defense counsel for the largest general court martial jurisdiction in Vietnam, II

Field Force Vietnam, numbering more than 80,000 soldiers. He also served as defense counsel on a temporary duty basis with the 101st Airborne, the 82nd Airborne, the 1st Infantry Division, the 1st Calvary Division, the 199th Light Infantry Brigade, the 11th Armored Calvary Regiment, and the 5th Special Forces.

His efforts in the defense of the commander of the Green Berets in Vietnam and some of his officers on a charge of murder and conspiracy to commit murder is the basis of his Vietnam memoirs, *Those Gallant Men* (Presidio Press), which was a selection of the Book of the Month by the Military Book Club. Other books he has written include *Darkness of Snow* (poetry), and he was the lead author of *Inside the Minds: Utilizing Forensic Science in Criminal Cases.*

After his duty in Vietnam, Berry served as chief defense counsel at the Presidio of San Francisco. His military decorations and awards include the Bronze Star, the Vietnamese Cross of Gallantry with Palm Device, the Vietnam Medal of Honor 1st Class (Gold), the Vietnamese Medal of Honor 2nd Class (Silver), the Vietnamese Civic Action Medal, and other awards and decorations.

Berry is a fellow of the American Board of Criminal Lawyers and past president of the Nebraska Criminal Defense Attorneys Association. He is also a member of the Melvin Belli Society and the Baker Street Irregulars.

Addicus Books True Crime

Visit our online catalog at www.AddicusBooks.com

Addicus Books
P. O. Box 45327
Omaha, NE 68145